The Siege of Derry 1689:
The Military History

THE SIEGE OF DERRY 1689: THE MILITARY HISTORY

by

Richard Doherty

SPELLMOUNT

First published 2008
This edition published by Spellmount in 2010

Spellmount Publishers
The History Press Ltd.
Cirencester Road, Chalford,
Stroud, Gloucestershire, GL6 8PE
www.thehistorypress.co.uk

Spellmount Publishers are an imprint of The History Press Ltd.

British Library Cataloguing in Publication Data.
A catalogue record for this book is available from the British Library.

ISBN 978 0 7524 5536 5

Typesetting and origination by The History Press Ltd.
Printed in India by Aegean Offset Printers, New Delhi

Dedication

For Danny McLaughlin
Who taught better than he knew, and enriched many young lives.

I'll have you learn to sleep upon the ground,
March in your armour through watery fens,
Sustain the scorching heat and freezing cold,
Hunger and thirst right adjuncts of the war,
And after this to scale a castle wall
Besiege a fort, to undermine a town,
And make whole cities caper in the air

Christopher Marlowe
(Tamburlane, to his sons)

Contents

By the same author

Wall of Steel: The History of 9th (Londonderry) HAA Regiment, RA (SR), North-West Books, Limavady, 1988

The Sons of Ulster: Ulstermen at War from the Somme to Korea, The Appletree Press, Belfast, 1992

Clear The Way! A History of the 38th (Irish) Brigade, 1941–47, Irish Academic Press, Dublin, 1993

Irish Generals: Irish Generals in the British Army in the Second World War, The Appletree Press, Belfast, 1993

The Williamite War in Ireland, 1688–1691, Four Courts Press, Dublin, 1998

Irish Men and Women in the Second World War, Four Courts Press, Dublin, 1999

Irish Winners of the Victoria Cross (with David Truesdale), Four Courts Press, Dublin, 2000

Irish Volunteers in the Second World War, Four Courts Press, Dublin, 2001

The Sound of History: El Alamein 1942, Spellmount, Staplehurst, 2002

The North Irish Horse: A Hundred Years of Service, Spellmount, Staplehurst, 2002

Normandy 1944: The Road to Victory, Spellmount, Staplehurst, 2004

Ireland's Generals in the Second World War, Four Courts Press, Dublin, 2004

The Thin Green Line: A History of The Royal Ulster Constabulary GC, 1922–2001, Pen & Sword Books, Barnsley, 2004

None Bolder. The History of the 51st Highland Division in the Second World War, Spellmount, Staplehurst, 2006

The British Reconnaissance Corps in World War II, Osprey Publishing, Botley & New York, 2007

Eighth Army in Italy: The Long Hard Slog, Pen & Sword Books, Barnsley, 2007

A Noble Crusade: The History of the Eighth Army, 1941–1945, Spellmount, Staplehurst, 2008 new ed.

Only the Enemy in Front. The Recce Corps at War, 1940–46, Spellmount, Staplehurst, 2008 new ed.

List of Maps

Acknowledgements

I owe thanks to a number of individuals and organisations without whose assistance this book would not have been possible. As the reader will note from the Introduction, I have had an almost life-long interest in the subject, an interest sparked by the late Danny McLaughlin in a school classroom almost a half century ago. Therefore, my first thanks must go to Danny McLaughlin for doing his job as a teacher so well.

More recently, but still almost twenty years ago, Michael McGowan and Frances Campbell welcomed me into the world of historical broadcasting with a series of contributions on the siege in Frances' BBC Radio Foyle afternoon programme, which was produced by Michael. In 1989, the tercentenary of the siege, I presented a radio series called *The Siege Chronicles*, which Michael produced. For their encouragement and support, I thank them both.

Although the siege occurred three centuries ago, there are many contemporary records still extant. These include a number of Admiralty records, among them ships' logs, relating to the maritime aspects of the siege. I was able to consult these at the National Archives at Kew where the staff were, as I have always found them, both professional and helpful. Other records survive in the House of Lords' Records Office, in the Palace of Westminster, and thanks are also due for the assistance I received there. Yet more contemporary documents reside in the Scottish Records Office in Edinburgh and I am especially indebted to Hazel Weir for her work on my behalf in that institution. The National Army Museum, Chelsea, was another valuable source of information which I acknowledge readily together with the National Gallery of Ireland, Dublin. Finally, I was able to consult contemporary copies of the *London Gazette* in the British Library Newspaper Library at Colindale, London.

The siege, and the war of which it formed part, spawned a number of books in an early manifestation of a now familiar phenomenon, the recording of participants' experiences. I am grateful to Mr Tony Crowe who lent me original copies of some of these books and to the Linenhall Library, Belfast and the Central Library, Foyle Street, Londonderry, for their assistance.

A very special word of thanks must go to St Columb's Cathedral and to the Very Reverend Dean William Morton, Dean of Derry, as well as Daphne and Gerry Gallick, Ian Bartlett and Billy Begley, for access to documents and books in the Cathedral's collection and also for permission to photograph exhibits in the Chapterhouse Museum; some of the photographs grace the pages of this book.

My publisher, Jamie Wilson of Spellmount was a great support, as well as being a good friend, and the editorial and production team, including Shaun Barrington and Clare Jackson, are to be congratulated on their efforts which have resulted in a fine volume.

To my wife Carol, our children Joanne, James and Catríona, and grandson Ciarán, I extend my thanks for constant support and understanding.

Introduction

It is often referred to as the greatest siege in British military history. Indeed, Macaulay called it the greatest siege in English history, going on to say that the wall of Derry 'remains to the Protestants of Ulster what the trophy of Marathon, or the pass of Thermopylae, was to the Athenians – a sacred spot dear to memory, and enkindling by its name the fire of patriotism'. The siege is recalled on an annual basis by the Apprentice Boys of Derry, who celebrate the 'shutting of the gates' in December and the relief of the city in August. It is also used as a shibboleth by politicians and others, while some academics consider that the siege continues in a psychological fashion to the present day, with the unionist community in Northern Ireland feeling the sense of isolation that was felt by the defenders of Derry in 1689.

My first awareness of the siege of Derry came as a schoolboy in the city fifty years ago. Our teacher, the late Danny McLaughlin, had written an account of the siege which he read to us on an instalment basis. I was enthralled with the tale he told and can still recall his telling us about Governor Lundy who was prepared to sell the keys of Derry, as Danny McLaughlin put it, 'for a bap', and of how Captain Browning, commander of the relief ship *Mountjoy* died, like Wolfe and Nelson, in his hour of glory and triumph. The school that I attended was St Eugene's Boys' Public Elementary school, although we all called it the Rosemount School, and its very name is a clear indication to anyone raised in, or knowing anything about, Northern Ireland that this was somewhere one would not normally expect the defenders of Derry to be lauded as heroes. And yet that is how they were presented to us in that classroom all those years ago, as individuals at the centre of a gripping story.

In the years since then I have continued to be enthralled by the story of the siege. As a military historian I am also intrigued by the way in which the events in and around Derry during that spring and summer of 1689 are celebrated and commemorated. At the risk of being accused of mixing metaphors it has become something of a tug-of-war with politicians of different hues using it to their own ends; and, of course, it has given Northern Ireland's unionists their rallying cry of 'No Surrender'.

But the siege of Derry is not a story that belongs exclusively to one element of our population. Rather it is part of the history of everyone who lives anywhere in Ireland and, indeed, throughout the British Isles, while it also has resonances further into Europe. What is often forgotten in our myopic view of 1689 is the fact that, for 105 days in that year, a small city on the very edge of Europe was the hinge on which the history of the continent swung. This was not simply a spat in a war between native Irish and planter Irish but also a crucial event in the second British civil war of the seventeenth century, and of an even broader struggle for the domination of Europe. It is my aim in this book to demonstrate that events at Derry were crucial to the outcome of each of those struggles and how the defeat of the Jacobite forces helped shape a continent for the centuries to come.

It is with respect and thanks that I dedicate this book to the memory of Daniel McLaughlin.

Richard Doherty

CHAPTER ONE

An Island City and Three Kings

The *Oxford Dictionary* defines a siege as a '(Period of) surrounding and blockading of fortified place' with the derivation of the word being attributed to the French *sege* or seat. It is in the nature of siege warfare that both sides spend much time sitting around and thus the entirely appropriate use of the word *sege*. Siege warfare has a long history, dating back to the first occasion on which people took refuge behind some form of fortification, and it continues even into our own times. During the twentieth century the trench warfare of the Great War was siege warfare in linear form and it required the development of siege-breaking techniques to bring it to an end. The Second World War also had sieges: the siege of Leningrad was the longest in modern history while another Russian city, Stalingrad, was also besieged, with the occupying Sixth German Army surrounded by Soviet forces. For the British forces, perhaps the most famous siege was at Tobruk in Libya, although the entire United Kingdom could be said to have been under siege for much of the war, while the siege of Malta led to the award of the George Cross to the island and its people. Over a decade later the French army suffered the siege of Dien Bien Phu in Indo-China, now Vietnam, while US forces were later also besieged in that country. Irish troops on United Nations duty came under siege in the Congo, at Jadotville, in 1961. Thus sieges, great or small – but usually small – have continued to be part of our history and the word has also come to describe a situation in which criminals or small groups of terror-ists hold out against the police or the armed forces. Examples of the latter include the siege of Sidney Street in London in 1911 and, much more recently, the Balcombe Street and Iranian Embassy sieges, also in London.

The evolution of warfare has brought with it a further evolution in the conduct of sieges, from both sides of the fortifications. While the conduct of a siege several centuries after the demise of the Roman Empire might still have been familiar to a Roman general, the introduction of gunpowder seemed to herald the end of siege warfare but, instead, brought only an adaptation of that warfare. By the late-seventeenth century a system of 'siegecraft' had been developed with its own rules and protocols – one might almost say 'etiquette' – and European armies were familiar with the rules for the conduct of a siege and the equipment and manpower needed to lay siege to a fortified town or city. Those fortifications had also changed, the tall thin walls and towers of earlier times giving way to squatter, stouter walls with bastions that allowed enfilading fire on the attackers.[1]

Those rules of 'siegecraft' had developed their own, military, definition of a siege, which would not coincide entirely with that laid down by the *Oxford Dictionary*. The surrounding of a fortified place, for example, required an army capable of reducing that fortified place, be it town, city or fortress, and this included sufficient artillery to create a breach in the defences, or walls, through which an initial attacking force of about twenty volunteer infantrymen – a 'forlorn hope' – could fight its way to achieve entry for even more infantry.[2] In terms of manpower, Napoleon believed that a besieging force had to be four times the size of the invested force to ensure success; in the seventeenth century, Vauban had advised that the besieging force had to outnumber the garrison by ten to one, with a minimum manpower of 20,000 if lines of circumvallation and contravallation were to be built. As well as artillery, engineers were also needed; their task was to provide gun platforms, or batteries, for the artillery, construct protection for those batteries, and develop other means of creating a breach, by use of mines under the defences and the digging of saps, which were tunnels or trenches, to allow access to where those mines were to be placed. Engineers were also responsible for the equipment needed to scale walls or cross defensive ditches; these included ladders and fascines, bundled branches with which to create a causeway over the ditches. Those engineers who planted mines needed to be expert in explosives. Their very risky profession had prompted Shakespeare to put the phrase 'for 'tis the sport to have the engineer hoist with his own petar' into Hamlet's mouth. The petar, or petard, was a mine placed under the fortifications, the premature detonation of which would see the miner, or engineer, blown up or 'hoist'.

Judged even by this very basic outline of siegecraft, what happened between April and August 1689, over a period of 105 days, at Londonderry does not appear to justify the term 'siege'. But, by the *Oxford Dictionary* definition, there was a siege, since the city was surrounded and blockaded during that time. Irrespective of these definitions, there is no doubt that there was considerable military activity at Londonderry during those months. Furthermore, the lack of artillery and engineering stores does not mean that the attacking army did not intend to besiege the city but rather that it lacked the wherewithal to do so effectively. The reasons for that will be discussed in a later chapter. Nor is there any doubt that considerable importance was placed on the city by both sides, nor that the echoes of those days over three centuries ago may still be heard today. So, let us examine those 105 days to see if we can define the truth of what occurred.

In the spring of 1689 the Protestant, or Williamite, population of Ireland considered itself to be facing dire threat. Most of Ireland was under Jacobite, largely Catholic, control, and Ulster and north-east Connaught were about to be attacked by Jacobite forces. Before long, the Williamite forces would be drawing back to Sligo, in Connaught, and Enniskillen and Londonderry, in Ulster, as they waited for relieving troops to arrive from Britain. Although Sligo would change hands, neither Enniskillen nor Londonderry were to fall to the Jacobites and it was their failure to take the latter that prevented the Jacobites pursuing the strategy of using the city as a stepping-off point to cross to Scotland, link up with Jacobite forces there and march south into England to restore James II to his kingdoms. Had that happened, the course of Irish, British and European history might have been very different. The Jacobite failure to take the city was a pivotal point in this second British civil war of the seventeenth century. But why was Londonderry important? That is the central question that this study of the siege will try to answer.

The seventeenth-century city of Londonderry sat on a site with a history that already stretched back more than a millennium. Although the popular belief is that the city was founded by a Donegal monk, Colmcille, and named Doire Cholmcille in his honour, the origins of the settlement predate his era and it is quite possible that Colmcille never visited the place.[3] There was an even older tradition that named the settlement as Doire Calgach and this tradition seems to date back to the first century AD. Calgach, it is believed, was a Celtic warrior and may even be the Galgacus mentioned by Tacitus as leading the Celts against Agricola's Romans at the battle of Mons Graupius, in modern-day Scotland, in AD 89; this was the belief of Dr John Keys O'Doherty, Roman Catholic Bishop of Derry from 1889 to 1907, who was an antiquarian writer.[4] As was so often the case, it may well be that the Christian church replaced the name of Calgach, which means 'sharp' or 'fierce', with that of Colmcille, the 'dove of the church', to rename the little settlement that sat on an island in the river Foyle.

As far as the name Doire is concerned, the received wisdom is that it means an oak grove. However, the word can also mean a small hill, as evidenced by the many small hills throughout Ireland that include the anglicized 'Derry' in their names; more than a thousand townland names include 'derry'. In the case of Doire Calgach, or Doire Cholmcille, this alternative translation as a small hill is more logical than oak grove, since it conveys the sense of an island rising from the waters of the river. Brian Lacy notes that the word frequently indicated an island that was totally or partly surrounded by peat bog and this would apply especially to Doire Calgach or Doire Cholmcille.[5] The Foyle once flowed around the island of Doire thereby making that feature of high and dry ground an attractive location for settlers who sought some degree of security, which the river would have provided. Even when the Foyle's westerly branch silted up, it reduced the surrounding ground to marsh or bog – and hence the term 'bogside' – which continued to provide some security from the west. In the late-seventeenth century, at the time of the siege, the marshy ground to the west was still a major obstacle to the besieging Jacobite army. One of the best descriptions of the city's location is provided by Avril Thomas:

> The site is visually striking – a clearly defined, oval-shaped hill of about 80 hectares in area and almost 40 m in height, with slopes that are steep at its broader northern end and more gradual as it narrows to the south in a wedge-like form. It is bounded on the east by the broad, deep and fast-flowing River Foyle, which is tidal at this point, and on the west by a former course of this river. Beyond these the ground rises to over 70 m rapidly on the east and less so on the west.[6]

The Foyle is formed at Strabane by the confluence of the Mourne and Finn rivers whence it wends its way northwards to flow into Lough Foyle at Culmore, some eighteen miles to the north-east as the crow flies but a few miles longer by boat due to the river's meanderings. Just south of the city the Foyle turns more sharply north-eastwards at the beginning of an arc around the one-time island before turning almost directly north whence it flows into Ross's Bay. From there the river enters a narrow section, some two miles in length, across which the Jacobite army sited its boom in 1689, before flowing into the lough. From Culmore Point to the city's quay in 1689 was a distance of a little more than four miles. Lough Foyle lies between County Londonderry, which forms its southern and eastern shores, and Inishowen in County Donegal, which forms its western shore. Strictly speaking, in 1689 all the waters of the lough were considered to be in County Londonderry, the western boundary of which was along the high-water mark on the Inishowen shore.[7] From Culmore to the mouth of the lough is over eighteen miles, while the maximum distance across the lough is some ten and a half miles. The mouth of the lough, from Magilligan Point in County Londonderry to Greencastle in Inishowen, is about a mile in width.

We do not know when the settlement at Doire began to attain importance. It was a monastic settlement, with the first monastery, known as the Dub Regles, or Black Church, in the area of the present Saint Augustine's church inside the city walls*, but the base of local military and political power was then at the settlement on Grianan hill, with its circular dry-stone fort, or cashel, which was the seat of the northern Uí Néill, some five miles to the north-west in the modern County Donegal and overlooking the neck of the Inishowen peninsula[8]. This ancient fortification, in ruins by the seventeenth century, was to oversee part of the stage on which the drama that was the siege was played out.

During the reign of Queen Elizabeth I, determined efforts were made to bring the province of Ulster under English control, and by the end of that long reign this had largely been achieved. Part of the process of subduing the Ulster clans had been to build a military base at Doire, in 1566, 'to check the increasing boldness of' Hugh O'Neill.[9] This was seen as a sound operational centre, with a good strategic location, and the new military establishment, under Edward Randolph, included a hospital. Randolph, who bore the title 'commander of the forces, and provost marshal of and within the province of Ulster', commanded a force of seven companies of foot and a troop of horse, about a thousand infantrymen and fifty cavalry, and made his camp on the monastery site, expelling the occupants. Defence works were built of earth, the first Derry walls, and the nearby Tempull Mór, the great church or cathedral – from which the modern parish of Templemore takes its name – was taken over to store the force's gunpowder, ammunition

---

*The monks of the Dub Regles adopted the Rule of St Augustine and the church became an Augustinian monastery, surviving as such until the end of the middle ages. The site, therefore, has an ecclesiastical history of some 1,400 years.

and provisions. Following a victory against the O'Neills some five miles from the city, the garrison appeared to be well established.[10]

However, Randolph was killed in another action against the O'Neills in November 1566 and was buried in Derry; he was succeeded as commander by Colonel Edward St Low. Although plagued by illness, which reduced its numbers, the garrison continued mounting expeditions against the local clans until its strength fell to such a point that a proposal was made that it should leave Derry and move to the area of Strangford lough. Before this plan could be executed, however, a fire broke out in the camp and spread to engulf all the buildings. Tongues of flame leapt to the great church which held the powder and 'the church and town (such as it was) were blown up, the provisions were destroyed, and many lives lost; in consequence of which the place was considered untenable'. The garrison was evacuated, the infantry sailing from the Foyle for Dublin and the cavalry travelling across country through Tyrconnell and Connaught. But the lesson of the value of a military base at Doire had not been lost.[11]

It was not long before a further expedition arrived at Doire. A new base was established which was intended to be permanent and it is to this establishment that the modern city owes its origins. At the time of the plantation of Ulster, in the reign of King James I, settlers were brought into the area and the new town of Doire, anglicized to Derry, or Derrie, was surrounded by a defensive wall. Before long, in 1604, the town became a city when James awarded it a royal charter;[12] thus it was the first city in the province of Ulster. Life was never secure for the people of the plantation who, it was said, lived with one hand on the plough handle and the other on the sword. And so it proved in May 1608 when Sir Cahir O'Doherty, lord of Inishowen, led his clansmen against the garrison and people of Derry and sacked the town. Having slaughtered the garrison of Culmore fort, Sir Cahir and his men 'hastened to Derry on the same night, surprised the garrison, slaughtered Paulett [the governor of the city], with his Lieutenant, Cosbie, and put every man to the sword; plundered the town and reduced it to ashes'. Sir Cahir was hunted down into Donegal where he lost his life in battle at Kilmacrenan. His pickled head was taken to Dublin to be displayed on a spike as a lesson to any who might be inclined to follow his example.[13]

This time the settlement was not abandoned. It had been recognized as an important military base, pivotal to the control of north-west Ulster, and O'Doherty's rebellion emphasized that value. Sitting on what was still almost an island, Derry separated the major clans of the region – the O'Cahans, or O'Kanes, to the east of the Foyle in what had been the county of Coleraine,* their neighbours in Tyrone, the O'Neills, and the O'Donnells to the west in Tyrconnell, with their allies, the O'Dohertys of Inishowen. And so it was decided that the city would be rebuilt but with much better defences than hitherto. The help of the City of London Guilds, or companies, was sought to provide investment capital for the project. Most of the guilds made contributions, albeit unwillingly in many cases, and a special investment body was created to oversee the work; this was to become the Honourable The Irish Society.[14]

To mark the role played by the London companies a new charter was granted to the city, combining the ancient name of the settlement with the name of London: London-Derrie.[15] Paradoxically, in the light of recent clamour by republicans and nationalists to change the name of Londonderry to Derry, the London prefix has a Celtic origin, and derives from two words meaning the 'fort of the ships'. The equivalent Gaelic words – dun, or fort, and long, or ship, are recognizable and, to add to the paradox, some five miles south of the city, beside the Foyle in County Tyrone, is the townland of Dunalong, 'dún na long', the 'fort of the ships', where, it is believed, Norse raiders came ashore from their longships and set up camp, giving the locality its name. A new coat of arms was granted to the new city; as with the name, this combined the arms of Derry with those of London, although an Irish harp was added to the cross of St George on the latter.

The city's new walls were intended to protect its inhabitants against another attack such as that launched by Sir Cahir O'Doherty since the main perceived threat came from local clansmen who would have had no artillery and none of the equipment needed to penetrate a walled city. Thus the walls, which were constructed between 1614 and 1619, included a six-foot-thick outer 'skin' of stone against a twelve-foot-thick earth wall although they did conform to contemporary standards of military engineering by being squat and stout, rather than high, with emplacements for cannon instead of the high towers of earlier times. Artillery for the walls was also provided by the City of London Guilds; six culverins, six demi-culverins and eight sakers were emplaced.[16] There was no inner stone wall to create a sandwich; the inner stone wall as seen today was a later addition. Four entrances

---

*The former county formed the basis of the new county of Londonderry. To Coleraine county were added parts of Counties Tyrone and Antrim as well as part of County Donegal in which sat the city of Londonderry.

to the city were made in the walls: Water Gate, later Ship Quay Gate, at the quay on the river; New Gate, later the Butcher's Gate, from which led the road to Inishowen, carried on a causeway or embankment over the bog; Bishop's Gate, facing towards the south; and the Ferry Gate, or Ferry Port, leading to the cross-river ferry. Each gate had a small fort to protect the gate guard and a drawbridge.

Within the walls was a thoughtfully-planned geometric city, possibly the first example of such in these islands, with the streets leading from the four gates converging on a central square in which a market house was built. In his book on the city's walls, Cecil Davis Milligan rejects the theory that there might have been a French influence in the design of the city. More recent research indicates otherwise. Brian Lacy has drawn attention to similarities between Londonderry and the French city of Vitry-le-François on the Marne, some one hundred miles from Paris, a possibility first noted by two American historians of town planning, Anthony Garvan and John Reps, in their research for the origins of plans for the early English settlements in the colonies destined to become the United States.* Vitry had been designed by an Italian engineer, Hieronimo Marino, for King Francis I; Lacy notes that the resemblance may be due to the fact that Vitry was completed during the reign of Francis II. The second Francis was married to Mary, Queen of Scots who, in turn, was the mother of King James VI of Scotland who became James I of England, the man responsible for the plantation of Ulster and the building of the new city of Londonderry.' Of course, when Marino was designing Vitry-le-Francois he was not concerned about town planning but in creating a frontier fortress and the inspiration for his design lay in the camps built by the campaigning legions of ancient Rome; he was reproducing their patterns rather than designing a new concept in towns. And whereas a Roman legion, of fewer than 5,000 men, could build its camp in hours, it took years to build the new city of Londonderry, which is probably the last example of a Roman camp to be built in Europe.

Captain Edward Doddington designed Londonderry's walls, adapting the Vitry plan to the local topography, and the surveyor was Thomas Raven, while Peter Benson took charge of the building with John Baker overseeing the work in the absence of Doddington.[18] At first the streets inside the walls were named Queen's Street, Silver Street, Gracious Street and the Shambles,[19] but these later became,

---

*Reps suggested that the original plans for Philadelphia had parallels with those for Londonderry.

respectively, Bishop's Street, Shipquay Street, Ferryquay Street and Butcher's Street. Within the walls a new Anglican cathedral, the first to be built specifically for the Anglican faith, was constructed between 1628 and 1633, and dedicated to St Columb, the same Colmcille so often regarded as the founder of the city. Described as 'a fair church', the cathedral was built in Gothic style, known as Planter's Gothic, at the expense of the Irish Society and cost £4,000. The Society anticipated the building of the cathedral by sending over a silver-gilt chalice and paten for the church; the chalice, referred to as the 'Promised Chalice' is still used for the celebration of Holy Communion during special services.[20] Another Anglican church, St Augustine's, was built nearby, on the site of the original monastic settlement, while a Free Grammar School was also to be found.* A more modern St Augustine's Church today stands on the site of the original.[21]

By 1689 the walls had not been improved in any way but rather had been allowed to deteriorate as the city fathers sought to save money in a manner that continues to be familiar to this day – by reducing the amount spent on defence. This would suggest that the Planter inhabitants of the city and its environs no longer felt it necessary to be ready to meet an armed rebellion at short notice; the days of sword in one hand and plough in the other seemed to be past. In spite of threats in the 1640s, the walls, and the cannon emplaced on them, continued to deteriorate; this lackadaisical attitude to the city's defences came close to gifting it to King James II's army in 1689. By another of those paradoxes which enrich history, that this did not happen was due largely to the energy and military skills of a man whose fate it has been to be denounced as a traitor for over 300 years: Colonel Robert Lundy.

Europe in the late-seventeenth century was in a state of unrest, characterized by a series of wars and alliances in which the principal power was France, whose monarch, Louis XIV, the 'Sun King', was acutely conscious, and jealous, of his nation's security. Hitherto, Spain had long been the dominant power on the continent, but the French were now in the ascendant and it was Louis XIV who was to be the key figure in the conflict that engulfed Ireland from 1688 to 1691 and brought two armies to the city of Londonderry in 1689. To understand how this occurred we must first take a brief look at developments in Europe in the years before the war in Ireland.

---

*Grammar schools were so called because their pupils were taught Latin grammar.

The son of King Louis XIII and Queen Anne, Louis XIV was born on 5 September 1638. By then France had been at war with Spain and Austria for three years and the religious conflict known as the Thirty Years War was entering its final decade. This war led to death and destruction on a huge scale across the mainland of Europe with the misery of war exacerbated by a series of epidemics of plague. As if that were not enough, the continent was emerging from what is now regarded as a mini ice age. Thus the France into which Louis was born was far from being a settled nation and this situation was exacerbated when the young prince was only five years old. It was then that Louis XIII died and Queen Anne became regent of France; she appointed a prime minister in the person of Cardinal Mazarin.

The Thirty Years War finally came to an end with the Treaty of Westphalia which followed the Prince de Condé's victory at the Battle of Lens in 1648. However, France was not to enjoy peace for, while Condé was battling at Lens, parliament in Paris was rebelling against Mazarin's rule. Queen Anne and ten-year-old Prince Louis were forced to flee from the city, quitting the Louvre palace on the night of 5–6 January 1649. Civil war, known as the Fronde, followed by the 1650 Revolt of the Princes, reduced Paris to a state of anarchy. By now Condé had gone over to the Spanish and, in July 1652, he captured Paris for his new masters. Outside the capital, most of France remained loyal to the regency, and anarchy was brought to an end quickly, allowing the royal court to return to Paris on 21 October. The experience of this period shaped Louis' future attitude to the security of the monarchy and of the country, with effects that would be felt as far away as the north-west of Ireland.

In 1653 France formed an alliance with the exiled British court against Spain. Five years later, Marshal Turenne – with Condé one of France's greatest generals – defeated Spanish forces in the Battle of the Dunes, near Dunkirk. During this battle a young British prince, James, Duke of York, distinguished himself, drawing Turenne's praise for his outstanding gallantry. November 1659 saw an end to the conflict with a negotiated peace. Condé was pardoned that same year by Louis who had been crowned as King Louis XIV on 7 June 1654, although Mazarin continued to hold the reins of power. When Mazarin died on 9 March 1661, Louis chose not to appoint a successor and assumed full power for himself. Thus began the process that would make the Sun King the most powerful monarch in Europe.

Considering that France's security depended on having defensible borders, Louis embarked on a series of military ventures aimed to create such frontiers. In 1672 his army crossed the Rhine into Holland.

Dutch resistance was led by William Henry Nassau, Stadtholder of the Dutch Republic, who was also known as the Prince of Orange. The tiny principality of Orange, in Provence, was annexed by Louis in the same campaign in an action that was both insult and injury to William since it was the possession of Orange that made him a prince. However, Orange was too isolated and France much too powerful for any possible military action to restore the principality to William's family. Two years later, Britain, now a monarchy again, made a separate peace with Spain, from which point both France and William of Orange sought to draw Britain into an alliance as part of the European conflict.

France remained at war for most of the decade that followed. During this period, on 22 October 1685, Louis XIV revoked the edict of Nantes of 1598, which had guaranteed religious freedom to the Protestants of France, the Huguenots.* French Protestants were ordered to convert to Catholicism, but many refused and were massacred. Others chose exile, fleeing to England and other European countries: their skills in many crafts and their intellectual achievements in many spheres were to benefit the countries that gave them refuge; the Irish linen industry and trade owed much to these refugees from persecution. Among those who sought safety in exile were some of Louis' generals, including the Duke of Schomberg, who would later command the Williamite army in Ireland. Included in the leaders of the campaign of persecution against the Huguenots was Marshal Conrad de Rosen, who would serve James II in Ireland and, for a time, command the Jacobite forces arrayed against Londonderry. One leading French commander, Marshal Vauban, estimated that some 600 first-class officers and about 12,000 good soldiers were among the Huguenots who fled France. They went to England, Holland and some of the German states, offering their services to their new countries and becoming some of the bitterest foes of Louis XIV.[22] Their military skills were also to add to the professionalism of the armies in which they now served.

Under Louis the army of France had changed dramatically. When the Duke d'Epernon, the Colonel-General of Infantry, died, Louis took over that office as well, having earlier identified the Colonel-General of Infantry as being more powerful than himself. Louis now held the authority to issue commissions in the Royal Army's infantry arm. Colonel-General appointments continued to exist in the army's other

---

*Their name derives from the German *eidgenossen*, men bound to one another by oath. France's Protestants originated in Switzerland and were followers of Calvin.

arms – cavalry, dragoons and Swiss troops – but their power was nominal. The king now possessed real power and began establishing the most powerful war machine seen in Europe since the demise of the Roman Empire.[23]

The concept of national armies is now so familiar that it is difficult to conceive of a time when they did not exist, but this was the case even in the France of Louis XIV where there were many local town forces under governors who enjoyed almost complete independence. Louis brought that situation to an end by cutting off the finance for local troops and rotating the postings of governors so that power and control shifted to the centre, to Louis himself. With that centralized power, Louis began reforming the French army, especially the infantry, which he noted, as late as 1666, was not very good.[24] As with other armies of the day, the French army was a collection of units rather than a cohesive force. Discipline was poor and often non-existent, while weaponry, organization, pay and clothing were far from uniform; a regiment might have several companies in different uniforms and of differing strengths. As for pay: sometimes it arrived and sometimes it did not, and this was one of the greatest causes of indiscipline.

The reform process was begun by Michelle le Tellier, Louis' secretary of war, but it was le Tellier's son, the Marquis de Louvois, who achieved his monarch's aim of creating a thoroughly professional and effective fighting force.[25] To Louvois and Louis belong the credit for creating the first truly modern army, to which most modern armies owe their genesis. In the new French army, discipline and loyalty to the monarch were core features; the corruption that had existed hitherto was stamped out by making examples of corrupt officers, and morale increased, especially when soldiers realized that their officers had to become conversant with the skills of warfare. No longer were commissions to be awarded as sinecures, and, since officers now recognized that their careers depended on demonstrating professionalism, the sales of military training manuals increased exponentially. Within the rank and file, soldiers took pride in their new uniforms and were pleased that their pay was arriving regularly. Thus both officers and other ranks were keen to become more professional.

This new era of professionalism was embodied in one commanding officer whose regiment became a byword for effective and disciplined service. This was Jean de Martinet, lieutenant-colonel of le Regiment du Roi (The King's Regiment). Martinet trained his regiment so well that it became an exemplar during the 1667 campaign, the War of Devolution, and its practices and procedures were commended to the rest of the army, both infantry and cavalry, and adopted as standard practice. Sadly for Martinet, his name has become synonymous with that form of rigid discipline that demands blind obedience, something with which he, and his soldiers, would have been unfamiliar.[26]

Expansion of the Royal Army was also facilitated by the practice of keeping officers of disbanded regiments in service with the Guards' units, thereby creating a cadre of professionals who could raise new regiments whenever necessary. In 1688 Louis also introduced conscription through what was known as a militia draft.[27] By the time the European war reached out to engulf Ireland, the Royal Army already numbered about a third of a million men and was destined to increase to almost 500,000, and the largest in Europe, by 1694. That figure would not be exceeded for a century until another French leader, Napoleon Bonaparte, created his Grande Armée.

This powerful Royal Army allowed Louis XIV to expand France's frontiers through military muscle. He was attempting to create a defensive buffer, or *ceinture de fer* (iron belt), around his country, in much the same manner as the Soviet Union's domination of Eastern Europe provided a defensive buffer for Russia in the decades following the Second World War. In Louis' view, the natural frontiers of France were formed by the Rhine to the east and the Pyrenees to the south with Spanish Flanders, present-day Belgium, as an integral part of France. Military power was used to dominate and intimidate Europe as Louis pushed to make France's frontiers more easily defensible, at less cost to France, by creating the *pré carré*, or square field.

Needless to say, other European states were not happy with French policy. The Dutch were especially reluctant to see Louis XIV's France try to establish dominion over the continent. They had but recently thrown off the control of the Spanish empire and were not willing to become a vassal of France. Regardless of his neighbours' views, Louis continued to expand to what he considered the natural and logical frontiers of France: Artois, Lorraine and Franche-Comté, all French-speaking areas, were annexed and integrated into France in spite of opposition from neighbouring states. Then, in 1681, Louis seized Alsace, an area that was German-speaking. In doing so, he set the trigger for a process that would create long-lasting alliances between states that shared few interests other than the checking of Louis' expansionist policy. Only through such alliances could the other states in Europe stand against France since the latter was by far the largest state in Europe: in 1661, when Louis took personal power, the population of France numbered some 18 million souls, whereas Habsburg

Austria had about eight million and both England and Spain some six million each. It did not require a Cartesian genius to realize that none of these states could stand alone against France.

Louis also succeeded in making an enemy of the Pope, Innocent XI, by his refusal to accede to a papal request to go to the assistance of Austria when Turkish forces laid siege to Vienna in 1683. Although the Austrians beat off the attackers – and celebrated their success by creating a new cake in the form of the Islamic crescent, the *croissant* – the Pope was not to forgive Louis, and friction between the pair increased in 1688 when Innocent refused to appoint a Frenchman to the archbishopric of Cologne. The man was Louis' candidate and the Sun King's anger led to the invasion of the Rhineland which, in turn, triggered William of Orange's invasion of England. By now, Austria, Sweden and several German states had formed the League of Augsburg – created in 1686 – to counter French expansionism. Also a member of the League was the Dutch Republic, and William of Orange was to become the leading figure of the League. William's invasion of England in 1688 was intended to bring that country into the League against France. Pope Innocent XI gave the League his blessing, thereby creating a Catholic-Protestant alliance against the world's most powerful Catholic monarch, and this in an age when religious affiliations were very important. Louis was left with only one ally in Europe, King James II of England, who was forced into exile after William's invasion of his country. James had supported Louis' candidate for the archepiscopacy of Cologne and thereby incurred the wrath of both the pope and the Austrian emperor.

It was the exiled James II who was to become Louis' surrogate leader in Ireland, rallying Irish Catholics and Jacobites in a campaign to take control of the island. (Louis' intentions, however, were limited to using James as a distraction to keep William away from the continent.) Ireland was to be the scene for a war that lasted some three years and which devastated much of the country. In Irish history the war has become known as the 'war of the two kings' but it ought, more accurately, to be styled the 'war of the three kings' for, although he was never present in Ireland Louis' was the hand that did most to precipitate that war.

Why had James II been forced into exile? Although the traditional answer is that he fled the country of his own volition and thus abdicated, the truth is not quite so simple. Since King Charles II had no legitimate male heirs, the crown was likely to pass to his brother, James,

Duke of York, unless James predeceased Charles. James had converted to Catholicism and there had been a move to exclude him from the succession in 1678 but this, the Exclusion Bill, had come to naught, being defeated in the House of Lords, and when Charles II died in 1685 James II's religious affiliation was not perceived as a threat by Parliament since he had no legitimate male heir to succeed him, thereby establishing a Catholic dynasty. Instead, the crown would pass to James' daughter Mary, who was married to James' nephew, William Henry Nassau, Stadtholder of the Dutch Republic and Prince of Orange.[28]

This state of affairs changed when James' second wife, Mary of Modena, gave birth to a son and raised the threat of Protestant England being ruled by Catholics.[29] Allegations were made that the queen had borne a daughter but that a boy had been smuggled into the royal bedchamber in a warming pan.* These claims were part of a propaganda campaign to deny the new-born Prince of Wales his birthright but even then the thought of a Catholic succession might have been tolerable had it not been for James' attitude to Parliament. Although his own father, Charles I, had been executed by Parliament for opposing that institution, James failed to appreciate the lesson of his father's fate: that, having shown its muscle already in his lifetime, Parliament was capable of repeating the performance. James seemed to believe in the divine right of kings and was determined to be the real power in the land, as was Louis XIV in France. The power struggle that ensued and which led to the war in Ireland, and Scotland, had much more to do with the rights of Parliament than with religion.

Although James was an enthusiastic Catholic, as is often the case with converts, the charges that he was a bigot are unfounded.[30] Although he proclaimed that he wished all his people to enjoy the Catholic faith as he did, he added the rider that 'our blessed Saviour whipt people out of the temple, but I never heard he commanded any should be forced into it'.[31] In his day James II was a man of considerable tolerance and while he is remembered for instigating a policy of reverse discrimination, placing Catholics in positions of influence and power where and when he could, it is forgotten that he also included non-conformists in that policy, as they suffered the same disabilities as the Catholics. James took care to advise his lord deputy in Ireland, Richard Talbot, Earl of Tyrconnel, to be generous to the Presbyterians

---

*This had a long-lasting effect which continued until the present reign which required all royal births to be witnessed on behalf of Parliament. This requirement has now been dropped.

of Ulster – advice that Talbot ignored with disastrous consequences for his and James' cause.[32] Implementing his new policy required the repeal of legislation that restricted the rights of Catholics and non-conformists, but this necessitated the support of Parliament. However, that body was composed entirely of Anglicans who benefited from those laws and were, therefore, unlikely to repeal them to their own detriment. To bring about the changes he wanted, James II would have to follow the example of Louis XIV by proroguing Parliament and assuming absolute power. Such a step was guaranteed to bring King and Parliament into conflict.

James' attitude to Parliament had created a momentum that threatened to lead to another civil war and his son-in-law, and nephew, William of Orange decided to travel to England to persuade his father-in-law to adopt a more conciliatory tone. William knew that none of his Catholic allies in the League of Augsburg, and especially Austria's Emperor Leopold, would tolerate the deposing of any monarch, above all a Catholic, by a fellow head of state; the one exception to this rule was, of course, Louis XIV. Events overtook both William and James as a small group of influential Englishmen invited William to come to England and take the throne. The invitation was not issued by Parliament, although it is a popular belief that such was the case. When William landed in Devon on 5 November 1688 at the head of an army of 15,000 men, the largest invasion force ever to land in Britain, James led his army to Salisbury to meet the invaders.[33] William might have expected a warm welcome from the people of the West Country, but if he did he was mistaken: following Monmouth's defeat in 1685 that part of the country had been ruled rigorously and the 'Bloody Assizes' had left such an impression that the reception for William was quite cool.[34] Had James seized the initiative 'and appealed to the national dislike of foreigners to rouse his subjects against the Dutch the issue would hardly have been in doubt'.[35] Instead he vacillated and appeared to be more concerned about gaining time for the Queen and the infant Prince of Wales to leave the country than in fighting the Dutchman. This lack of resolution, which he attributed to a nosebleed, lost him the confidence of his commander in chief, John Churchill, later the first Duke of Marlborough. Churchill decided that he was on the losing side, and switched his allegiance to the Dutchman leaving James' army in turmoil; a third of its officers followed Churchill, another third remained loyal to James, and the remainder resigned their commissions. Nor had the Royal Navy, of which James had been high admiral, been able to stop the Dutch fleet due to adverse wind conditions; it was said that a 'Protestant wind' brought William to

Britain. Betrayed by his commander in chief and, apparently, failed by his navy, James II panicked and fled for refuge to France.

The king's panic-stricken departure left London in a state of anarchy with rioters attacking Catholics and burning buildings and the homes of foreign diplomats; the Spanish ambassador's home was among three that were destroyed. To try to restore the situation, a group of peers, under the presidency of the Marquis of Halifax, who was to become Lord Privy Seal, met at London's Guildhall and, on 21 December, twenty-nine of the peers declared that they would unite themselves with William of Orange and undertake to maintain order until his arrival in London. James' departure allowed a constitutional settlement to be reached quickly. An election was held and the convention formed thereby began the work of reaching a settlement. This was not a proper parliament since there had not been a royal summons but it was understood that its work would be affirmed later by a regular parliament. It was this convention that declared that James had abdicated and which, on 23 February 1689, invited William and Mary to take the throne. William had refused to hold any position that would make him subordinate to his wife and this ruled out the option of Queen Mary with a prince consort, or of William as a regent. The coronation followed on 11 April 1689, by which date James was in Ireland, where, because of the separate Irish Parliament, he was still legally the monarch.[36] However, William, now William III, was able to proclaim that he had been given the crown rather than having taken it.

James arrived in Ireland on 12 March 1689, landing at Kinsale, the nearest major port to mainland Europe.* He found considerable support since Richard Talbot had created a Catholic army and a Catholic civil service. In addition, he had the support of Louis although, as already noted, that support was limited to using James' presence in Ireland to distract William from the conflict on the European mainland. A Jacobite army in Ireland, with James at its head, and the backing of France, meant that William would have to guard his back and undertake a campaign in Ireland, albeit unwanted, to contain James' army. That campaign would mean the deployment of many English troops who might otherwise have joined the forces of the League of Augsburg on the mainland. And there was a bonus for Louis in that James also enjoyed considerable support in Scotland – he was, after all, a Stuart – and success in Ireland would allow James to move to

---

*Although this may be seen as a significant event in Irish history there is nothing in Kinsale today to mark the arrival of King James

Scotland, thus increasing the threat to England. Louis' strategy was working well.

The new joint monarch of England and Scotland, William III, was a paradoxical figure. He came from Europe's only republic, The Netherlands, where he had been born, less than forty years before, in 1650, in the Binnenhoft Palace in The Hague. His mother was Charles II's daughter but William never knew his father who died before his only child was born. William's great-grandfather was William the Silent, the man who had led The Netherlands to independence from Spain; this began a family tradition of being champions of Protestantism. Following a lonely childhood and a strict religious education, William Henry Nassau* became a gifted statesman as well as Stadtholder of the Dutch Republic. His qualities as a statesman are illustrated by his cementing the League of Augsburg, an unlikely and disparate alliance, and by his success as stadtholder, where he worked in union with the States General, the Dutch ruling body. Arguably, he was the most suitable candidate to be a constitutional monarch, which is what he became in Britain. In fact, William III saved the monarchy and created the institution that we know today. This is often forgotten amidst the claims that William secured civil and religious liberty in Britain. His true legacy is the modern monarchy. With James in exile, Parliament could have deposed him as it did with his father and declared a second British republic in less than fifty years. Few wanted that, however, and William proved to be the ideal compromise as a monarch who would rule with Parliament, allowing precedence to the latter.

These were the three kings who would bring war to Ireland, a war that included the famous siege of Londonderry. By the end of 1688, with William already in England and James in exile in France, war had already broken out in Ireland and the people of Londonderry felt threatened.

Notes

1: Hughes, *Military Architecture*, Ch 3 'Renaissance Fortifications' deals with this change but see especially pp. 62–77.
2: Chandler, *The Art of Warfare in the Age of Marlborough*, p. 69

---

*William's family held large estates in Nassau and were counts of Nassau. In spite of his religious upbringing, William was a very tolerant man and made no distinctions between Catholics and Protestants; his Blue Guards were mostly Catholic and their loyalty to William was unquestioning.

3: Lacy, *Siege City*, p. 19
4: Ibid, p. 10
5: Ibid, p. 8
6: Thomas, *Derry-Londonderry*, p. 1
7: NA Kew, ADM1/11935
8: Lacy, op cit, pp. 9–32
9: Simpson, *Annals of Derry*, p. 19
10: Ibid; Lacy, op cit, p. 68
11: Simpson, op cit, p. 19; Lacy, op cit, pp. 69–70
12: Simpson, op cit, pp. 21–3; Lacy, op cit, pp. 72–7
13: Simpson, op cit, pp. 25–6; Lacy, pp. 78–80
14: Lacy, op cit, pp. 81–87; Simpson, op cit, pp. 28–33; Macrory, *The Siege of Derry*, pp. 68–80
15: Simpson, op cit, pp. 34–5
16: Scott et al, *The Cannon from the City of Derry*, p. 118
17: Lacy, op cit, pp. 90–1
18: Milligan, *The Walls of Derry*, p. 33
19: Ibid, p. 122
20: Lacy, op cit, p. 100; further information from St Columb's Cathedral.
21: Ibid, p. 25 & p. 95
22: Chartrand, *Louis XIV's Army*, p. 11
23: Ibid, p. 8
24: Ibid, pp. 7–8
25: Ibid, p. 8
26: Ibid, p. 10
27: Ibid, p. 11
28: Harris, *Revolution*, pp. 1–2
29: Clark, *The Later Stuarts*, p. 117
30: Ibid, p. 127
31: Stewart, *The Narrow Ground*, pp. 63–4
32: Quoted in Maguire, *Kings in Conflict*, p. 54
33: Ibid
34: These were the Earls of Devonshire, Danby and Shrewsbury, the Bishop of London, Henry Compton, Lord Lumley, Edward Russell and Henry Sidney. Harris – op cit, p. 3 – describes their letter as 'incredible' since it was 'an invitation to a foreign power from high-ranking political and religious figures to invade their own country'.
35: Clark, op cit, pp. 138–9
36: Ibid, p. 139
37: Ibid
38: Ibid, pp. 142–153

Ireland in 1689

✕   Major battle

Atlantic Ocean

Rathlin
Island

Coleraine

Newtownlimavady

Londonderry

Foyle

Carrickfergus

Killybegs

Donegal

*Lough
Neagh*

Ballyshannon

*Lower
Lough
Erne*

Charlemont

Belfast

Bangor

Sligo

Enniskillen

*Upper
Lough
Erne*

Newtownbutler

Dundalk

Drogheda

*Irish
Sea*

*Lough
Ree*

Boyne

*Lough
Corrib*

Aughrim

Athlone

Dublin

Liffey

Galway

*Lough
Derg*

Wicklow

Shannon

Barrow

Limerick

Kilkenny

Tralee

Wexford

Waterford

Cork

Kinsale

Bantry Bay

CHAPTER TWO

The Closing of the Gates

When King James II came to the throne in 1685 on the death of his brother Charles II, there were expectations in Ireland that the social and political situation of the country's Catholics might improve. Those Catholics who had lost land and property during the Cromwellian period had hoped that the restoration of the monarchy would see a reversal of the confiscations that had taken place under the Commonwealth with a repeal of the Acts of Settlement that, in 1652, had gifted land to supporters of the parliamentary cause and placed two-thirds of all the land in Ireland into Protestant hands. But Charles II, although sympathetic to the plight of the Catholic gentry – who had, after all, provided him with much support and many officers for his army in exile – adopted a pragmatic stance. Realizing that he had been restored to the throne by the army of the Commonwealth and that to upset the parliamentarians could well lead to a second, and possibly permanent, spell of exile, Charles chose to do little and his Irish Catholic subjects were disappointed.

The little that Charles did do was enshrined in a declaration of 30 November 1660 by which those Cromwellian adventurers and soldiers who had been given land in lieu of pay that was due to them were allowed to hold whatever estates were theirs on 7 May 1659. Nonetheless there were some exceptions: Ormonde and other loyalists were to have all their property restored and the Church of Ireland was to be treated likewise, as were all Anglicans who had lost property. Some Catholics, those who had remained loyal to the crown since 22 October 1642, were also to have their property restored while those Cromwellians who had been in possession of it were to receive compensation. Sir Charles Petrie considered that Charles would never have signed the declaration 'had his information concerning conditions in Ireland been more accurate, or had he paid the briefest of visits to the country'. Petrie provided no evidence to substantiate his theory.

But King James II was considered to be a very different individual. As Duke of York he had adopted Catholicism with enthusiasm and much was hoped from him. There were signs that he might be willing to improve the situation of Catholic landowners whose property had been confiscated under Cromwell. Such hopes may have been raised when James removed the incumbent viceroy, the Duke of Ormonde, and replaced him with Henry Hyde, second Earl of Clarendon and his own brother-in-law. A contemporary commentator wrote that

> The Duke of Ormonde, lord-lieutenant of Ireland, is removed from that government, and two lords justices appointed for that purpose at present: his [Ormonde's] regiment is given to Col. Talbot: the privy council is dissolved, and a new one appointed, and some talk as if there were a design for the papists regaining their estates in that kingdom.

The two lords justices were the Archbishop of Armagh and the Earl of Granard. The Colonel Talbot to whom Ormonde's Regiment was given was Richard Talbot, of Malahide,* a close friend and confidant of James II. Ormonde had expected to be succeeded by Laurence Hyde, Earl of Rochester, but the latter showed no desire to take up the appointment, which then passed to his elder brother Henry. Not only was Richard Talbot given command of Ormonde's regiment but he was also ennobled as Baron of Talbotstown, Viscount Baltinglas and Earl of Tyrconnel. It was by the last title, which had once belonged to The O'Donnell, that Talbot was to be best known and remembered. He was also promoted to the rank of lieutenant-general and appointed commander-in-chief of the army in Ireland.

Clarendon and Tyrconnel were not men who could work together. The former lacked his father's ability but had inherited his narrowness of mind while harbouring a dislike of Irishmen and Catholics in general and of Talbot, now Tyrconnel, in particular. Some contemporaries felt that James intended that the two should neutralize each other but 'the elevation of Tyrconnel to the peerage and to the rank of Lieutenant-General was as far as James felt he could safely go for the moment . . . it was only the first step in a revolution of the Irish administration'.

Initially, Tyrconnel did nothing overt against Clarendon who did not travel to Dublin until January 1686. Thereafter there was friction between the pair, with Tyrconnel doing his utmost to undermine Clarendon and force James to recall the viceroy. In February 1687 the

---

*Talbot belonged to 'a Pale family of Anglo-Irish stock' and was part of what is sometimes called the 'new Irish'.

viceroy resigned but, although Tyrconnel hoped to be appointed in his stead, James was unwilling to give him that title. Rather Tyrconnel was made lord deputy in Ireland but since, effectively, he was the viceroy, he set about reforming the military and civil services in the country. Whereas James had instructed Tyrconnel to treat Catholics and Protestants alike, the lord deputy had his own agenda and began purging both the army and the administration of Protestants, replacing them with Catholics. Tyrconnel, 'a fighting man, truculent and ambitious', was the brother of a former Catholic archbishop of Dublin and was married to Frances Jennings, a sister of Sarah, later to be the first Duchess of Marlborough. A very ambitious individual, Tyrconnel 'worked whole-heartedly . . . to build up the royal power in Ireland; but on a catholic basis'. In the long term, however, he did more to bring about James' defeat in Ireland than almost any other individual or factor.

One of Tyrconnel's first measures as lord deputy was to reform the councils and corporations of Ireland which were entirely Protestant in their composition with Catholics denied seats. At first Tyrconnel suggested that Catholics and Protestants should have equal representation on councils but when this proposal was rejected he invoked the royal prerogative to issue an order in council that called in the charters of the towns and cities. Most councils accepted this, but among the few that did not were those of Londonderry and Dublin. The recalcitrant councils were brought into line by the courts, which decided that the king could do as he wished with their charters as he had awarded them in the first instance. James commented that there was 'no great trouble except at Londonderry (a stubborn people, as they appeared to be afterwards), who stood an obstinate suit, but were forced at last to undergo the same fate with the rest'. Tyrconnel issued another order in council that warned those clerics who pronounced from the pulpit on matters political that there would be penalties should such oratory persist.

The Irish army was a separate establishment from that of England – and a further discrete establishment was maintained in Scotland – and was paid for from the monarch's personal purse rather than by Parliament which voted the funds for the English army.[1] In 1684, the year before James came to the throne, the army of Ireland included a troop of Horse Guards, the Regiment of Guards in the Kingdom of Ireland, twenty-four troops of cavalry and seventy-five companies of infantry, giving an overall force of some 1,400 horse and 6,400 foot soldiers.[2] The Irish army was deficient in artillery, the third major arm or fighting element, but contemporary practice was to raise a train of artillery for each campaign or war rather than to maintain a permanent body of artillery. In England the artillery was the responsibility of the Board of Ordnance rather than the army and came under command of the Master-General of the Ordnance;[3] a similar arrangement existed in Ireland where Lord Mountjoy was Master-General of the Irish Ordnance.[4] The English Board of Ordnance equated to a department of government and the Master-General of the Ordnance had responsibility for all matters related to the artillery and those services associated with it: manufacturing, testing and maintaining the weapons; recruiting and training gunners and their teams; ensuring the availability of munitions and other necessary stores.[5] His responsibility extended to engineering services and supplies as well as the upkeep of fortresses (the letters BO can be seen to this day on many such buildings) and to the Royal Navy, for which he also oversaw the provision of weaponry and other associated stores. During 1684 the Irish army was reorganized into regiments so that when James became king in 1685 there were three cavalry and seven infantry regiments in his army in Ireland. Some permanent Irish artillery had been formed under Mountjoy's command (he assumed his post in 1684) but the Irish Board of Ordnance was subject to that in London. In 1685 a regiment of dragoons was also added to the Irish army's order of battle.[6]

The officers and soldiers of the Irish army had not been confined to service at home. Since the monarch had more discretion in the employment of his Irish forces than those in England, some of his Irish troops had seen service on the continent, often on loan to other monarchs, and even in Tangier.* Irish forces had also been prepared for service in Scotland on two occasions; these expeditions, which were cancelled, would have seen them fight against the Covenanters. However, the army's primary employment had been as a police force within Ireland; soldiers were posted in small groups throughout the country to combat tories, or thieves. Thus it was not an effective military force; it was considered inefficient and was, at times, close to mutiny, although poor pay may have provided much of the reason for this latter state. Prospects for this army being successful in action were poor; the contrast with the contemporary French army could not have been greater.[7]

---

*Three central figures in the siege, Robert Lundy, Henry Baker and Jonathan Mitchelburne, had served in Tangier, while Percy Kirke, who commanded the relief force, was another Tangier veteran.

With Talbot's appointment as lord deputy, the army was faced with further changes as a purge of Protestant officers and soldiers began. This followed the disbandment of the militia which had been almost entirely Protestant.[8] By the time James landed at Kinsale in March 1689 Talbot had removed more than 4,000 Protestants, about a tenth of whom were officers. Talbot's plan to convert the Irish army to a largely Catholic force was pushed through in quick time. In 1685 there were fewer than a thousand Catholic soldiers but their numbers had increased almost fivefold by the end of 1686, a period of only eighteen months. One of the last regiments that Talbot set out to purge was the garrison regiment in Londonderry, commanded by William Stewart, Lord Mountjoy, of Ramelton in County Donegal, which was ordered to Dublin in November 1688. Mountjoy's lieutenant-colonel was a Scot, Robert Lundy, who had seen much service and was to be one of the central figures of the siege. We shall see later how the attempted replacement of Mountjoy's Regiment with the Earl of Antrim's Regiment was a major factor in events at Londonderry.

William III disbanded the Irish army, which was now James' army anyway, with the exception of a single regiment which had been deployed to England. The latter was Forbes's Regiment, later to become the Royal Irish, the senior Irish line infantry regiment* of the British Army, from which William removed all Catholics. Similar purges of Catholics took place throughout the English army. Although William might have declared it disbanded, the Irish army continued in existence and began expanding its infantry establishment; there were thirty-five regiments by May 1689. The normal complement of a regiment was thirteen companies, each nominally sixty strong, but many mustered fewer men. This Irish Jacobite army also included two battalions of foot guards, seven regiments of horse, seven dragoon regiments and a troop of horse grenadiers. By the time that Londonderry became the front line in the war in Ireland the Jacobite army had increased to about sixty regiments, with some infantry units having as many as forty-five companies, an unmanageable order of battle. A process of rationalization in 1689 reduced this figure to forty-five infantry regiments, nine cavalry, including a Life Guard, and eight dragoon regiments. One contemporary account suggests that the army increased to 60,000 soldiers before being reduced to 35,000.

---

*The infantry arm included two elements: the foot guards and the infantry of the line.

A similar situation had arisen with the English army which had lost most of its officers following John Churchill's defection to William. With only one-third of its experienced officers remaining in service, the army faced many problems, especially as it tried to expand, and, during the Irish campaign, these had often appalling consequences for its soldiers while testing the faith of William and his Dutch commanders in their English soldiery.

Needless to say, the rapid expansion in the Irish army also caused many problems, not the least of which was in supply. It is hardly surprising that logistics were to prove the greatest weakness of the Jacobite army at war. Many Jacobite soldiers were neither equipped nor clothed properly, with contemporary accounts showing that large numbers went to war in their everyday clothing while carrying cudgels, sticks and a variety of agricultural implements as weapons.[10] Training also suffered, there not being sufficient time, nor enough instructors, to drill them in all the skills necessary for waging war, although some summer camps of instruction were held. Small wonder that this army was described as a 'rabble' by friend and foe alike. However, during 1689 standards improved considerably, in some part due to a decision by Patrick Sarsfield to dismiss all those who did not meet his standards; Sarsfield's action followed the 1689 campaign and thus did not affect events at Londonderry. These comments apply only to the Jacobite infantry since the cavalry was a very different story and, from the start, Jacobite cavalry were recognized as the match of anything that any other European nation could put into the field. As the cavalry were seen as the *arme blanche* of most armies, commissions in cavalry regiments were the most attractive to officers, and those regiments tended to number the socially elite in their ranks.[11] This was also the case with the Jacobite cavalry with many officers drawn from those Irish Catholics who had served Charles II but who had been sent to the continent to do so; perhaps the best-known example of one of these men was Sarsfield, who was to earn distinction as one of the outstanding soldiers of his generation.[12]

In spite of its shortcomings, when the Jacobite army first took the field it enjoyed significant success. Much of this might have been due to the even greater shortcomings of the army's Williamite opponents, but the morale effect of that success should not be understated. We have already seen that James, having fled into exile in France, had arrived in Ireland on 12 March 1689, landing at Kinsale. He had the support of Louis XIV and also found that Talbot had created a Catholic army and

Catholic civil service in Ireland, James, however, was now becoming a pawn in the European power struggle in which the two principal figures were Louis and William. Although James hoped to regain his kingdoms, this was not an inherent part of Louis' strategy. The latter saw James' presence in Ireland, with a large army and French support, as something to distract William from the main conflict in Europe.

The French monarch's strategy would compel William to guard his back. He would be forced to undertake a campaign in Ireland to contain the threat from James and would have to deploy English forces that might otherwise have reinforced the armies of the League of Augsburg on the mainland. And, of course, as we have seen, the Jacobite threat was not confined to Ireland since James also enjoyed considerable support in Scotland – where he was King James VII. Success in Ireland would allow James to move to Scotland, thus increasing the threat to England. This was to be James' strategy, which he hoped would lead eventually to his return to London. Louis had every reason to be happy with his strategy.

By the time James arrived in Ireland his forces had enjoyed considerable success in Ulster. Early the previous December, an anonymous letter, addressed to Lord Mount-Alexander and dated 3 December, was, allegedly, found in Comber, a small village in County Down. Written in a semi-literate hand, or the hand of someone wishing to be considered semi-literate, the letter read:

> Good my Lord, I have written to you to let you know that all our Irishmen through Ireland is sworn that on the ninth day of this month they are to fall on to kill and murder man, wife and child; and I desire your Lordship to take care of yourself and all others that are judged by our men to be heads, for whosoever can kill any of you, they are to have a captain's place; so my desire to your honour is to look to yourself and give other noblemen warning, and go not out either night or day without a good guard with you, and let no Irishman come near you, whatsoever he be; so is from him who was your father's friend, and is your friend, and will be, though I dare not be known as yet for fear of my life.[13]

The 'Comber letter', as it became known, has long been considered a hoax but it was a very dangerous hoax in the atmosphere of the time in Ulster. Memories of the 1641 rebellion and the atrocities that accompanied it were still very strong and there were many still living who could remember those days. Thus the letter served to increase fears that a similar rebellion was in the planning and Protestants felt especially vulnerable since the changes effected in the army by Tyrconnel left them without any guarantee of protection from that body.

News of the 'Comber letter' spread across Ulster very quickly. Panic followed, and many Protestants opted to flee the country, joining relatives in England or Scotland, where their imported panic spread along with frightening stories of the fate of their co-religionists left behind in Ireland. However, the majority of Ireland's Protestants remained in the country and made ready to defend family, home and land against whatever might befall them. Tyrconnel had tried to call in all the arms in the country but many weapons remained in Protestant hands and the Protestant people of Ireland had the consolation that almost every gunsmith in the country was of their faith.

Copies of the 'Comber letter' were circulating throughout Ulster and beyond. Some copies reached Dublin and led to such shock and anger that Tyrconnel called the city's leading Protestants to Dublin Castle. At this meeting he denied the existence of any plot such as that suggested in the letter and called the wrath of God down on his own head if the letter was anything other than a 'cursed, a blasted, a confounded lie'. His protestations did him no good. If anything, they added to Protestant fears since Tyrconnel was already regarded as an untrustworthy individual, with the soubriquet 'Lying Dick'; many were prepared to believe that a denial by such a man was proof positive that the threat contained in the letter was real.

A copy of the letter had been sent to George Canning of Garvagh, in County Londonderry, who sent a copy to Alderman Tomkins in Londonderry and to George Phillips in Newtownlimavady.* Phillips received his copy of the letter on 6 December and must have felt that it contained the truth when he heard that Antrim's Regiment, en route to Londonderry to replace Mountjoy's, was about to arrive in his town. Antrim's Regiment, known as the Redshanks, was to stay overnight in Newtownlimavady. The unit must have been an impressive sight; it numbered some 1,200 men recruited from the glens of Antrim and the Scottish highlands.

George Phillips, who had been governor of Londonderry, immediately sent two messengers to the city to warn Alderman Norman to gather 'the sober people of the town and to set out the danger of

---

*The village of Limavady (Leim an Mhadaidh, the dog's leap) was also settled in the plantation and a new town created in 1624. The prefix 'Newtown' was applied to the existing name. During the nineteenth century the prefix fell out of use but still appears in the coat of arms of the local council

admitting such guests among them'. It appears that Phillips believed that his first message was not worded strongly enough since the second messenger's despatch advised that the city's gates should be closed against Antrim's men. This would amount to an act of rebellion. Furthermore, Phillips told Norman that he and his friends would come to the city the following day to join the local people and stand by them.[14]

Phillips' first messenger reached the city as Alderman Tomkins was reading his copy of the Comber letter to a gathering of concerned citizens. Their concern increased considerably when Phillips' warning arrived. The people of the city were now faced with a dilemma: the letter warned of a massacre of Protestants that would begin on 9 December, and the impending arrival of Antrim's Regiment suggested that they might prove to be the first victims of that massacre with the earl's soldiers the instrument of slaughter.[15] Thus admitting the Redshanks to the city might lead to mass murder but refusing them entry would be an act of rebellion that might be put down by military action. After all, the soldiers and their commanding officer were acting on the orders of Tyrconnel who was the king's lord deputy, and James II was still the only lawful king. Denying James' soldiers entry to the city might bring upon the townspeople the fate that had befallen the Duke of Monmouth's followers in 1685 since shutting the gates against Antrirn's men would make rebels of the Protestant citizens of the city. Had not Lord Mountjoy, in answer to a deputation from Enniskillen seeking his advice, recommended that they submit to the king's authority since 'the King will protect you'? For people conditioned to accept lawful authority the suggestion that they refuse to do so represented a major dilemma.

But refuse to accept lawful authority they did. However, the story is not quite as simple as that statement suggests. Those who refused to accept the lawful authority were not the men of means and middle age who held authority in the city and who normally made civic decisions. These worthies debated the problem as is the habit of such men the world over, and members of the city's corporation and the Anglican bishop, Dr Ezekiel Hopkins, advised that Antrim's Regiment should be allowed into the city. The bishop argued that these were the king's soldiers and, since the king was God's anointed, an affront to the soldiers would be an affront to the king. Presumably the bishop also felt that it would be an affront to God; he was a believer in the divine right of kings. Bishop Hopkins' views would have been shared by most of the city's secular leaders and prominent citizens since these men would all have been members of the Anglican communion. Presbyterians, or Dissenters, held a social standing similar to that of Catholics, and it is unlikely that many Presbyterians were involved in the debate. However, the argument was taken, literally, out of the hands of the civic and religious leaders. A group of young men, apprentices in the city, seized the keys to the city's four gates and, shutting each of the gates, locked them against the soldiers.[16]

By that time the leading elements of Antrim's Regiment had crossed the Foyle by the ferry and were approaching the Ferry Gate. These were the officers and men of what today might be known as the commanding officer's reconnaissance, or R, group. In fact, two of Antrim's officers were already inside the city walls and were involved in discussions with some of the citizens. As with Caesar's crossing of the Rubicon, the apprentices had cast the die for their city; the first irrevocable act of defiance had been taken against the rule of King James II in Ulster.

What of the boys who had closed the gates? They were apprentices, and their names are known to history, but those names are usually subsumed in the corporate identity of 'the apprentice boys of Derry'. In number they were thirteen and their names were William Cairnes, Henry Campsie, William Crookshanks, Alexander Cunningham, John Cunningham, Samuel Harvey, Samuel Hunt, Alexander Irwin, Robert Morrison, Daniel Sherrard, Robert Sherrard, James Spike (or Spaight) and James Steward.[17] Little is known about them but they were probably Presbyterians who were not convinced as deeply of the concept of divine right as their Anglican brothers and it is also possible that their act of defiance may have been sparked by the Reverend James Gordon, a Presbyterian minister, who had called for the gates to be closed as had a small number of other citizens.[18] Their action may also have been initiated by the arrival of George Phillips' second messenger with the order to close the gates.

A further possible spur to their actions, or perhaps a result of their actions – we do not know the exact time frame – came from another citizen, James Morrison, who was standing on the walls at the Ferry Gate at about the time that gate was shut. Morrison called on the Redshanks below to be off and is said to have barked an order to bring 'a great gun' to the gate.[19] Whatever the truth of the Morrison story, those soldiers outside the gate did return to the quay, boarded the ferry and crossed to the east bank of the Foyle to rejoin the remainder of Antrim's Regiment. Had there been any intention of massacring the citizens one would have expected Antrim to order his men to assault the city, which could not have provided much resistance, and wipe out its people. That this did not happen would suggest that the fears of local people were unfounded and that the Comber letter was a cruel hoax.

What did happen at this stage was that Tyrconnel had a rethink of his plan to Catholicize Mountjoy's Regiment, most of which was ordered to return to Derry. Mountjoy came back to the city with his regiment but did not remain there. While Mountjoy returned to Dublin, on Tyrconnel's orders, the regiment came under the command of his lieutenant-colonel, the Scot Robert Lundy, who was well known to the local citizenry; his daughter, Aromintho, had been baptized in St Columb's Cathedral on 17 May1686.[20]

Having seen off Antrim's Regiment, the people of Derry were in no mood to accept Mountjoy's Regiment at face value and when it arrived at the city its soldiers, too, found the gates closed against them.

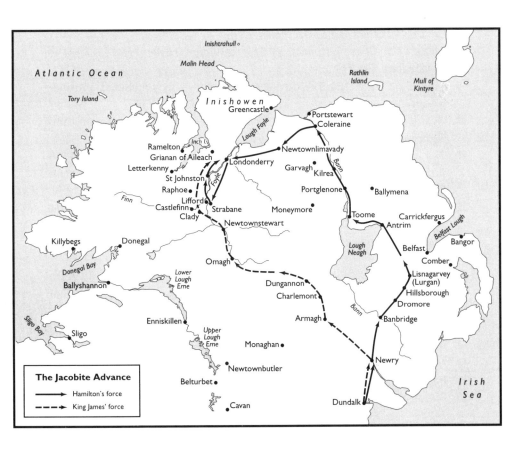

Notes

The principal source in this chapter for information on constitutional developments is *The Great Tyrconnel: A Chapter in Anglo-Irish Relations* by Sir Charles Petrie and, particularly, Chapters V, VI and VII. All other sources are as noted below.

1: Doherty, *The Williamite War in Ireland 1688–1691*, p. 23; Murtagh & Murtagh, *The Irish Jacobite Army*, 1689–91, Irish Sword Vol XVIII, No. 70, p. 32; Bartlett & Jeffery, *A Military History of Ireland*, p. 189; Childs, *The Army of Charles II*, p. 196.

2: Murtagh & Murtagh, op cit, p. 32; Doherty, op cit, p. 23;

3: Wilson, *The Story of the Gun*, p. 14; Murtagh, *Jacobite Artillery*, 1689–91, *Irish Sword* Vol XXIII, No. 94, p. 383.

4: Murtagh, Jacobite Artillery, 1689 – 91, op cit, pp. 383–4.

5: Chandler, *The Art of Warfare in the Age of Marlborough*, p. 154.

6: Murtagh & Murtagh, op cit, p. 32; Murtagh, *Jacobite Artillery*, op cit, p. 383.

7: Bredin, *A History of the Irish Soldier*, p. 98.

8: Petrie, *The Great Tyrconnel*, p. 153; Milligan, *History of The Siege of Londonderry*, pp. 7–9.

9: Bredin, op cit, p. 100; The final establishment in 1689 included a further ten infantry regiments (Murtagh & Murtagh, op cit, p. 33).

10: Avaux makes many references to the lack of uniform, weaponry and equipment among the Irish soldiery.

11: The combat strength of the Irish cavalry was between 2,500 and 4,000 during the war and there was a similar number of dragoons. (Murtagh & Murtagh, op cit, pp. 34–5).

12: See Piers Wauchope's biography of Sarsfield: *Patrick Sarsfield and the Williamite War* (Dublin 1992)

13: Mackenzie, *Memorials of the Siege of Derry*, p. 8

14: Ibid, p. 9

15: Ibid

16: Ibid, pp. 9–10; Milligan, op cit, pp. 26–7; in contrast see Walker's version in his *True Account*, pp. 16–17.

17: Their names are recorded by Mackenzie, p. 10. That Walker did not record their names supports the contention that they were Presbyterians.

18: Mackenzie, op cit, p. 9

19: Ibid, p. 11

20: St Columb's Cathedral baptismal register

CHAPTER THREE
Disaster in Ulster

The suspicions that the people of Londonderry felt about Mountjoy's Regiment were based on the fact that they knew there to be a large number of Catholics in the regiment since it had been stationed in the city for some three years. Furthermore, the regiment had returned from Dublin on the express orders of Tyrconnel 'to use our [endevours] with the [citizens] of that place to [receive] us as a gareson'. Letters were also received from Dublin to the effect that 'Lord Tyrconnel had ordered the Lord Mountjoy and Lieut-Colonel Lundy, with six companies of their regiment, to come down and reduce this city to its former obedience. But our friends there [in Dublin] cautioned us against the receiving of them.' One of the officers of Mountjoy's Regiment was to play a major role in the siege but when Jonathan Mitchelburne was serving as an acting company commander in Dublin in late-1688 'he thought it not his interest to continue among the Irish that were enemies to his religion and country; quitted his command . . . and made his way to Londonderry'. His escape was made by disguising himself as a Scottish highlander and riding away with the only English grenadier still under his command.[1] Mitchelburne's evidence suggests that a considerable proportion of Catholics were in the ranks of Mountjoy's Regiment, which accounts for the stand-off when that regiment returned to the city.

Mountjoy, however, was able to resolve the situation by reaching an agreement with the city fathers that two companies, about 120 men, under Lieutenant-Colonel Robert Lundy, could enter the city on condition that only Protestant soldiers should be included in their ranks. These were Lundy's own company and that of Captain Stewart. Furthermore, it was agreed that no other troops should enter the city before 10 March and should Lundy receive orders to march off before then he was 'to leave the town to themselves as I found it'. Lundy marched into the city with his two companies on 22 December. The remainder of Mountjoy's Regiment was ordered into quarters at

Strabane, Newtownstewart and Raphoe until the other companies could be purged of Catholics.[2]

By now the Catholic corporation created by Tyrconnel had ceased to function and members of the previous corporation, under Phillips, had retaken control of the city; they constituted what was effectively a military government.[3] Before departing for Dublin, whence he had been recalled by Tyrconnel, Mountjoy saw Lundy appointed as military governor of the city, responsible for its defences. His was now the task of making the city defensible since it was virtually certain that action would be taken against the rebels of Londonderry. By his own account, Lundy called a meeting of the corporation on the 24th at which he told the civic leaders that he found the city's defences in poor condition, a situation that would have to change since he believed that their actions 'had given [distaste] to the Government' which was then arming and regimenting the Irish 'without [employing] a Protestant'. It was his view that Londonderry would become a target for the Irish, thus making it imperative that the city's defences be repaired.

It might be imagined that the city's walls already provided sturdy defence against an attacker. However, the walls and the cannon upon them had been neglected by the city authorities for many years and Lundy was faced with a daunting task, made more onerous by the continued restriction on entry to the city of any more than two companies of his soldiers. He now impressed upon the corporation the need to spend money on the city's defences and outlined those areas on which work had to be done. At that meeting voluntary subscriptions raised £700 which was soon being used to make good deficiencies in the defences. Many of the cannon had defective carriages which needed replacing or repair while level firing platforms, or batteries, had to be constructed. Although the money had been raised and the work begun, not all the city's cannon were given new carriages, and it would not be until the siege had been underway for over two months that the remaining cannon were made fully fit for their role.

Among the other tasks carried out at this time was one which is almost unbelievable to a twenty-first century mind. This was occasioned by the presence of what Lundy described as 'two grait dunghills without the walls almost as high as themselves'. Local residents had been in the habit of throwing their night soil over the walls and this practice had created the two huge middens that would have made admirable, if unpleasant, ramps for attacking soldiers to reach the tops of the walls. These two mounds of ordure were removed. The city walls themselves had fallen into a state of disrepair and work had to be carried out to bring them up to an acceptable standard. Likewise, repairs were carried out to the city's gates.

Within the city was a magazine, or storehouse, in which Lundy discovered some 500 old musket barrels. Since these could be made usable he bought stocks for the weapons as well as a supply of powder, without which all weapons were useless, while an additional 500 matchlock muskets were bought from the castle at Stirling. (The muskets found in the magazine were almost certainly matchlocks also.) Some fourteen barrels of gunpowder were recovered from thirty that had been stranded at Strangford, while a supply of cannonballs was also obtained; these, and the muskets from Stirling, were paid for by an additional subscription of £400 raised by the city fathers in mid-January. Recruiting efforts brought in additional soldiers and new companies were formed. Lundy had found six companies already raised within the walls by David Cairnes, obviously from citizens of military age;[4] a further five were raised from residents of the liberties, who were issued with the old muskets to which new stocks had now been fitted. The officers of the six companies formed by Cairnes are recorded: the first company was commanded by Captain Samuel Norman with Lieutenant William Crookshanks and Ensign Alexander Irwin; the second by Captain Alexander Lecky with Lieutenant James Lennox and Ensign John Harvey; the third by Captain Matthew Cocken with Lieutenant Henry Long and Ensign Francis Hunt; the fourth by Captain Warham Jemmet with Lieutenant Robert Morrison and Ensign Daniel Sherrard; the fifth by Captain John Tomkins with Lieutenant James Spaight and Ensign Alexander Cunningham; and the sixth by Captain Thomas Moncrieff with Lieutenant James Morrison and Ensign William Mackey.[5] (Of these officers, at least six – Crookshanks, Cunningham, Irwin, Morrison, Sherrard and Spaight – were among the thirteen apprentices who had shut the city's gates while two others, John Harvey and Francis Hunt, may also have been of that group although the apprentices were named Samuel Harvey and Samuel Hunt.) By mid-January the four companies of Mountjoy's Regiment that had been kept outside the walls had become entirely Protestant and Lundy was asked to bring them inside the walls where he noted that they did equal duty with his soldiers.

Nor had Lundy been slow in carrying out this work. His energy had inspired the townspeople with confidence and ensured that an otherwise penny-pinching corporation would spend money on improving the city's defences. He had done wonders for morale in the city, according to one contemporary commentator, who noted that 'The Opinion they had of his Experience in War, and Zeal for the Cause they were to Maintain, gave all the People great Expectation from his Conduct.[6] The writer of those words was the Reverend George Walker, rector of Donoughmore near Dungannon in County Tyrone, who was recounting his experience when he made a visit to the city in March 1689. On that occasion Walker was seeking assistance for Dungannon from Lundy and he was successful in his mission, recording that Lundy 'approves and encourages the design, sends two files of his disciplined men to Dungannon, and afterwards two troops of dragoons'.[7] Walker was later to become a governor of the city during the siege and to produce the first account of that siege. By contrast, Lundy is remembered more commonly as a traitor with a name that has become synonymous with treachery, in Ulster at least. But it is a simple fact of history that the work carried out to the city's defences at Lundy's behest and under his supervision was responsible for the city being able to stand against the Jacobite army. One recent writer on the siege avers that apart from 'the building of a ravelin in front of the Bishop's Gate, [Lundy] had done little to improve the defences'.[8] As may be seen, this assessment is far from accurate.

Lundy had also made appeals for assistance to several noteworthy figures including the Duke of Ormonde, the Earl of Clarendon (the former lord lieutenant of Ireland), Admiral Herbert, commanding the Royal Navy, and Major-General McKay in Scotland. To each of these he had written 'begging of them' to represent the condition of the Protestants of Ireland 'to his Highness the prince of Orange'. In his appeal he made it clear that 'without a speedy supply of men money arms and ammunition . . . they [were] all lost'. He had also remonstrated against any precipitate action that might bring the fury of Tyrconnel on the city while it was still in a state unfit to meet an assault. Thus when the gentry of the counties of Londonderry, Tyrone and Donegal had a meeting in the city on 16 January to discuss a letter from their counterparts in Antrim and Down proposing that they all entered into an association 'for defence of the Protestant religion', Lundy opposed the idea, saying that it was a downright defiance to the government and that they were in no fit condition to be provoking the government in such fashion at that time. This association was the Council of the North, which we shall meet later. Lundy counselled that the Protestants of the north-west should continue to prepare themselves for defence 'but with little noise, for fear of bringing an Army amongst them'.

Following Lundy's advice, the gentry of the north-western counties began raising regiments: County Londonderry was able to raise one dragoon and three infantry regiments and also chose Lundy as governor of the county. In Tyrone one dragoon and two infantry regiments were added to the Williamite order of battle while Lundy and Colonel Hamilton were made joint governors of the county. For its part, Donegal, which elected Colonel Hamilton as governor, contributed another three infantry regiments as well as one of dragoons. Lundy appointed majors to each of these regiments from Protestant officers of Mountjoy's Regiment who had laid down their commissions from Tyrconnel and come back to the north.

Robert Lundy might have been the principal architect of the city's defences but he was not alone in his efforts on its behalf. Captain John Forward,* sheriff of Donegal, brought in a shipload of arms and powder from The Netherlands while, as we have seen, other landowners in Counties Donegal, Londonderry and Tyrone strengthened the local garrison with their newly-raised regiments.[9] John Forward had also ignored Tyrconnel's order to disarm the Protestants of Donegal and was thus able to ensure that the men of his county were prepared for the forthcoming conflict. He had been active from the beginning of the crisis and with William Stewart had 'brought about two or three hundred horse into the city' on 10 December. John Cowan, from St Johnston in County Donegal, had also brought a company of foot soldiers to the city, and these, with Forward and Stewart's horsemen, were offered to the city fathers to assist the defence. Further troops came from Limavady where Philips recruited 'about three or four hundred horse', while William Hamilton of Moyagh brought in another two hundred.[10]

The corporation had already chosen David Cairnes, a local lawyer and uncle to one of the apprentices who had shut the gates, to obtain help for the city from England. As we have seen, Cairnes had helped to organize the existing garrison into six companies before departing for London on 11 December to make an appeal to the Irish Society for arms and ammunition to defend the city they had adopted. He carried 'a large letter of credence, and full instructions under the hands and seals of the chief then in town ... [and] also a letter to the [Irish] Society in London'. A private cypher was devised so that Cairnes might correspond securely.[11]

In County Fermanagh the people of Enniskillen and the surrounding area had also taken steps to protect their interests against a Jacobite attack. Although Enniskillen was a small town, really only a village of about

---

*Forward's family is remembered in the name of the townland of Castleforward, outside Newtowncunningham, in east Donegal. Newtowncunningham, in turn, was a plantation village, originally called Cunningham's New Town

eighty dwellings, outside a castle, it had become a stronghold for the Protestants of the region of south-west Ulster and north Connaught. On 16 December 1688 an act of defiance by the Enniskillen men had caused a Jacobite force to retreat into Cavan to be 'seen no more'.' Enniskillen and Derry had become rebel strongholds but in the rest of Ulster the prospects for the Protestant people seemed much less auspicious.

Tyrconnel wrote to the exiled James II in France, using Mountjoy as the bearer of the letter, suggesting that he (Tyrconnel) could lay waste to Ireland for James but that preserving and making use of the country for the king was not possible. The Lord Deputy was having a crisis of loyalty, if not of conscience, and was considering the possibility of a compromise with William that would give Catholics in Ireland more justice than they had seen under Charles II. Using Mountjoy as a messenger also served to get the latter out of Ireland, as Tyrconnel suspected his loyalty following the compromise that Mountjoy had arranged at Derry. But Mountjoy did not make his journey to Paris alone. He was accompanied by Stephen Rice, Chief Baron of the Exchequer Court, who, unknown to Mountjoy, carried another message to James, indicating that the latter was a traitor and the leader of Ireland's Protestants. Otherwise, Tyrconnel advised James, Ireland was firmly on the king's side and would rise in arms if he were to come to Ireland with a French army. James was happy to allow Mountjoy to return to Ireland but Louis XIV took a different view and ordered the earl to be locked up in a Paris prison where he remained for the next three years.*[14]

Louis now saw the advantage of supporting James in Ireland but with the limited objectives that we have already noted, whereas James saw Ireland as a stepping-off point for Scotland. There, Claverhouse, 'Bonnie Dundee', was also ready to rise in arms in support of James who, with Ireland and Scotland behind him, could march south to London and be restored to his kingdoms. James' strategy was to make Derry a critical objective in any Irish campaign since from there he could transport an army to Scotland.

Meanwhile Tyrconnel was also negotiating with William, who had no desire to become involved in military action in Ireland and, in any case, had no troops to spare for a campaign there, such was the state of the English army. With Tyrconnel hinting that Ireland might come over to William's cause there seemed every reason for negotiations. An intermediary was found in the person of Richard Hamilton, an Irish

---

*Not long after his release *Mountjoy* was killed at the battle of Steenkirk while fighting in William's army.

Catholic officer in one of the regiments previously deployed to England but who had become a prisoner of William. Hamilton told William that he knew Tyrconnel, which was true, and that he believed that he could persuade the latter to change sides. Having spoken to Tyrconnel, Hamilton undertook to return to England to report to William, and with the help of John Temple, an officer in William's service, who vouched for him, travelled to Ireland with William's offer to Tyrconnel and the Irish Catholics. We do not know if Hamilton's original intentions were honest, or if Tyrconnel would have accepted William's terms, since events now moved so quickly that the Irish Catholics would accept no compromise. Tyrconnel had set rolling a ball that had now achieved its own momentum over which the Lord Deputy had little control. For the unfortunate John Temple the apparent treachery of Hamilton led to his taking his own life rather than face dishonour. He was to be but one of the many casualties that the course of events in Ireland was to cause.[15]

By the time James landed at Kinsale in March, Tyrconnel had already decided that he would remain true to the Jacobite cause and called for support for his master throughout Ireland. A banner displayed on Dublin Castle bore the legend 'Now or Never! Now and for Ever'. Any man who could raise a body of troops for the army was offered a commission; this had a huge response with some sources putting the number of troops raised as high as 100,000.[16] This is a most unlikely figure and a maximum of 50,000 is more plausible. The Protestants of Leinster, Munster and Connaught suffered attacks and outrages that included the theft or destruction of property on a massive scale. Louis' ambassador to James' court, Comte d'Avaux, reported that more than 5,000 cattle had been slaughtered by thieves in a six-week period; Macrory records this as 50,000 cattle and 300,000 sheep although Avaux's 'plus de cinq mille boeufs', with no mention of sheep, leaves little doubt of the figure. Livestock was stolen and killed for no purpose other than to remove the hides of the beasts, which were then left to rot in the countryside. Milligan suggests that Avaux noted that since the cattle 'were mostly killed during Lent' their carcasses were left untouched. Once again, this is a complete departure from the original. However, Avaux did reckon that Ireland would need ten years to recover from the depredations of six weeks, which suggests that the problem was more than 5,000 slaughtered cattle. He also wished to have provost companies assigned to dealing with the thieves who plagued Ireland.[17]

By the time James came ashore there was no opposition outside Ulster. Less than a week later, Avaux was writing from Cork to tell Louis that Tyrconnel believed that the Irish Protestants would fall back on Londonderry, a strong town in Irish terms, and that this might lead to an encounter that would last several days. That same day, however, he was writing to Louvois, Louis' war minister, with the information that Tyrconnel believed that besieging Londonderry would be more difficult than had been imagined.[18] On 15 April a Mr Evans, 'lately come out of Ireland', gave evidence to the House of Commons of James' arrival in Ireland 'with two and twenty ships; accompanied by Count Davaux, and other French officers, to the number of two hundred; and of his going to Cork and Dublin; and his intentions to go Northwards, and into Scotland; and of the seizing of the Duke of Ormonde's estate, and the stocks of the Protestants'.[19] Evans appeared to be very well informed. Tyrconnel had travelled south to bring his king the news that opposition outside Ulster was non-existent, but he also assured James that the opposition in Ulster was being dealt with; already Lieutenant-General Richard Hamilton had marched north from Dublin leading a force of 2,500 men, as many as Tyrconnel could spare from the capital, to deal with the Ulster rebels. This was the same Richard Hamilton who had travelled from London as an emissary to Tyrconnel from William.

In his report to James, Tyrconnel noted that the army was not yet battleworthy, a view supported by Avaux in many of his letters.[20] However, the anonymous Jacobite author of *A Light to the Blind* had a higher opinion of the same army and wrote that:

> Of battering cannon, of field pieces they had enough to their purpose . . . Of small arms they had some store; they had iron and artificiers to form a sufficiency in a short time, as also to cast mortars and bombs, pikes, half pikes, scythes, spades, pickaxes, and other utensils of war they might have in abundance.[21]

That this assessment was foolishly optimistic was to be proved beyond any doubt when the Jacobite army laid siege to the city.

What of the French support that arrived with James? This had been much less than might have been expected and the arms supplied were of poor quality, probably weapons of which the French quartermasters wished to dispose. However, James was accompanied by some 200 officers, both British and French, as Evans had told the House of Commons. These included James' illegitimate sons, the Duke of Berwick and the Grand Prior, the former born in 1671 and, therefore, only eighteen, the latter some two years younger, as well as men of experience, commanders and advisers such as John Drummond, Earl of Melfort, a Scot, and Henry Jermyn, Lord Dover. His military commanders included

Patrick Sarsfield, John Wauchope and William Dorrington. Among the Frenchmen in James' entourage was le Comte d'Avaux, Louis' ambassador, Conrad de Rosen, the French commander, and several senior army officers. The latter included Maumont, Pusignan, Lery and the Marquis de Pointis; the last named was a naval officer but also an engineer and artilleryman.[22]

In Dublin James summoned the Irish Parliament to meet on 7 May but, before that, he made a speech in the capital in which he outlined his policy in Ireland. He promised religious freedom for everyone and asked that nothing should be preached or taught that might 'alienate the hearts of our people from us'. Appealing to those Protestants who had fled the country to return to Ireland within forty days, he guaranteed that they and their property would receive full protection.[23] James was sincere in his appeal and probably believed that his Protestant subjects would accept his promises and guarantees. In that judgement he was completely out of touch with the levels of suspicion, distrust and hatred that prevailed across the land.

Richard Hamilton's army was already making war in Ulster and thereby ensuring that James' promises and appeals would fall on deaf ears. Londonderry and Enniskillen were the major Protestant strongholds in Ulster but not the only ones. Ulster's Protestants had heard stories of the size of the army that Tyrconnel had mustered, stories that were exaggerated as is the nature of such things, and felt that it would not be long before this army would be used against them. No Protestant is likely to have believed that the army existed for the safety or advantage of their community.

At this stage, John Hawkins, a young Protestant of some means, helped galvanize the defensive spirit in Ulster, persuading both Protestant and Dissenter that they should arm and come together to defend both their persons and their homes.[24] In January 1689 the aristocracy of the north-eastern counties had appointed Lord Mount-Alexander, he to whom the Comber Letter had been addressed, as leader of all Protestant forces in the counties of Antrim, Armagh, Down and Monaghan. By mid-January, the gentry of these four counties had formed the Council of the North, which met at Hillsborough, and made approaches to the Protestants of the other Ulster counties. The Council had also approached the Earl of Clarendon for support in asking William for troops, arms and equipment as well as money to defend Ulster against the Jacobite threat. Their requirements included 10,000 infantry, 1,500 cavalry and 20,000 muskets for local volunteers. Mount-Alexander had written to Robert Lundy, telling him of the preparations being made for a Jacobite expedition into Ulster and asking that Lundy should join forces with the Council's army.

Lundy's reply to Mount-Alexander showed a strategic awareness of the overall situation in Ulster and the importance of Londonderry:

> I writ him word that I could not come to join him in his country as he desired, for fear of the Irish marching straight to Derry, but as soon as was possible I would march with all the forces I could make and 2 field pieces and all the ammunition I could spare to Dungannon, which was the pass in to our north and in case the Irish Army [marched] straight to him if he would keep the pass of Portadown for me I would march that way to join him, and that in the meantime I had posted Captain Stewart at Dungannon with 3 troops of dragoons, 100 detached Red Coats and 6 country companies* to make that pass good and keep the garrison of Charlemont in [as] they had been very troublesome to the country by plundering them of their goods and cattle.

Thus it appears that Lundy was well informed on what was happening elsewhere in Ulster, even to the extent of knowing that the Jacobite garrison of Charlemont was making nuisance raids throughout the surrounding countryside, stealing cattle and provisions. But he continued to hold paramount the integrity of Londonderry and hence his reluctance to move his force away from the city. It is unlikely that such a move would have met with the approval of the local gentry in any case, leaving Lundy able only to field a small force.

The news that William and Mary had been proclaimed as joint sovereigns in England seems to have lulled the Council of the North into a state of inertia. Believing that this news meant that Tyrconnel would come to terms with William, the Council lost any sense of urgency and, in spite of the exhortations of John Hawkins, seemed to think that the crisis was over. A few companies of soldiers were mustered and deployed to various points but the earlier plans to gather and store weapons, ammunition and other military equipment now seemed to be of passing interest. In the light of what was about to happen it was as well that Lundy had not sent any troops to join them.

Paradoxically, the Council now decided that it was time to evict Tyrconnel's troops from Carrickfergus and launched an attack on the town. This amounted to little more than a skirmish, and the attackers

---

*'The 'Red Coats' were regular infantry while the 'country companies' were from the locally-raised forces

withdrew. But both sides had parleyed and agreed to despatch an account of the battle to Tyrconnel. For the attackers this was a serious mistake since the agreed bearer of the message was a friar, Father O'Haggerty. The latter had observed the Council's forces during the encounter at Carrickfergus and was able to tell Tyrconnel that they were ill-prepared for war, with few experienced officers, and with soldiers scattered across the region in numbers far below that which had been 'confidently reported in Dublin'. Moreover, they were also short of ammunition and of the stores needed for any length of campaign.

Armed with this intelligence Tyrconnel issued a proclamation on 7 March in which he offered a pardon to anyone who laid down his arms while threatening those who persisted in what he described as 'their wicked designs and treasonable practices'. Those who fell into the latter category would be treated as rebels and traitors but the king's soldiers would treat the innocent well. Ten men were stated to be unpardonable.

> But in regard Hugh Earl of Mount-Alexander, John Lord Viscount Mazareen, Robert Lord Baron of Kingston, Clotworthy Skeffington, Esquire, son to the Lord Viscount Mazareen, Sir Robert Colvil, Sir Arthur Royden [Rawdon], Sir John Magill, John Hawkins, Robert Sanderson, and Francis Hamilton, son to Sir Charles Hamilton, have been the prime actors in the said Rebellion, and the persons who advised and fomented the same, and inveigled others to be involved therein; we think fit to except them out of this our Proclamation, as persons not deserving His Majesty's mercy or favour.[25]

By now Tyrconnel was a much more confident man than hitherto; his flirtation with a compromise with William was over and he knew that James was on his way to Ireland from France with Louis' backing.

Hamilton's expeditionary force to Ulster, which Tyrconnel told James numbered 2,500 men, was estimated by others at 7,000 strong with five field guns.[26] As this force marched north, an emissary from Tyrconnel was also sent northwards with a peace offer to the Council of the North. The emissary was a Presbyterian minister, the Reverend Alexander Osborne, who met the Council at Loughbrickland on 9 March. The peace offer was really Tyrconnel's proclamation of the 7th to which Osborne added that the alternative was destruction by Hamilton's army which would then sweep through the rest of Ulster, rolling over any opposition at places such as Coleraine, Enniskillen and Londonderry. Moreover, while Hamilton's troops were reducing the opposition in such manner, the native Irish of Cavan, Monaghan,

Tyrone and Londonderry would 'upon the approach of the army and resistance thereunto made, immediately enter upon a massacre of the British in the said counties'. Osborne reported that Tyrconnel regretted that he would be unable to prevent such a massacre occurring.[27]

However, Osborne was able to provide the Council with some valuable intelligence on the Jacobite army, just as O'Haggerty had been able to provide Tyrconnel with similar military intelligence. The Jacobite army, said Osborne, was short of ammunition and 'though their horses are good, yet their riders were but contemptible fellows, many of them having lately been cowherds etc'. This latter observation was a very inaccurate assessment of the Irish cavalry and suggests that Osborne was allowing some of his own prejudices to colour his judgement. The Council, said Osborne, should resist rather than accept Tyrconnel's promises since the latter would certainly renege on these and make paupers and slaves of Ulster's Protestants. As if to support Osborne's comments on the untrustworthiness of Tyrconnel, the emissary the Council had sent to William had just returned with a promise of support and assistance to 'rescue you from the oppressions and terrors you lie under'. The message from William and Osborne's recommendations combined to strengthen the resolve of the Council, which chose to send a message to Tyrconnel saying that they would not lay down their arms but that they would negotiate with the Lord Deputy. Such negotiation would be conducted only on terms that recognized their rights and allowed them freedom of religion and civil liberty.[28]

The Council had made one major error. Its members, deeply involved in debate and politicking, had failed to heed Osborne's warning that Hamilton's army was closing on them. Now they learned to their collective horror that Hamilton was almost upon them. Sir Arthur Rawdon, known as the 'Cock of the North' and one of the men deemed unpardonable by Tyrconnel, led a small force of yeomanry cavalry to meet Hamilton at the nearby village of Dromore in County Down.

Rawdon's soubriquet suggests that he may have been a man who exuded confidence and he certainly seems to have been considered a leader. Whatever his qualities, these proved of no avail in the encounter with the Jacobite army which became a débâcle. Rawdon's force had formed a blocking line, intended to deny passage to Hamilton, but on sighting the Jacobite army the Ulstermen panicked and fled the field. This was a clear case of raw, unblooded soldiers, with inadequate leadership, losing confidence when faced with the enemy. Their natural instinct for survival took over and their horses carried them away from instead of towards the enemy. Robert Lundy recorded that he had an 'express' – an urgent despatch – from Sir Arthur Rawdon on about 11 or 12 March telling him that Rawdon's soldiers had run away at 'the sight of a few troops of the vanguard of the Irish Army' at Dromore.

Jacobite cavalry chased the fleeing Ulstermen through Hillsborough. Some hundred yeomen were lost, and resistance in the area simply melted away. Rawdon told Lundy that his men at Lisnagarvey – modern Lisburn – and Hillsborough had fled when they saw their comrades retreating in haste from Dromore; at neither place did the Williamites even see a single Jacobite soldier. Of those who had been in Rawdon's force, many made for their own homes and accepted promises of protection from Hamilton. This humiliating defeat for the Ulstermen was quickly dubbed the 'Break of Dromore' and led to Jacobite domination of almost all of east Ulster.

Following the Break of Dromore many Protestants from the eastern counties of Ulster took ship to Scotland or England, believing that their cause in Ireland was lost.[29] These included 'many of the officers', among whose number was Lord Mount-Alexander. But Arthur Rawdon was made of sterner stuff and was determined to continue the fight, gathering together a force of several thousand men and leading them to Coleraine. The level of panic among Ulster's Protestants was indicated by the thousands of refugees who were also making for the protection of Coleraine, as their predecessors had done nearly fifty years before. Coleraine was not the sole objective for refugees since many more were tramping the roads for Enniskillen and Londonderry. Macaulay provides a description that is at once harrowing and vivid:

> The flight became wild and tumultuous, the fugitives broke down the bridges and burned the ferryboats. Whole towns, the seats of Protestant population, were left in ruins without one inhabitant. The people of Omagh destroyed their own dwellings so utterly that no roof was left to shelter the enemy from the rain and wind. The people of Cavan migrated in one body to Enniskillen. The day was wet and stormy. The road was deep in mire. It was a piteous sight to see, mingled with the armed men, the women and children, weeping, famished and toiling through the mud up to their knees.[30]

Rawdon and his men reached Coleraine on 15 March where they prepared to meet the expected attack by Hamilton. However, the threat was not quite as imminent as the defenders might have thought since the Jacobites were indulging in a frenzy of looting.

Learning from Rawdon of the retreat, Lundy had countermanded his earlier orders for Dungannon and sent a message to Captain Stewart to withdraw his party from there, leaving only an officer and forty or fifty men in the castle. The remainder Stewart was to lead to Coleraine. However, most of the troops under Stewart's command refused to follow him to Coleraine when they learned of the extent of the Jacobite advance; the bulk of these men returned to their own homes. Lundy also wrote to Rawdon to tell him that he would join him at Coleraine the next day and expressing sympathy for his plight and sorrow at the cowardice of his men. And he ordered troops to deploy to Portglenone to cut the bridge there.

At the same time Lundy called a meeting of the leading citizens of Derry, telling them of the enormity of the strategic situation. It was now inevitable that a Jacobite army would march on the city and preparations had to be completed. Chief among these preparations was the storing of 'provisions of all kinds'. Although there was no money to pay for these, there was a promise of £30,000 to come from England and, on the basis of that promise, he had appointed four 'known men' as storekeepers while proclamations were to be made by beat of drum throughout the town asking people to bring in provisions for the store. Although there were as yet no funds to reimburse them, they were asked to have faith that they would be paid from the first money that became available.

Lundy's inspections of the city walls now led him to persuade the corporation to order the demolition of buildings immediately outside the walls, thereby preventing attackers from using them as cover under which to approach and scale the walls. If this were not done, he warned, attackers could lodge themselves within ten yards of the walls and the city could not be held in such circumstances. The demolition of these buildings would also provide the defenders with a clear field of fire. Lundy was proving that he had the eye of a professional soldier. A further innovation at his behest reinforces that perception of the Scot.

For much of their length the city walls created a formidable obstacle to an attacker because of the topography of the one-time island on which the city stands. Even today the observer on the walls can see this. On the east side, between the Coward's Bastion and the Water Bastion, the Foyle made it undesirable to launch an attack since this would have to be by boat, would be obvious long beforehand and would have to be carried out in the face of heavy fire. From the Coward's Bastion to the Double Bastion the ground fell away below the walls, creating a steep, natural glacis that would have forced attackers to approach through a hail of fire. The same held true for that section of wall from the Water Bastion to the Ferry Gate. Only the length of wall from the Ferry Gate to the Church Bastion and then across by Bishop's Gate to the Double Bastion remained and it was the area most vulnerable to attack. Moreover, the most likely direction from which an attack might come was from the south, thereby further emphasizing this stretch of wall as the city's weakest point; the wall from the Church Bastion to the Double Bastion faces southwards.

Recognizing this factor Lundy proposed that 'a ravelling must be mad out at Bishop's Gate which was the weakest place of the towne, considering the high ground that was without it'. What Lundy was suggesting, the construction of a ravelin, was a relatively new concept in military engineering, which would increase and project the defences of the city in that area. The ravelin, or half-moon, fortification was the brainchild of the leading military engineer of his day: Sébastien le Prestre, Seigneur de Vauban, who later became a marshal of France. In spite of the term half-moon, a ravelin was a triangular-shaped fortification; the base of Lundy's ravelin was against the city walls with its apex some distance forward.* Vauban is acknowledged as one of the greatest names in siege engineering; only Archimedes compares with him. In proposing the construction of a Vauban-type work at Bishop's Gate, Lundy was not only demonstrating that he had a good eye for ground but that he was au fait with the most modern ideas in military engineering. These facts suggest that Lundy was a thoroughly professional soldier, something that should be borne in mind when considering future developments in this story.

On the day after the meeting Lundy had the ground marked out for the ravelin and also ordered men to begin demolishing the houses close to the walls. Officers were appointed to oversee the work. But the work on the southern defences of the city was not restricted to building the ravelin. Lundy pushed the defences out even farther with the construction of a line of outworks in the area of Windmill Hill and between that hill and the river Foyle. Having ensured that the work had begun and having appointed the overseers, Lundy then 'took horse with Colonel Hamilton for Coleraine'. En route they met Sir Arthur Rawdon, who must have been on his way to Derry but who turned back to Coleraine with them.

In Coleraine Lundy had all the officers in the garrison gathered together and emphasized the necessity to re-organize the broken forces

---

*The outline of the ravelin was discovered during an archaeological dig in the area in 1999.

that had fallen back on the town. Once their numbers were known, these men should be formed into companies and battalions with officers appointed to command them; of the nine regiments that retreated from Down and Antrim, the colonels of only two had thus far come to Coleraine. Lundy assured them that the forces of Derry, Donegal and Tyrone were marching to support them and that Lord Blaney with his men was also on the march, from the south of the province. Once these units were in place there would be a considerable body of men in Coleraine which Lundy considered 'a good post and easy to be kept, considering their number and the strength of the place'.

A plan for the defence of the town was drawn up. While a garrison would be posted in Coleraine itself, the remainder of the force would deploy along the Bann to oppose the Jacobites if they attempted to cross the river. The latter element should be no more than an hour's march away so that it could move quickly to Coleraine if the town were to come under attack. Lundy's proposals seem to have impressed the officers so much that they urged him to stay and command the garrison as governor but he told them that he could not do so, although Colonel Hamilton would return to command in two days' time. This seemed to pacify the bulk of the officers.

However, not everyone was happy, and some of the subaltern officers* and almost all the soldiers 'began to be very troublesome'. The soldiers claim to have been betrayed by their officers and drew up the drawbridge to prevent Lundy leaving the town, even threatening him with their weapons. Showing considerable coolness, Lundy asked them to put up their arms and explain their grievances to him. They had no satisfactory answer although the bridge was let down. Lundy was compelled to stay all day to pacify the garrison and commented that he had never seen such disorder and distraction with 'everybody running up and down like mad men'. Next day the garrison was still mutinous but under arms, and Lundy, keen to return to Derry, had to ask Rawdon to place some of his reliable men on the bridge so that he could leave. Rawdon did so, but it was not until that night that Lundy was able, with considerable difficulty, to get away from Coleraine. He rode all night to get to Derry where he impressed upon the civic leaders the importance of supporting Coleraine. Should the latter fall, declared Lundy, the enemy would be at the gates of the city in four days. A sum of £300 was raised to be sent to Coleraine with Colonel Hamilton who

---

*These are the officers below the rank of captain although at this time the term may also have included captains.

'in a short while put the men on a good foot for they began to obey, they being under pay'. It seems that one of the main grievances of the Coleraine garrison was that they were being asked to risk their lives to 'preserve their landlords' estates for nothing'.

At Coleraine the figure of Jonathan Mitchelburne appears once again. Commanding Skeffington's Regiment, Mitchelburne had driven Colonel O'Neill from Toome castle before escorting Clotworthy Skeffington's wife and niece from Antrim to Coleraine, for which service Skeffington gave Mitchelburne command of his regiment and presented him with his charger, 'Bloody-bones', and his scimitar. Having done so, Skeffington then fled Ulster for safety in England. But, although present when the Jacobites first attacked the town, Mitchelburne disagreed with Gustavus Hamilton about the defence of Coleraine and marched off with his regiment towards Londonderry.[31]

On 8 March, the day after Tyrconnel issued his proclamation with its offer of pardon or promise of retribution, at Whitehall in London, the Secretary of State, Lord Shrewsbury,* was writing a letter to Robert Lundy:

I am commanded by the king to acquaint you that his Majesty's greatest concern hath been for Ireland, and particularly for the province of Ulster, which he looks upon as most capable to defend itself against the common enemy. And that they might be the better enabled to do it, there are two regiments already at the sea side ready to embark, in order to their transportation into that province, with which will be sent a good quantity of arms and ammunition. And they will be speedily followed by so considerable a body, as (by the blessing of God) may be able to rescue the whole kingdom, and re-settle the protestant interest there. His Majesty does very much rely upon your fidelity and resolution, not only that you shall acquit yourself according to the character he has received of you, but that you should encourage and influence others in this difficult conjuncture to discharge their duty to their country, their religion, and posterity, all which call upon them for a more than ordinary vigour, to keep out that deluge of Romish superstition and slavery which so nearly threatens them. And you may assure them, besides his Majesty's care for their preservation, who hath a due tenderness and regard for them, (as well in consideration that they are his subjects, as that they are now exposed for the sake of that

---

*Charles Talbot, Duke. of Shrewsbury, had been a minister under James II. He had converted to Protestantism and was now in favour with the new regime, having been one of the seven men who had invited William to come to England.

religion which he himself professes,) the whole bent of this nation inclines them to employ their utmost endeavours for their deliverance; and it was but this very morning that his Majesty hath most effectually recommended the case of Ireland to the two houses of parliament. And I do not doubt but they will thereupon immediately come to such resolutions, as will show to all the world that they espouse their interest as their own.

As to your own particular, you will always find the king graciously disposed to own and reward the services you shall do him in such a time of trial.[32]

It took some time for this letter to reach Lundy but it was in his hands, as we shall see, by 21 March. It was also to be read at the council of war convened in the city on 10 April, just over a month after Shrewsbury put pen to paper. Much happened during that month.

Richard Hamilton's army reached Coleraine on 27 March. The garrison was now commanded by Gustavus Hamilton and the town's defences had been improved, although they were still not impressive, in spite of Lundy's earlier comments, and the Williamite soldiery had been given time to regain some confidence. This appears to have been an aspect of Coleraine's defence that Richard Hamilton had not bargained for; his army was not prepared for a siege and carried only sufficient provisions for two days.[33] The Jacobite commander, having seen the rout at Dromore, must have expected a similar reaction at Coleraine. But the defenders were determined to put up a better fight than at Dromore and now had the advantage of some fixed defences. The first Jacobite attack was repulsed. There followed an exchange of fire between the artillery on either side as well as between the opposing infantrymen. But with reinforcements on their way, the advantage lay with the Jacobites, and Hamilton decided that he would leave the reinforcing regiments to mask, or contain, the Coleraine garrison and move against Derry with his main force. This, he reasoned, would force Gustavus Hamilton to abandon Coleraine for fear of being cut off from Derry. In this thinking the Jacobite Hamilton was proved right.[34]

There followed a brief campaign along the river Bann, which marks the boundary between the counties of Antrim and Londonderry. After almost a week Jacobite troops forced the Williamite garrison, under Rawdon, out of Moneymore on 4 April; three days later, Richard Hamilton's men crossed the Bann at Portglenone. Bad weather conditions, including persistent rain – and it had even been snowing when the Jacobites first reached Coleraine – played havoc with the health of the soldiers, including the officers. One Williamite officer, Colonel Edmonstone, the commander at Portglenone, died from a fever contracted in the trenches there, while Sir Arthur Rawdon was also taken ill and, although he made his way to Londonderry after the defeat at Moneymore, had later to be evacuated to England due to his illness.[35]

With the Jacobites on both sides of the Bann, Gustavus Hamilton decided that he had no choice other than to evacuate Coleraine since the town now faced a full-scale siege which it could never have withstood. Williamite detachments along the Bann were withdrawn and the entire force began its march to Londonderry before the Jacobite army could cut it off. This move brought much criticism down on Gustavus Hamilton, with one Williamite writer alleging that Coleraine fell because of a shortage of good officers, while the garrison was described as a rabble that retreated in considerable disorder allowing many of its weapons and horses to fall into enemy hands.[36] However, the writer failed to indicate what alternative there might have been for the Coleraine garrison.

As the soldiers trudged along the road to the longed-for safety of Ulster's only city, they were caught up once again in a stream of refugees. The Reverend John Mackenzie, one of the chroniclers of the siege that was to follow, wrote of them that they 'came towards Derry as their last refuge'.[37] This last refuge, the last walled city built in Europe, was now a refuge for Ulster's Protestants, a regional stronghold for them and a strategic defence for Protestantism and King William's cause in Ireland. It thus fulfilled all three possible roles for fortifications as recognized by military theorists.[38] As a refuge the city provided the perceived protection of its walls, although these had not been intended to withstand modern artillery, while those same walls became the stronghold for most Protestants in north-west Ulster, as well as from east Ulster. Perhaps its most important role was as a strategic defence for the cause espoused by the Protestants of Ulster, which included allegiance to William III. Nowhere else was there a location that would permit the Williamites to seek defence but also maintain lines of communication with England that offered the prospect of allowing a relief force to arrive by sea.

And so it was that the city of Londonderry became the major battleground in Ireland in 1689. All possibilities of a negotiated peace had vanished in the havoc of war, and preparations were underway to increase both the level and tempo of military activity in the country. In late-March, as Coleraine teetered, Parliament in London voted to allocate finance for a relief force for Ireland with a sum of over £300,000 for a campaign of six months' duration; an additional £100,000 was granted to cover the costs of transportation and to provide an artillery train. Should the Irish campaign last more than six months then more provision was to be made in the form of an additional £300,000.[39] This financial allocation marked an important moment in parliamentary history since it indicated that the monarch had to approach parliament to secure the finance with which to wage war. The money was to be raised, in part, by a Poll Bill which proposed imposing taxes under twenty-three different heads; all but one of these – a tax on fee farm rents 'now paid and not otherwise charged' – was agreed by the Commons on 4 April. Among those to be taxed were judges, nobles, baronets, esquires or reputed esquires, widows, gentlemen having an estate of £300 and 'dignified' clergy.[40]

In spite of his earlier proclamation to bring in provisions, Lundy found that the response in the city had been poor and 'therefore by force [he] obliged all the merchants' to hand over provisions to the city's stores. Salmon, butter and cheese were confiscated. The outlying landowners were ordered to have their tenants bring in all the grain that they could on the promise that they would eventually be paid for it. Should they fail to do so they would certainly lose their grain 'for if our own men or the Enemy came amongst them they would take it for nothing'. Lundy also encouraged the landlords to take grain in lieu of rent and then send that grain into the stores. This would also be a good way for the tenant farmers to pay their rents as they had no cash to do so. Whether the landlords considered this a good idea we do not know.

On 20 March Lundy received a letter from Captain James Hamilton, aboard the merchant ship *Deliverance*, which had been escorted by the frigate HMS *Jersey*,* under Captain Beverly, and which had brought arms, ammunition and some money 'for the use of Derry'. The latter sum totalled £598.16s.8d which Hamilton had received from the collector of customs at Chester, Mathew Anderton, who had been instructed to provide £1,000. It seems that Lord Shrewsbury's letter of 8 March was also delivered by Hamilton.

However, Hamilton had orders not to unload anything into Lundy's care until the governor had taken the oath of allegiance to King William and Queen Mary. Lundy therefore boarded the *Jersey* where Hamilton 'tendered me the oath'. This was to be a subject of controversy in the days ahead with some claiming that Lundy had never taken the oath at all and demanding that he do so again. Against this, Lundy noted that,

---

*The first of eight ships of this name to serve in the Royal Navy, *Jersey* carried forty-eight guns. The ship was captured by the French in the West Indies in December 1691.[41]

on 21 March, he 'had all the people of quality and officers of [the] town assembled and tendered them the oath [and] in the afternoon [he] had their Majesties proclaimed King and Queen' with all the solemnity that circumstances in the city permitted. Subsequently, a House of Commons committee was told that Colonel Stewart, Captain Mervyn and Captain Corry were all present when Lundy took the oath 'to be true to King William before his commission was delivered to him: But the Mayor of Londonderry was not present, being gone into the Irish Army; And the Deputy Mayor was suspected for a Papish at that time'. Presenting his evidence to the same committee Sir Arthur Rawdon claimed to have been put out of the cabin with Captain Beverly and 'divers others'. It was on this same day that a Declaration of Union (see Appendix Two) was made by 'the nobility and gentry of the neighbouring counties, and of the citizens and garrison of Londonderry'.[42]

Following this the arms and ammunition were landed and distributed although some 600 weapons of the 1,600 unloaded were defective; it was said that there were weapons for 2,000 men. Some 480 barrels of powder were included in the cargo that was landed. It is unlikely that Hamilton would have permitted this unloading to take place had Lundy not taken the oath. There was considerable consternation at both the quantity and quality of the weapons supplied. The muskets were matchlocks rather than the more modern flintlocks and there must have been a feeling that the city was being fobbed off with obsolescent weapons. Not surprisingly, Lundy recorded that this bred much ill-feeling that led to many leaving the country who would previously not have considered doing so.

Once more Lundy took up his pen to write an appeal for assistance. His letter, addressed to Shrewsbury, detailed the sad condition of the city, the great disappointment felt at the supplies that had arrived with *Deliverance* and HMS *Jersey*, the pressing need for money and arms, and general officers to command the garrison. Without these, he argued, the town would almost inevitably fall into Irish hands. He was also concerned about the soldiers of the garrison who were 'negligent and would do nothing', a complaint that seems to relate to the locally-raised units. Without money to pay these men there were no sanctions with which to punish or discipline them. His ordeal at Coleraine seems to have caused Lundy to look on the Londonderry garrison with a more jaundiced eye. But, he told Shrewsbury, the most urgent need was for provisions 'considering the great numbers of people that flocked from all parts to Derry, being chased there by the Irish from their own homes'. Even while appealing for provisions for his own town, Lundy was sending powder – twenty barrels with ball and match – to Coleraine as well as two guns, and food. But Coleraine was soon to capitulate, as we have seen, allowing Richard Hamilton to march for Derry with his army.

This caused Lundy to write yet another letter to Shrewsbury in which he told his lordship, who held one of the highest offices of state and might be equated to the modern home secretary if not the prime minister, that the situation was becoming desperate, the soldiers were 'downright [mutinous] and would do nothing but what they pleased'. Unless a general with an army and provisions was despatched forthwith to relieve Ireland, it would be too late. In spite of their truculent state, Lundy 'drew out 19 companies of those that came from Coleraine' (about 1,050 men) and brought them into the city to strengthen the garrison, giving them provisions from the stores and supplying their officers with some money to pay them. The remainder of the Coleraine force was sent into the Laggan valley, an area of highly fertile farmland between the city and Letterkenny, where they were allocated quarters. However, the Coleraine commander, Hamilton, was so incensed at what he saw as the cowardice of his men that he refused to stay any longer. Lundy comments wryly that a great many followed Hamilton's example and went off.

Two Jacobite forces were now making their way towards the Protestant stronghold of Londonderry. Richard Hamilton's force was approaching from Coleraine while the force that had been marching to reinforce him was en route from Charlemont in Tyrone. But there was no agreement on overall strategy within the Jacobite high command. Both King James and Lord Melfort had planned that a campaign in Scotland should follow the fall of the city. One senior Jacobite, Justin McCarthy, felt that the only real difficulty with that plan was in finding the shipping to transport the army from the Foyle to Scotland since the French fleet, having brought James to Kinsale, had sailed for home, leaving only three frigates for James' use. This absence of a strong French naval presence was to be crucial to the Jacobite army at Derry and later in the Irish campaign.

While James and Melfort seemed optimistic, the principal French representatives did not share that feeling. Avaux, the senior French adviser, and Conrad de Rosen, the senior general, were pessimistic; the former's reports back to Louis told of shortages of trained soldiers, horses, money, military equipment and provisions.[43] This was hardly a situation in which confidence could be felt. And matters were complicated by Tyrconnel's attitude to Melfort. He distrusted the Scot's influence with James, a distrust also felt by Avaux who, by contrast, considered Tyrconnel a trustworthy ally. These tensions did nothing for morale at the top of the Jacobite command while the shortages did little for morale at the lower end. However, the news that Hamilton had pushed the Williamites back to Derry raised confidence in Dublin. That was tempered by further news that a relief force was being made ready in north-west England with a fleet assembling in Liverpool to carry it to Londonderry. On 2 March the Navy Board had received orders that

> Vessels be immediately hired at Liverpool or where it may be most conveniently done for transporting two battalions of soldiers consisting of about 1200 men with their accoutrements from this port to London Derry in Ireland, and that they be victualled as can best be done at the said place of their embarking.[44]

This made the seizure of the city the most important strategic objective for James and his forces. It also made that seizure a matter of great urgency.

Notes

Much of the material in this chapter is based on documents in the National Archives of Scotland. These are: GD26/7/37 – 1, Case for Lundy and letter giving details of preparations at Derry; GD26/7/37 – 2, Account of Lundy's proceedings in Ireland since 13 December 1688; GD26/7/37 – 3, Draft petition to the Privy Council defending his conduct. In most cases it will be clear to the reader that the source is one of these documents and thus these are not normally annotated.

1: Mitchelburne, *Ireland Preserv'd*.
2: Mackenzie, op cit, p. 14
3: Milligan, op cit, p. 42
4: Mackenzie, op cit, p. 13
5: Ibid
6: Walker, *A True Account of the Siege of London-Derry*, pp. 19–20
7: Ibid, p. 20
8: Seymour, p. 108
9: Mackenzie, op cit, p. 13, refers to Forward's arrival with that of two other Donegal landowners.
10: Ibid
11: Ibid
12: Witherow, *Derry and Enniskillen*, pp. 212–7
13: Gilbert, *A Jacobite Narrative of the War in Ireland*, p. 43

14: Ibid

15: Macrory, pp. 138–9

16: Finlay, *The Siege of Londonderry*, p. 13. Finlay used figures and comments made by Macaulay.

17: Avaux, *Négociations*, p. 85; Milligan, op cit, pp. 112–3; Macrory, pp. 142–3. Although Macrory cites Avaux as his source the details he gives do not chime with the Frenchman's report.

18: Avaux, op cit, p. 37 & p. 44

19: House of Lords Record Office (HLRO): *House of Commons Journal (HoCJ)*, 15 April 1689

20: For examples see Avaux, op cit, pp. 74–5 on general shortages and p. 82 on the lack of weaponry in infantry units.

21: Gilbert, op cit, pp. 47–8

22: Ibid, p. 46; Avaux, op cit, p. 11. The former does not mention Lery but he is included as a cavalry brigade commander in Louis' orders to Maumont, reproduced in Avaux's records.

23: Doherty, op cit, p. 38

24: Macrory, op cit, pp. 143–4

25: Quoted in Mitchelburne, op cit

26: See Gilbert, p. 45, where the army is estimated at 3,500.

27: Macrory, op cit, p. 146

28: Ibid, pp. 147–8

29: HLRO, *HoCJ*, 15 April 1689. On this date it was agreed to appoint a committee 'to consider of the distressed condition of the Protestants of Ireland fled from Ireland; and of a way how they may be relieved'.

30: Macaulay, *History of England, Vol. III*, p. 55

31: Mitchelburne, op cit. See also Wauchope Colonel John Mitchelburne, *Irish Sword*, Vol. XX, No. 80, p. 138.

32: Quoted in, inter alia, Simpson, op cit, p. 96

33: Avaux, op cit, p. 60

34: Macrory, op cit, pp. 149–151; Doherty, op cit, p. 43

35: Macrory, op cit, p. 151; Doherty, op cit, p. 44

36: Quoted in Macrory, pp. 151–2

37: Mackenzie, op cit, p. 28

38: Keegan, *A History of Warfare*, pp.139–40

39: HLRO, *HoCJ*, 24 March 1689

40: Ibid, 3 April 189

41: Colledge & Warlow, *Ships of the Royal Navy*, p. 179

42: Simpson, op cit, pp. 100–1

43: Avaux, op cit, as for note 20.

44: NA Kew, ADM2/1743

CHAPTER FOUR

No Surrender!

As the refugees from Coleraine streamed across the mountain to Newtownlimavady and thence to Londonderry, the defences of the latter had been improved almost beyond recognition since the shutting of the gates in December. Much of this was attributable to the city's new governor, Lieutenant-Colonel Robert Lundy. A Scot, Lundy knew the city well and had been stationed there for some time. He had a lengthy military career behind him and had served with the Royal Regiment of Foot in Tangier, which had been under an almost constant state of siege.[1] Moreover, he was acquainted with the latest concepts in military engineering as had been proved by his building of the ravelin at Bishop's Gate. Lundy knew that the French were the most sophisticated military engineers of the day and that, should the city come under siege, it was likely that French engineers, or men familiar with their ideas, would be among the besiegers.

But we have noted that Lundy was frustrated at the attitude of many of the garrison and at the lack of assistance that seemed to be forthcoming from England. Had he known how the situation was being viewed in London, his frustration might have been even greater since the House of Commons appeared to be taking an almost casual approach. On 4 April it was decided that a committee of the whole house would be established 'to consider the state of this Kingdom, and of Ireland'. That the plight of Ireland's Protestants was known in London is evidenced by the same house, on 15 April, appointing a further committee 'to consider the distressed condition of the Protestants of Ireland fled from Ireland; and of a way how they may be relieved'. This latter committee was to have its first meeting on the 16th but its work thereafter seemed to lack any sense of urgency as did that of the first committee.[2]

Nor do the citizens of Londonderry seem to have responded as well as Lundy had hoped to his earlier call to store provisions in anticipation of action against the city. When he sent for the storekeepers to make an inventory of what was in the stores and the quality thereof, he found that the two principal storemen had gone, taking their ledgers with them. So Lundy went to the stores, accompanied by Captain James Hamilton, who had arrived on the *Deliverance*, to see what was there and was surprised to find nothing approaching the quantity of meal that he had expected. This prompted him to requisition all the provisions in private homes, a move that can have done very little for his popularity among the townspeople. Another proclamation was made, offering ready money for all the hay that might be brought in from the country, since there was little left in the town.

Lundy now issued an order that was to make him equally unpopular in the countryside around the city. He told the commanding officers of four horse or dragoon regiments – Lord Blaney, William Stewart, James Hamilton and Sir Arthur Rawdon – to disperse their men into the countryside and bring to the city's stores 'all the meal and oats hay' that they could find, leaving only sufficient for the use of families. Parties of dragoons and infantry were also sent out from the city on the same task. Since these units could have covered a large area, it seems that many people in outlying areas, certainly as far as Raphoe and Letterkenny, would have had their stocks requisitioned. This order incensed many in the rural areas against Lundy; they claimed that he 'was worse than the enemy could be' and reacted by burying grain to preserve it from the governor's foraging parties. Obviously the land-owners and their tenants had a good system of communication that allowed some at least to save much of their crop from the soldiers.

John Mackenzie commented on the availability of food at this time. He notes the goodly supply of food available on 9 April and the prices thereof:

> It was providentially arranged that at this time food was exceedingly cheap and plentiful in the North of Ireland. Thus it happened that Derry was supplied with stores, which sustained the inhabitants during the siege. The following account of the prices of various articles about the time when the Irish army sat down before the city is worthy of record. 'A salmon, about two feet long, may be bought for a penny or twopence. Forty-five eggs for one penny. A fat goose for threepence. A fat turkey for sixpence. A fat hen for threehalfpence. A fat lamb or kid for a groat.*[3]

---

*A groat was a silver coin worth four pence (4d), less than 2p in today's coinage.

There was still work to be done in the city, and the early days of April were spent levelling the suburbs and completing the ravelin as well as in bringing in provisions from the surrounding area. Every effort was being made to put the city in the best condition for defence and Lundy wrote a third letter to Shrewsbury. Once more he emphasized the needs of the city, urging that these requirements be sent speedily but especially general officers, provisions, money and tools for working on the defences. Added to the city's artillery was a great gun from Culmore Fort, while sixty barrels of salmon were brought from Lord Massereene's fish houses.[4]

Lundy's efforts in bolstering the city's defences had earned him praise. We have already noted what George Walker wrote of him in March, but another, anonymous, witness has left a further glowing testimonial to the man who was to become one of the most despised figures of Irish history. On 10 April, the day before the coronation of William and Mary, an unnamed Ulsterman gave evidence before a committee of the House of Lords about the situation in his native province. He told the committee that

> The number of Protestants in the North of Ireland were [estimated at] not much less than 100,000 men, some whereof have left the kingdom, others have taken protections; but generally ill-armed, want arms and ammunition and have no moneys [and] ... are thronged into a small corner of the country near Londonderry where (without the walls) there is little safety and, within, the room for about 3,000 men at most (when I came away)...
>
> [Colonel Lundy is] very much esteemed not only for his forwardness in their Majesties' service but for his military knowledge and courage and his extraordinary care and vigilance.[5]

The witness's comment that there was 'room for about 3,000 men at most' within the walls raises an interesting question: how many people were inside the walls during the siege? This estimate of there being room for no more than 3,000 is obviously far from accurate – there were over 7,000 in the garrison alone – but can Walker's overall figure of 30,000, including the soldiers of the garrison, be taken as any more accurate? The witness in the House of Lords might have intended his estimate to relate to people in addition to the normal population of the city, but even this leaves a great disparity between the two sets of figures. There is no doubt that the city was vastly overcrowded during the siege but it is all but impossible to imagine 30,000 within the walls, an area of no more than 500 yards by 300 yards. Without taking into consideration the space occupied by buildings, that would have allowed only five square yards per person. When one studies photographs of the crowds that gathered in front of the modern Guildhall on 30 November 1995 for the visit of the US President Clinton, even more doubt is cast on Walker's figure. (On that occasion the crowd was estimated at more than 20,000.) Walker goes on to say that 10,000 people deserted the city to take advantage of 'a declaration of the enemy to receive and protect all that would desert us, and return to their dwellings', while many more left later.[6] Even if such a reduction had occurred, the city would still have had an incredible overcrowding problem.

On that same day, 10 April, a council of war was held in the city at which a defence strategy was drawn up. The senior officer present was Robert Lundy. At the meeting it was agreed that the council's decisions should be posted at the town house for all to see and should also be read out to the soldiers of the battalions in the city. Clearly stated were the duties of the officers of the garrison, while it was noted that a 'thousand men shall be chosen to be part of this garrison, and joined with the soldiers already herein, to defend the city'. Further defensive works were to be undertaken which included the demolition of all houses and ditches outside the walls; this was in addition to the levelling of buildings close to the walls which had already taken place. That discipline was to be enforced was made clear by the order to erect 'a pair of gallows . . . in one of the bastions upon the south-west of the City, whereupon all mutinous or treacherous persons of this garrison shall be executed, who shall be condemned thereunto by a court martial'. In contrast, generous provisions were made for feeding the garrison with

> every soldier of the garrison, and non-commissioned officer, . . . weekly allowed out of the magazines eight quarts of meal, four pounds of fish, and three pounds of flesh for his weekly subsistence.
> . . . every soldier and non-commissioned officer . . . allowed a quart of small beer per day, as soon as the same can be provided, until some money shall come to allow them pay.*[7]

---

*The full text of the articles adopted by this council of war appear as Appendix Three. Small beer was a brew that attracted a lower excise duty than the full-strength brew and it continued to be produced until the duty on it was raised to the same as the full-strength product. The closest modern equivalent would be low-alcohol beer.

It was on that day, also, that David Cairnes returned from London, bringing with him a letter containing instructions for Governor Lundy.[8]

Meanwhile Lundy was deploying some of his new troops on tasks that were part of the city's preparations. Some of the cavalry from Coleraine and elsewhere in the county had arrived at the Waterside on the 9th; Lundy ordered these men to Strabane in County Tyrone, the neighbouring town of Lifford in County Donegal, and Letterkenny, also in County Donegal. These horse soldiers subsequently returned to the city with stores of meal and other provisions from the foraging expeditions earlier ordered by Lundy. On the 13th, and shortly before some Jacobite troops, described as 'a considerable body of King James's troops', arrived at the Waterside, Lundy ordered the destruction of houses there; these were to be set alight. The Jacobites who appeared at the Waterside that day were the first soldiers of James' army, other than Antrim's Regiment in December, to approach the city. Lundy comments that there were three squadrons of horse and that he supposed that he had a gun fired at them which caused them to retreat. Although some of the Jacobites, presumably those Lundy ordered to be fired at, found boats, they made no attempt to cross the river and withdrew that evening to Ballyowen on the road to Newtownlimavady. There they set up camp for the night. In contrast to this account, the House of Commons committee was told by Daniel Sherrard, on 12 August, that, when the enemy first appeared at the city on 13 April, the gunner, Mr Watson, had no ammunition.[9] Sherrard commented that it had been the gunner himself who had given him this information, which seems not only to contradict Lundy's evidence but much of what we know about the state of preparedness of the city. None of the local accounts mentions the shot or shots that Lundy ordered to be fired, although Ash recounts that the Jacobites fired on the city.[10] However, in the light of subsequent events it seems implausible that the city's artillery could have been without ammunition at this time. There are two possible explanations for Sherrard's comment. The first is that he was indirectly accusing Lundy of incompetence, or worse, while the second is that the guns facing the river might have had ammunition of the wrong calibre. Of the two suggestions the former is the more likely; Daniel Sherrard was one of the apprentices who shut the gates in December 1688 and he was later commissioned as ensign in Captain Jemmet's company, one of those formed by David Cairnes.

Those behind the city walls realized that their situation was at its most serious. A further council of war was called which appointed

Lundy to the post of commander in the field.[11] This appointment was made in spite of the fact that some in the city were now opposing him. Later it would be argued that some were already beginning to doubt his loyalty to the Williamite cause. One writer noted that:

> Lundy ... was at this time encouraging the principal officers to leave, telling them that the city was untenable and the belief became current that he had designs to give it up. It was because of this that many people, discerning his treacherous intentions, were unwilling to remain and be betrayed into the hands of the enemy.[12]

Such retrospective wisdom must be treated with scepticism and it is more likely that Lundy continued to enjoy the confidence of most of the townspeople and of his colleagues, although the confiscation of supplies would not have helped his popularity. It was this council of war also that made the decision that the local forces should take the field against the Jacobites before the latter could close on the city. In fact, this decision was made on Lundy's advice. Speaking to all the officers he told them that they were 'all drive[n] in to a little place' where, due to the great numbers present, they must perish by starvation but there was still the opportunity to drive off the Irish army. This could be done at the pass of the Finn water, 'which had always been fatal to the Irish' and since this was the last chance to beat the Irish 'we ought to venture all rather than suffer them to pass'. Lundy said that he would accompany the army as it tried its fortune in a battle, and this was approved by all. It was resolved that:

> on Monday next, by 10 o'clock, all officers and soldiers, horse and foot, and all other armed men whatsoever, of our forces and friends enlisted or not enlisted, that can or will fight for their country and religion, against a common enemy, shall appear on the fittest ground, near Claudy ford, Lifford and Long-Causeway, as shall be nearest to their several and respective quarters; there to draw up, in battalions, to be ready to fight the enemy, and to preserve our lives and all that is dear to us, from the enemy.[13]

Each officer and soldier was to bring with him a week's provisions and 'as much as they can' for the horses, indicating that a quick battle was not expected. The other armed men, described as 'enlisted or not enlisted', were to include 'all from sixteen to sixty' years old.

Lundy's name appears as the first signatory of this order. This would be expected from the man who was now commander in the field as well as governor of the city but, since he had the greatest military experience of anyone present at the council, it is also clear that the entire plan was his. (Only Henry Baker and Jonathan Mitchelburne would have had military experience that matched Lundy's but neither was at the council of war, although the latter, who arrived in the city about a week before the siege began, was at the subsequent battle.) The first battle for Derry was to be fought some dozen or so miles from the city's walls; Lundy obviously believed in the concept that the best form of defence is attack, and that forward defence is preferable to close defence.

The deployment to Claudy-ford, which is at the modern village of Clady on the Tyrone–Donegal border, Lifford and Long-Causeway, north of Lifford near Porthall, may seem strange to modern eyes but it must be remembered that there was no bridge across the Foyle at the city, nor was the river fordable. An attacker would have had to use boats to cross, and this would have been too dangerous, even if boats had been available. The closest point to the city at which a large force of troops, with their weaponry and impedimenta, could cross the river was in the area of Strabane, close to where the rivers Mourne and Finn converge to form the Foyle. This was the logic behind the southward deployment, a logic proved on 14 April when a large Jacobite force passed the city on the other side of the Foyle en route to Strabane.

Lundy had already given orders to demolish the bridge at Clady, and some of its arches had been knocked down the week before while a breastwork had been built on the Donegal side, probably from the rubble of the bridge. With this and his deployments of troops, Lundy hoped to secure the crossing points along the Finn, and 'Major Crofton and Captain Hamilton, with a party at Lifford, were engaged all night, and repulsed the enemy in every attempt they made to cross the ford.'[14] These clashes occurred between advance parties from both armies and, at this stage at least, the Williamites were holding their own. On the 15th Lundy led out of the city the main body of the troops who were to meet the Jacobites at Lifford and the other fords. Several accounts put the strength of Lundy's force at 10,000 men, it having been reinforced on its march south to Lifford when 'great numbers of other Protestants did meet thereabouts'.[15] However, the overall figure of 10,000 is probably an exaggeration: a contemporary Jacobite account puts its strength at 7,000 and even that must be treated with some caution since it is in the nature of warfare that the strength of opponents be exaggerated so that the achievements of one's own side may be enhanced.[16] Mitchelburne reckoned the Jacobite army to be about 5,000 or 6,000 strong.[17]

As the Williamite force was setting out on its march to Lifford, the promised relief fleet from Liverpool arrived in Lough Foyle and dropped anchor off Redcastle.[18] The fleet included eleven ships and carried 1,600 infantrymen; these were ten merchant ships escorted by the Royal Navy 40-gun frigate HMS *Swallow*,* commanded by Captain Wolfranc Cornwall.[19] Captain Ash wrote that they dropped anchor at Ture, which is much closer to the city than Redcastle, and further commented that when the two commanding officers eventually returned to their ships these were then near Culmore; Ture is less than three miles north of Culmore.[20] Mitchelburne suggested that, at one point, the ships were at Quigley's Point, between Redcastle and Ture.[21] Obviously, the vessels were making their way up the lough and closer to the city. Three messengers, Major Zachariah Tiffin, who would later command an Inniskilling regiment, with Captains Lyndon and Cornwall, came ashore at different times to ride to Derry to meet Lundy with the news that reinforcements had arrived. These officers were to obtain Lundy's instructions for the landing and deployment of the troops.[22] When it was appreciated that Lundy had already quit the city to lead a field force, Colonel Cunningham, the senior of the commanding officers with the relief force (the other was Colonel Richards), wrote a despatch for direct delivery to the governor offering Cunningham's two well-disciplined regiments to support the local garrison at the fords, stating that:

> I am sure they will be of great use, on any occasion, but especially for the encouragement of raw men, as I judge most of yours are; therefore it is my opinion, that you can only stop the passes at the ford of the Finn until I can join you, and afterwards if giving battle be necessary, you will be in a much better posture for it than before. [23]

The despatch was received by Lundy at 9 o'clock that evening by which time any reinforcement of his force at the fords was out of the question. By then Lundy's command had been broken and was in retreat towards the city. Lundy replied to Cunningham:

---

*Since there was then a joint monarchy of William and Mary the warships of the Royal Navy ought to have been referred to as Their Majesties' Ships (TMS) rather than His, or Her, Majesty's Ship (HMS) but such a practice was not adopted and ships' logs of the time continue to refer to vessels as His Majesty's Ships. However, in his account of the siege, Cecil Davis Milligan uses the abbreviation TMS for Royal Navy ships.

I am come back much sooner than I expected when I went; for, having numbers placed on Finn water, as I went to a pass where a few might oppose a greater number than came to the place, I found them on the run before the enemy, who pursued them with great vigour, and, I fear, will march on with their forces, so that I wish your men would march all night in good order, lest they should be surprised; here they shall have all the accommodation the place will afford. In this hurry, pardon me for this brevity; the rest the bearer will inform you.[24]

In a postscript Lundy added the exhortation, 'If the men be not landed, let 'em land and march immediately.' The letter had already been sealed when Lundy decided to add that postscript; he opened the missive again with his own hand to add the additional words.[25]

What had happened to Lundy's soldiers? He certainly had the numbers to meet the Jacobites at the fords and, in and near the city, he had strong defences; but even the best of the engineer's science and the choicest of equipment make up only part of a commander's needs. In a later century Napoleon was to assess the value of morale to an army; but this was a truth already known. The French army of the late-seventeenth century knew the value of morale as did Robert Lundy, but he had now seen the morale of his army shattered in quick time in the area of Strabane and Lifford. And as the esprit of his command collapsed so, too, did that of Lundy.

Morale depends on a number of factors, among them good training and discipline. Lundy's army lacked both. It had been cobbled together in reaction to a crisis with no time for training. Contemporary military practice was for new recruits to be assigned to the regiment with which they would serve and be trained by that unit; there were no dedicated training establishments nor any system of regimental depots as would be developed in later centuries.[26] Thus training was the responsibility of individual commanding officers who needed a core of experienced officers and NCOs to discharge that task.[27] This was difficult enough at the best of times, but became almost impossible if training was to be carried out on campaign; and it was made even more difficult, if not close to impossible, if there was no strong core of experienced training staff.

Even though he had complained of lack of discipline, perhaps this had not troubled Lundy too much since he knew that the Jacobite army was afflicted in like manner. Some three-quarters of a century later Maurice de Saxe was to describe discipline as 'the soul of armies,'[28] and Lundy seems to have considered that both armies were short on soul.

Certainly he appeared quite confident of success when he deployed his troops about Long Causeway, through Lifford and thence to Clady. His men were fighting for their survival, a major spur to the morale of any military organization, and would have the benefit of choosing the ground and holding defensive positions; these two latter points gave a distinct advantage to the Williamites. But Lundy made one fundamental error in his assessment of the enemy army, and this was to be his undoing, and the undoing of his force at the fords. The Jacobite cavalry, as we have already seen, was of a much higher standard than Lundy believed. He considered the entire Jacobite army to be a rag-tag organization, with inadequate equipment, few weapons, no training and indifferent leadership.

None of these was true of the Jacobite cavalry. James' mounted troops were excellent and were probably the equal of any contemporaries in Europe.[29] It was this same Jacobite cavalry force that was to inflict a humiliating defeat on the Williamites in this encounter and that force would remain formidable throughout the war of the kings, causing especial distress to William's troops at the Boyne in 1690. At the fords the Jacobite cavalry had the additional benefit of being commanded by highly-experienced French officers: Rosen recorded that Maumont was the first to enter the river.[30] The accounts written by George Walker and John Mackenzie both blame Lundy for the débâcle that followed, one of the few points on which these two men agreed. Walker and Mackenzie point out the numerical superiority enjoyed by Lundy at Cladyford, where the Jacobites chose to launch an opposed crossing, and in this observation they are accurate.[31] Of the rout at the fords Lord Blaney told the House of Commons that 'the Protestants all run in great confusion; no order was either given or observed'.[32]

Other than Blaney, none of these commentators was a military man and their analysis of the situation at the fords cannot be taken as a serious dissection of the battle. To begin with, Lundy had deployed troops to cover several crossing places as a result of which his men were spread out over a line that extended almost eight miles. In such circumstances it was not possible for the commander to exercise full control over all his forces, and he was compelled to rely on the competence of those who acted in his stead at the various points of contact between the two sides. It is invidious to try to place all the blame for this defeat at Lundy's door.

Some of Lundy's units acquitted themselves admirably: Colonel Skeffington's Regiment, now under command of Mitchelburne, stopped a Jacobite party that tried to ford the river near Castlefinn, some miles beyond Clady, driving them back with many casualties. About thirty dragoons of Stewart's Regiment, commanded by Captain Adam Murray, a local man of whom we shall see more shortly, fought valiantly at Clady, holding back the foe until their ammunition was spent.[33] But there was an inevitability about the Williamite defeat. Infantry might hold back infantry, while dragoons, who were really mounted infantry and dismounted from their horses to fight, might do likewise, but the entry of heavy cavalry into the equation meant that there could be but one outcome.

Heavy cavalry, known as 'horse' at this time, provided the shock troops of a seventeenth-century army, the 'shock and awe' of a more recent American definition. Even a troop of horse at the charge was an impressive and frightening sight, especially for an infantryman who was asked to stand and face it. A squadron was even more impressive, and frightening, while a complete regiment would have been terrifying. Since the river was in flood the Williamites might also have expected this to be a protection against enemy attack and the psychological effect of the cavalry charge must have been heightened as a result. How strong was the Jacobite cavalry at the fords? Rosen later wrote an account of the battle for Louvois in which he indicated that Hamilton had three squadrons of cavalry and two of dragoons which were reinforced by additional cavalry from James' escort, deployed from Omagh, plus additional cavalry and dragoons under Lieutenant-General Pusignan.[34] Thus the Jacobites were able to deploy a sizeable body of cavalry, perhaps over 450 men, against the Williamite positions; this equates to a regiment. Furthermore, Rosen, Maumont and Lery took the time to make a detailed reconnaissance of the Williamite defences before launching their assault.[35] The adage that 'time spent on reconnaissance is seldom wasted' was obviously one in which these men believed. Accordingly, they were able to identify their opponents' weaknesses and use the speed of cavalry to exploit them.

The development of the infantry square to meet a cavalry charge was a relatively recent innovation from the Dutch, although its origins can be seen in the Spanish tercio, and the drill evolutions needed to move a battalion into square took a long time to learn and practise.[36] There can be no doubt that the Williamites at the fords had no idea of how to form a square. Had they been able to do so they might still have been performing a pointless exercise. The deterrent effect of the square lay not so much in its appearance to the cavalry trooper but in its appearance to that trooper's mount. A properly-formed square presented a hedge of steel to the horses prompting them to veer away from it, since the pikemen, normally placed behind the musketeers, would have taken their places in the square's front ranks.

But the Williamites could present no hedges of steel since they lacked the basic element of that hedge, the pike. A standard infantry battalion at the time had a balanced proportion of musketeers and pikemen, normally one pike to every five muskets. Pikemen carried sixteen-foot-long ash staves tipped with steel points which were driven into the ground at an angle of about forty-five degrees to create the hedge. Even before learning how to form square, the pikeman had to learn basic foot drill and then 'the postures' that governed his use of his weapon. Of these there were thirty-six separate drill evolutions.[37] It was small wonder that the few Williamite pikemen at the fords proved of little value. The introduction of the bayonet eventually rendered the pikeman obsolete since the musket-equipped infantryman could simply fix his bayonet to his weapon to produce the effect of a short pike.* But although the bayonet had already been introduced into English regiments, it had then been withdrawn, and no Williamite unit at the fords would have been equipped with bayonets. Thus most of the Williamite infantry had only its basic firepower to deter the Jacobite cavalry; Skeffington's Regiment was an exception and seems to have had a strong proportion of pikemen. This regiment marched back to Derry 'with flying colours and drums beating a march', and although attacked three times by Jacobite cavalry under Colonel Dominic Sheldon it beat off each attack, perhaps by deploying the pikemen to perform their tactical role or by good use of the musketeers.[39] The author of *Ireland Preserved* puts these words in Sheldon's mouth:

> I charged their rear three times, and each time the Commander drew off his shot, fired upon us, and put our men in disorder, we could do no good with him, whosoever he is, he has not his trade to learn.[40]

Another Jacobite commander, Dorrington, comments:

> This is the third time he brought up the rear of their flying army. He has his men in as good discipline as any of us; he marches with flying colours and cares not a pin for the government, regards not the Lord Tirconnel's proclamation a farthing. There's a spark for you.[41]

---

*Fitted with a plug bayonet, the standard English matchlock measured an inch short of seven feet, less than half the length of a pike. The flintlock was two inches shorter again.[38]

Although some Williamite foot soldiers were entrenched along the river banks by the fords, they could do little to repel an attacking cavalry force. Even the accusation that Lundy had failed to resupply his troops with ammunition is almost irrelevant: the speed of a cavalry charge across what was, and is, a narrow waterway, allowed no time for reloading; the task of reloading a matchlock, or the more modern flintlock, musket was a lengthy one, and raw soldiers could not have fired any more than one round per minute, and that is probably a generous estimate. Thus, as the Williamite soldiers watched the cavalry on their huge horses charge into the water on the opposite bank they would have been terrified. The noise of the charge alone was terrific, not to mention the fact that each individual – and these men would still have thinking as individuals rather than reacting as a disciplined and trained unit – saw several very large horses powering towards him as three ranks of cavalry, swords drawn, splashed into the river. Their reaction would have been the most natural of all: to survive; and to do so meant running for their lives. It was the effect of the Irish cavalry, more than any other factor, which led to the rout of the Williamites at the fords. Once the cavalry had made a successful crossing, the Williamite situation was bleak, since untrained infantry could do nothing to stop cavalry rolling up their positions from the flanks as well as hitting them in frontal attacks.

We have already seen that some individuals in the city were losing confidence in Lundy and were even regarding him as a traitor. The flight of the field force from the fords added to the strength of their accusations. It was claimed that Lundy was the first member of that force to reach the city's gates, thus further detracting from his reputation as a soldier. Even if this accusation was true, the fact remains that Lundy was still conscious of his duties for he added a further postscript to his despatch to Cunningham.

> Since writing this, Major Tiffin is come here, and I have given him my opinion fully, which, I believe, when you hear, and see the place, you will both join me, that without an immediate supply of money and provisions, this place must fall very soon into the enemy's hands. If you do not send your men here some time to-morrow, it will not be in your power to bring 'em at all.[42]

Lundy also told Tiffin to let Cunningham know that the city had no more than ten days' provisions for 3,000 men, although all unnecessary personnel had been told to leave and private supplies had been gathered into public stores.[43] (In contrast to these figures, Mitchelburne suggests that there was sufficient for 10,000 men for three months.[44]) Furthermore, he asked both Cunningham and Richards to come to the city with some of their officers, leaving their men on board, to 'resolve on what was best to be done'.[45]

Both men arrived in Derry the following day, the 16th, with some of their officers and learned that King James, with some 2,500 men, was approaching. Another council of war was decided upon. This seems to have been an entirely military affair from which local civilians, including George Walker, were excluded, thus giving further ammunition to Lundy's enemies. Even some soldiers were excluded: these were Colonels Chicester and Hamilton as well as Major Henry Baker. The council issued a declaration that read:

> Upon inquiry, it appears, there is not provision in the garrison of Londonderry for the present garrison and the two regiments on board, for a week or ten days, at most; and it appearing that the place is not tenable against a well appointed army, therefore, it is concluded upon and resolved, that it is not convenient for his Majesty's service, but the contrary, to land the two regiments under Colonel Cunningham and Colonel Richards, their command, now on board in the river of Lough Foyle; that considering the present circumstances of affairs, and the likelihood the enemy will soon possess themselves of this place, it is thought most convenient that the *principal officers shall privately withdraw themselves*, as well for their own preservation, as in hopes that the inhabitants, by a timely capitulation, may make terms the better with the enemy; and this we judge most convenient for his Majesty's service, as the present state of affairs now is.[46]

Following this declaration, the two commanding officers returned to their ship which set sail two days later, 'leaving the citizens to sink or swim'.[47] Strangely, Lundy had been issuing orders for quarters to be provided for the soldiers of the two regiments from the ships, but, while doing so, found himself surrounded by angry civilians and was unable to proceed further. He was also unable to leave the city and sent a despatch to Richards telling the latter to leave without him. To some, his being seen to issue orders for the quartering of fresh troops was a contrivance to cover his own treachery.[48]

Although it is often assumed that the ships sailed off with the provisions intended for the city still on board, Lundy was told by Cunningham that there were neither provisions nor money on the vessels. The story of the ships' cargo was to become a scandal and the agent responsible for providing and victualling the ships, as well as the cargo of provisions for the city and money for the garrison, Mathew Anderton, the collector of customs at Chester, was later accused of inefficiency. Although ordered to appear before the House of Commons to answer the charges laid against him, Anderton did not do so, pleading medical grounds, although his two sons did appear in his place and defended their father with some vigour.[49]

Among the charges made against Anderton were that he did not provide enough shipping; that the biscuit, on which the soldiers were to live, was 'very bad', as was the beer, which led some men to drink salt water instead and others their own urine. It was claimed that the beer, as well as being poor, was also about twelve to fourteen inches from full in each barrel. However, it seems that the cheese provided was good, although this can have been little consolation to the soldiers, some of whom died on the voyage from Hoylake to the Foyle while many others were sick.[50] That voyage took six days, and to the soldiers' complaints about the food and drink were added others about comfort. Not that soldiers expected to be comfortable on a sea voyage, but this seemed to be a situation worse than normal without any of the customary sleeping platforms on which to repose. Needless to say, all these problems were laid at the door of Mathew Anderton.[51]

Anderton was also suspected of the much more serious offence of peculation: he had been instructed to hand £2,000 to Cunningham for the subsistence of the soldiers and the defence of Londonderry. This was later increased to £4,000, of which £500 was to be paid to Colonel Lundy. The latter sum was intended as a reward to Lundy for his faithful services. It will also be remembered that James Hamilton was to have brought £1,000 to Lundy from Anderton in March but had received less than £600. In defence of their father, his sons told the House of Commons' committee that he had handed over to Colonel Cunningham every penny of public money that had been in his possession at the time. Cunningham's comment to Lundy that there was no money on the ships suggests that what Anderton had handed over had been far short of the £4,000 expected. Since there is no record of any further action being taken against Anderton, it would seem that his sons were giving accurate evidence and that the collector had had no public funds in addition to those monies he gave Cunningham.[52]

That same Cunningham was not impressed by the city although it was said in England 'to be one of the strongest places in the world'. Instead he considered it a town that could not keep out an army that had cannon. Neither did the garrison impress him 'for he had heard of all their cowardice'. Cunningham knew Derry well since he had been at school there and had visited it several times as an adult; he had never considered it 'to be a place of any strength'. At the time of his visit to Lundy, Cunningham had a brother still living in the city and may be presumed to have had information from him.* Who the brother was we do not know although there were several Cunninghams among the defenders; it is possible that his brother was Captain Michael Cunningham of Prehen, an officer in Skeffington's Regiment, but Captain John Cunningham who was killed at the battle of Windmill Hill on 6 May is another possibility as are Archibald, a signatory to the corporation commission of 1690, James, who was later to 'invent' a starch/tallow mix that allowed the garrison to eke out their supplies, and Alexander, one of the apprentice boys.[53]

Thomas Cunningham and Solomon Richards were later dismissed from the army, but it is significant that this did not happen until the siege had ended and the city had been relieved. Richards, who had been under Cunningham's command, was granted bail in July following a ruling by the House of Commons that there 'does not appear to be any evidence that [he] . . . was guilty of any miscarriage'.[54] Had the city fallen immediately to the Jacobites, it is quite possible that neither man would have suffered the disgrace of being cashiered, although command of their regiments was given to other officers soon after their return to England. The effects on these regiments were almost non-existent: in 1751 they became the 9th and 17th Regiments and, later, the Royal Norfolk and Royal Leicestershire Regiments; both are now subsumed in the Royal Anglian Regiment.

But while the relief fleet sailed off back to England there was further debate in the city. The council of war attended by Cunningham and Richards had also resolved to send messengers privately to King James, offering to surrender the city the following day.[55] When this plan became known to some of those excluded from the council's deliberations, there was much anger, with Sir Arthur Rawdon and others averring that 'deserting Derry would, in their opinion, be deserting the kingdom and the Protestant interest'. Not everyone shared this anger as some of the citizens recommended 'yielding to necessity'. On the other hand, many felt that those who would betray them should

---

*It is possible that it was a branch of Cunningham's family that gave the village of Newtowncunningham and the neighbouring Manorcunningham, in east Donegal, their names.

be shot.[56] And Lundy was the prime target for this communal anger. 'There is great notice taken of his dilatory proceedings; he does not at all answer the character most people give him.'[57]

It was only some six weeks since George Walker had formed such a high opinion of the governor, and only days since that unnamed witness had spoken so highly of him to the House of Lords' committee. How had Lundy gone from hero to villain in such short time? It seems that his morale had shattered in recent days and that he no longer possessed the stomach for a fight. After all, he had just witnessed a numerically superior force, in defensive positions, suffer humiliating defeat and dash into headlong retreat. On his return to the city he must have re-assessed its ability to withstand attack, especially when he now believed that his troops were not reliable in battle. Remembering that Lundy had also requested that general officers be deployed to the city, it is possible that he considered himself to have insufficient experience of command for the task that faced him. Doubtless, also, the performance of the Jacobite cavalry, some of which he must have seen in action, made him change his opinion of King James' army and he might now have considered that the Jacobites stood a good chance of taking the city. Could men who had suffered defeat after defeat - at Dromore, Coleraine, Portglenone, Moneymore, and, most recently, at the fords – really defend Londonderry? Was there any hope at all for the city?

Remembering that Lundy was still one of the few in the city with a true appreciation of what faced them, his doubts can be understood. What chance had Derry and its garrison of holding out should a Jacobite army appear, complete with an artillery train and all the equipment needed to mount a siege? The city walls had been designed to keep out Irish clansmen rather than a modern army with siege artillery, and the men who would be defending those walls had, so far, shown little real mettle as soldiers. Another factor was Lundy's estimate of the size of the Jacobite army, which he believed to number some 25,000 men. In his account Walker states there were 20,000 Jacobites. In fact the Jacobites could not have numbered any more than 10,000 and the true figure was probably even lower. However, commanders under attack have always been prone to exaggerate the strength of their enemies, thereby providing a better excuse for failure or to make success appear even more admirable and, perhaps, the result of military genius when obtained against superior numbers.

All these factors probably played a part in Lundy's loss of conviction. To the citizens of the city, who believed that they faced the prospect of annihilation, none of this would have mattered. In their eyes Lundy was a traitor: he later said that the rabble swore that he had 'sold them and the town to King James for 1700 pound'. Many, thinking that their cause was lost, left the city; these included members of the garrison. Some of those who had taken refuge in the city and some of the merchants were so concerned about the behaviour of the rabble following the defeat at Clady bridge that they left the town and boarded ships for England, paying what rates were demanded for their passage. Some of those refugees and merchants were on board the vessels that carried Cunningham and Richards' Regiments away from the Foyle. 'Great droves for England now are fled and gone/And in deep despair leaves us thus forlorn' is how Mitchelburne summed up the rush of evacuees in *Ireland Preserved*.

Rumours must also have been rife about the approach of King James. The monarch had left Dublin for the city although his principal French adviser, Avaux, recommended that he remain in the capital.[58] But James was bull-headed in his intentions and set off for Ulster. By 14 April the royal entourage was in the ruins of Omagh, where Avaux made another attempt to dissuade James from his plan to travel to Derry.[59] Once again he was rebuffed but then came the news of the relief fleet that was approaching Lough Foyle and of the Williamite intention to give battle at the fords. There seems to have been a remarkable flow of intelligence, but there is no indication from the various contemporary accounts whether this was from spies or simply from observation; that the king knew of the intention to give battle at the fords the day before Lundy marched out of Derry suggests the presence of spies in the city. By the same token the Williamites seem often to have had good intelligence on their opponents. One conclusion must be that there were many individuals who were determined to emerge safe from the crisis no matter what its outcome.

This new information brought about a change of heart in James who decided that he would retrace his steps, quitting Omagh for Charlemont the following day. His generals, including Conrad de Rosen, were ordered to make their way to join the Jacobites advancing on the fords. Whatever relief Avaux might have felt at James' change of mind must surely have evaporated at Charlemont where a messenger from the Duke of Berwick, one of James' illegitimate sons, reached him. Berwick's man had news from the army now close to Londonderry.[60] The decision by the council of war of the 16th to open secret negotiations with James led to a delegation visiting Hamilton's camp at St

Johnston where they, wrongly, believed James to be present. Learning of the discussions, Berwick sent his messenger to Charlemont where he told James that the gates of Derry would be opened should he appear in front of them. This seems to have fitted in with what James had long believed, and he also wanted to make it clear that rumours of his death in France were without foundation. So, once again, the King set his face towards Derry.[61]

In the meantime, Hamilton had made an arrangement with the city's leaders that the Jacobite army would not approach within four miles of the city while terms for the city's surrender were being considered.[62] Walker wrote of these terms that 'There was no doubt, but upon surrender of the Town, King James would Grant a General Pardon, and Order restitution of all that had been Plunder'd from them'.[63] Many, it seemed, were keen that these terms should be taken seriously. The unfortunate Lundy appears to have taken a back seat at this stage although he was still governor of the city. But now King James rode into the situation. During James' short reign, events seem to have conspired against him, while his communications with his advisers frequently left much wanting. The king's intentions were often misunderstood but never more so than on the April day that he appeared with his escort before Bishop's Gate.

James made good speed from Charlemont and arrived at Derry early on Thursday 18 April. With General Conrad de Rosen, and a small escort, he rode up to the city walls at about 10 o'clock, confidently expecting to see Berwick's prediction come true: that the gates of the city would be open to the monarch as the citizens came to their senses and realized that the king had no ill intentions for them.[64] James did not know that Hamilton had agreed a *cordon sanitaire* around the city while the leading townspeople considered the proposals he had made. Now the defenders on the walls and many of those who had sought refuge within the city walls saw James and his entourage approach. What they saw was not their monarch come with good intentions but a symbol of Jacobite treachery, a breaking of General Hamilton's word and a sign of the treachery that might govern their treatment should they surrender. Those defenders believed that James had been at St Johnston with his army, and there was a great surge of anger at what was seen as duplicity. This anger came close to having fatal consequences for James.

As the monarch and his most senior military commander rode towards the Bishop's Gate there was apprehension within the walls.

Upon the 18th of April [James] advances, with his Army, before our Walls, with Flying Colours.

Orders were given, that none should dare to fire till the King's Demands were first known, by another Messenger to be sent to His Majesty for that purpose; but our men on the Walls, wondering to see Lieut Gen. Hamilton (contrary to his Engagement, not to come within four Miles of the Town) approaching our Walls in such order, they imagining they were by some means or other betrayed, thought it reasonable to consider their own safety, and to keep the Enemy at distance, by firing their Guns upon them, which they accordingly did.[65]

There is no evidence that Hamilton was with the king but the result was the same since

In an instant a discharge of musketry and cannon from the troops stationed in the church bastion, was directed against the enemy, proclaiming defence and hostilities with the triumphant shout of 'No Surrender'.[66]

One of James' aides-de-camp, Captain Troy, a dragoon officer, was struck by a cannonball and killed. Troy was at the king's side. Other members of the party were also fatally injured. James chose discretion and retreated out of range of the angry defenders on the walls.[67] Safe from cannon fire, he spent the rest of the day on Foyle Hill, near the modern Carmelite monastery at Termonbacca, gazing at the city and watching the Williamite gunners vent their anger and frustration on their foes. For James it was a miserable situation, made more miserable by the rain that was now falling steadily. While that rain presented an augury of James' hopes being washed away, it also provided a foretaste of the conditions his soldiers were to endure around the city for the next 105 days.

Towards the end of what, for him, must have been a most inauspicious day, James withdrew to the small castle at Mongavlin, some eight miles to the south in County Donegal.[68] It is to his credit that he continued to maintain communication with the leaders in the city; he made four attempts to agree terms with its defenders. He must have impressed those leaders who even sent an apology to the king for opening fire on him; this was accepted by James.[69] While such gentlemanly conduct might be dismissed as being expected of that period, it does suggest that hope continued, on both sides, of agreeing terms and thereby saving Derry from the trauma of a siege. But those now negotiating from within the walls were no longer representative of the bulk of opinion in the city; the more radical leaders and many of the inhabitants were determined not to negotiate with James. Their view was represented in a letter to the king.

> Sir: The cause we have undertaken, we design for ever to maintain, and question not, but that powerful providence which has hitherto been our guardian, will finish the protection of us, against all your attempts, and give a happy issue to our arms. We must let you know, that King William is as capable as rewarding our loyalty as King James; and an English parliament can be just as bountiful to our courage and suffering as an Irish one: and that in time we question not, but your lands will be forfeited rather than ours, and confiscated into our possession, as a recompense for this signal service to the crown of England and for this inexpressible toil and labour, expense of blood and treasure, pursuant to their sacred Majesties declaration to that purpose; a true copy whereof we herewith send you to convince you how little we fear your menaces.[70]

The cry of 'No Surrender' shouted from the city's walls that morning was echoed in that letter which made clear to James that the city would not submit to him. James now decided that matters at Derry should be left in the hands of his generals, Hamilton, Maumont, Pusignan and Pointis, while he returned to Dublin, accompanied by Rosen and Melfort.[71] He left no specific orders about attacking the city, besieging it or blockading it. He did, however, decide to promote Rosen to the post of Marshal General of his armies and of his kingdom of Ireland as Rosen reported in a letter from Lifford to Louvois.[72]

Not only had James angered the defenders of the city but he had also caused considerable frustration within the ranks of his own supporters, one of whom wrote:

> You observe here the return Londonderry made the king for all the paths he had taken in travelling so far, in order to gain those rebels with lenity. But 'tis what he always gets from Protestants generally. No experience will make him behave himself towards those traitors as he should do. He spoiled his business in Ireland by his over great indulgence towards them. He was infatuated with this rotten principle – provoke not your Protestant subjects – the which hindered his majesty from drawing troops sooner out of Ireland into England for the security of his person and government; from making up a Catholic army in England; from accepting those forces the most Christian king [Louis XIV] had offered him.[73]

Any military headquarters must be able effectively to command, control and communicate. James' headquarters had been shown as sadly deficient in communications, so deficient in fact that it might well have drafted the death certificate for James' hopes and his strategy of using Ireland as a stepping stone to Scotland. Although the Williamite narrative quoted earlier (p. 76) suggests that Richard Hamilton was included in the king's party at Bishop's Gate, and thus indicts Hamilton of being untrustworthy, there is no evidence that Hamilton was present. In all probability the king's approach was planned so hastily, and by so few individuals, that Hamilton was unaware of what was happening. He would have been shrewd enough to have realized that such a venture could only destroy any hopes of a negotiated settlement.

James' precipitate action had delivered a blow to the morale of his own army. Now, by default, he was to choose the worst of the three options that, but days earlier, had been open to that army. The first of these was to advance rapidly on the city while its garrison and the refugees were still in shock from the defeat at the fords and storm it. Had his army done so it would almost certainly have succeeded and Derry would have fallen, leaving James free to embark for Scotland, if he could obtain sufficient transports, to continue his quest to be restored. His second, and more feasible, course of action was to mask Derry by leaving a token force there to contain the garrison while the rest of the army took the field to clear the remainder of Ulster or, again, crossed to Scotland. (The port of Derry was not essential as the boarding could have been carried out in Lough Foyle at Redcastle or farther north at Greencastle.) But James was now forced into the least desirable of options: to lay siege to the city to bring about its surrender. This seems to support the comment about James' lack of decision made by Comte d'Avaux in his first despatch from Ireland: 'Our chief difficulty will be the irresolution of King James, who often changes his mind, and then decides not always for the best.'[74]

Why was laying siege to the city the worst option available to the Jacobite army? The answer is simple: that army had not come north with the type of organization necessary for a prolonged siege operation.* As well as being deficient in artillery, James' army also lacked engineering resources. When, before the army left Dublin for Ulster, the Jacobite command tried to obtain the tools and equipment needed for siege warfare, they found that 'there was nothing at all of what was required'. Looked at in its overall structure and organization, James'

---

*See Appendix Seven for Vauban's time scale for preparing a siege.

army included a weak infantry arm, lacking training and weapons and with poor leadership, while its artillery was inadequate, and the engineers even more so. All this stands in stark contrast to the cavalry, which was of high quality with good officers and which had already demonstrated its mettle. Such evidence suggests that King James and his staff had hoped for a rapid conclusion to the Ulster campaign, with a short war of movement rather than the static situation that was now emerging.

One of the accusations levelled against Robert Lundy was that he attempted to surrender the city by entering into negotiations with the Jacobites. In fact, by so doing, Lundy probably saved the city since, by involving the Jacobites in negotiations, he bought more time for the garrison and prevented a rapid Jacobite advance after their victory at the fords. It is also possible that Richard Hamilton was happy to enter into talks with the Williamites because he believed that Cunningham's and Richards' regiments were now included in the city's garrison. Equally, of course, Hamilton might simply have been unhappy about storming the city because he knew that such an operation depended on his infantry and he would have been very aware of the shortcomings of that particular arm of his army. Whatever the underlying reason, Hamilton's failure to make an immediate advance on the city cost the Jacobites the real fruits of the victory at the fords.

But Lundy's time as governor was now all but over. Too many in the city not only lacked confidence in him but also blamed him for their current ills. Lundy provided a ready scapegoat: all such situations require such an individual, and the unfortunate Lundy was to become immortalized as the man who attempted to betray the city. Strangely, he found some support, even at this late juncture, from an unlikely source: George Walker. The latter claimed that he and Henry Baker tried unsuccessfully to persuade the Scot to remain as governor.[75] Baker was a professional soldier and was to become governor, with Walker as his deputy, on Lundy's departure. If Walker's version of events is accurate, then it suggests that Lundy still had supporters in the city and that these included Baker. Since Baker knew the profession of arms it is likely that he had a much better appreciation of what was happening, that he could read between the lines where others could not, and that he felt that Lundy had been doing his best. Neither Baker nor Lundy would have seen the garrison's surrender as the final defeat of the Williamite cause in Ireland, as would most of the citizens. To them the established military protocols of siege warfare would have been coming into play. Surrendering the city did not mean surrendering the garrison since the defending troops would have been allowed to march out of the city and been accorded the honours of war. They might even have been allowed to take the field again in support of King William.

What were these protocols of siege warfare? They had developed over a long period of time and were to remain in practice until the early-nineteenth century when Napoleon brought them to an end by threatening to treat as traitors those of his fortress commanders who followed them. The first convention to be observed was the offer of terms to the fortress or town about to be invested. At this point the defending commander could accept the terms, which were usually quite generous and allowed the defending garrison to leave the fortress with colours flying, drums beating and honour unblemished. They might also be allowed to retain their arms and might join in battle elsewhere, although to do this was not considered honourable.

If the garrison chose to refuse this initial offer then the business of a siege began. This was a very exact military science which, by this time, had burgeoned in terms of military engineering. Artillerymen and engineers now came into their own with the latter preparing the way for the heavy guns to be brought ever closer to the walls; the preferred effective range was from 600 yards down to 100 yards, from which distance the guns could bombard the walls until the structure began to crumble. Once a useable breach had been created another offer of terms was made. Acceptance meant that the garrison would be accorded the same respect as if they had agreed to the initial call to surrender the fortress; but should the second offer be rejected, it was recognized that no quarter would be given in the ensuing assault, nor could it be sought, and that the entire garrison would perish. Civilians within the fortress might also die in the fierce fighting that would follow an assault through the breach, and this had to be considered by the commanders of the fortress.

However, all of this was irrelevant to the people sheltering behind Derry's walls. They had no real concept of what was happening, or about to happen, and no knowledge of the protocols recognized by soldiers. To them the situation was one of mortal peril, and Derry was the last place in which they could seek refuge. This was a clear matter of survival, and such was their fear that they were no longer prepared to trust James, or any of his representatives, whether soldiers or courtiers.

And so Lundy made his escape from the city, aided by Walker and Baker. Tradition has it that he climbed down a pear tree close to the walls while wearing the garments of a private soldier and carrying on his back a load of fuze cord, or match. It is said that the pear tree was still present many decades later but the story is doubtful: had not the walls been cleared of anything that would have assisted a Jacobite assault? Perhaps the pear tree later grew near the walls with the story of Lundy's departure amended to give it a key role in that flight from the anger of the besieged. One account indicates that 'Lundy, one Gilner Brasier* and Lieutenant Wildman made their escapes in disguise and went down to [Culmore] with Benjamin Adair, who came for powder to the town, and so got off to Scotland'.[77] Adair was one of the officers of the garrison of Culmore Fort, so it would seem that Lundy and the other pair left the city disguised as soldiers taking munitions to Culmore with Adair. That Lundy took ship to Scotland rather than slipping across to the Jacobite lines suggests that he had never been a Jacobite agent; this is strengthened further by his inclusion in a list of traitors attainted by the Irish parliament in May 1689. Why attaint a Jacobite agent?

As Lundy departed, so a new heroic figure took centre stage in the city. This was a local man, Adam Murray, who had already distinguished himself at the head of a cavalry unit at the fords. Murray had returned to the city and then taken a small force to Culmore. His return from Culmore to Derry coincided with James' approach to Bishop's Gate on 18 April, and while he was en route to the city Murray received a despatch from Lundy ordering him to take his troops (as well as his cavalry he also had 1,500 infantry) to Cloughglass, about two miles north-west of the city. However, Murray learned from the messenger who carried Lundy's despatch that negotiations for surrender terms were underway and he made straight for Derry instead of moving to Cloughglass. En route his men fought a brief skirmish with Jacobite dragoons before Murray entered the city by the Ship Quay Gate and then made for the council meeting. Once there, he accused Lundy and others of treachery before going outside to address the townspeople and soldiers whom he urged to hold out, assuring them that such was his own intention.[78] Murray's intervention at this point prompted those seeking terms to leave the city and was probably the final factor in Lundy's decision to quit.

---

*Gilner Brasier, or Kilner Brazier, is said by Young to have been in the city throughout the siege. From Rath in County Donegal, he was promoted colonel. After the war he was MP for Dundalk (1698–9), St Johnstown (1703–13) and Kilmallock (1715 until his death). There is no evidence that he fled the country with Lundy although he seems to have assisted the Scot's escape.[76]

Adam Murray, not surprisingly, was offered the governorship but turned down the appointment, saying that he preferred to serve the city as a soldier, judging 'himself fitter for action and service in the field, than for conduct or government in the town'.[79] However, he did accept an invitation to attend what ought to have been a gathering of all the officers of the garrison to choose a new governor. In the event there were only about fifteen present and the gubernatorial nominations were Major Henry Baker, Major Jonathan Mitchelburne and Lieutenant Colonel Richard Johnston. Henry Baker received the majority of the votes and was elected as governor but declared that 'the work they had now laid on him was too much for him to discharge, and therefore [he] desired they would allow him an assistant for the stores and provisions'. And it was then that the Reverend George Walker became assistant governor, on the proposal of Baker. The latter was to control all matters of a military nature while Walker was the civil administrator and had charge of the stores.[80] Walker's version of events is that the garrison 'unanimously resolved to choose Mr Walker and Major Baker, to be their Governors during the Siege', which puts a different complexion on the outcome of the election.[81] With this change in control of the city began the period of 105 days known as the Siege of Derry and described by Macaulay as the most important siege in English history. The paradox of the siege is that Derry could never have held out had it not been for Robert Lundy, who was now fleeing the city in ignominy.

Notes

Once again the NAS documents on Lundy provide much of the information on which this chapter is based and their use will be clear to the reader.

1: Dalton's Army List
2: HLRO, *HoCJ*, 4 April & 15 April 1689
3: Mackenzie, op cit, p. 29n
4: In view of the later frustration suffered by those involved in the defence of the city in trying to obtain compensation for their losses, it is enlightening to note that Massereene was paid £900 for his salmon on the orders of King William.
5: Quoted in Macrory, op cit, p. 152
6: Walker, op cit, p. 30
7: Simpson, op cit, pp. 97–99
8: Mackenzie, op cit, p. 29
9: HLRO, *HoCJ*, 12 August 1689

10: Ash, *A Circumstantial Journal of the Siege of Londonderry*, p. 62

11: Simpson, op cit, p. 105

12: Milligan, op cit, p. 70

13: Simpson, op cit, p. 104

14: Ibid, p. 105

15: Ibid; Walker, op cit, p. 22; Ash does not give a figure for the size of the Williamite force but notes that it outnumbered the Jacobites by five to one (p. 62).

16: Gilbert, op cit, p. 45

17: Mitchelburne, op cit

18: Simpson, op cit, p. 106; Walker, op cit, p. 23; Mackenzie, op cit, p. 30. Ash mentions the arrival of this fleet as an afterthought, following his diary entry for 1 July.

19: Powley, *The Naval Side of King William's War*, p. 92. Powley gives Captain Cornwall's forename as Wolfran.

20: Ash, op cit, pp. 83–4

21: Mitchelburne, op cit.

22: Simpson, op cit, p. 106

23: Ibid, pp. 106–7

24: Ibid, p. 107

25: Ibid; HLRO, *HoCJ*, 12 August 1689

26: Chandler, *The Art of Warfare in the Age of Marlborough*, p. 102

27: Ibid

28: Quoted in ibid, p. 105

29: Murtagh & Murtagh, op cit, p. 41; Avaux, op cit, p. 461

30: *Franco-Irish Correspondence*, pp. 86–9: letter and report, dated 29 April, from Rosen to Louvois from the Jacobite headquarters at Lifford.

31: Mackenzie, op cit, p. 31; Walker, op cit, pp. 21–3

32: HLRO, *HoCJ*, 12 August 1689

33: Simpson, op cit, p. 105; Mitchelburne, op cit

34: *Franco-Irish Correspondence*, pp. 86–9: letter and report, dated 29 April, from Rosen, op cit

35: Ibid

36: National Army Museum, London (NAM). Letter to author.

37: Chandler, op cit, p. 102

38: Ibid, p. 137

39: Mitchelburne, op cit

40: Ibid

41: Ibid

42: Simpson, op cit, p. 107

43: Ibid

44: Mitchelburne, op cit. This is supported by the evidence of Cornet Nicholson to the House of Commons: *HoCJ*, 12 August 1689.
45: Simpson, op cit, p. 108
46: Ibid; HLRO, *HoCJ*, 12 August 1689; Walker, op cit, p. 23; Mackenzie, op cit, p. 32
47: Simpson, op cit, p. 109
48: HLRO, *HoCJ*, 12 August 1689
49: Ibid
50: Ibid
51: Ibid; Powley, op cit, p. 268
52: HLRO, *HoCJ*, 12 August 1689
53: Young, *Fighters of Derry*, pp. 71–2
54: HLRO, *HoCJ*, 6 July 1689
55: Simpson, op cit, p. 109
56: Ibid
57: Mitchelburne, op cit
58: Avaux, op cit, p. 59
59: Ibid, p. 73
60: Ibid, pp. 99–103
61: Ibid
62: Simpson, op cit, p. 110; Gilbert, op cit, p. 62
63: Walker, op cit, p. 24
64: Gilbert, op cit, p. 62
65: Walker, op cit, pp. 25–6
66: Simpson, op cit, p. 112
67: Ibid; Gilbert, op cit, pp. 62–3
68: Milligan, op cit, p. 126
69: Walker, op cit, p. 26
70: Quoted in Milligan, op cit, p. 130
71: Ibid; Gilbert, op cit, p. 63
72: *Franco-Irish Correspondence*, pp. 86–9: letter and report, dated 29 April, from Rosen, op cit
73; Gilbert, op cit, p. 63
74: Avaux, op cit, p. 23
75: Walker, op cit, p. 28
76: Young, op cit, p. 157
77: Mitchelburne, op cit
78: Simpson, op cit, pp. 111–112
79: Mackenzie, op cit, p. 37
80: Ibid, pp. 37–8
81: Walker, op cit, p. 29

CHAPTER FIVE

Guarding Derry's Walls

In the days following 18 April the city, its garrison and inhabitants, and the soldiers of the Jacobite army settled into a state of uneasy warfare. No one could be certain of what would happen next, or where it might happen. The one certainty within the walls was that Londonderry had to be ready to meet an attack at any time. To meet that prospect the defending regiments were mustered with each company, of about sixty men, allowed to choose its own captain and each captain in turn permitted to select the colonel under whom he and his men would serve.[1] It was a very unmilitary procedure that led to disparities in regimental strengths. These were recorded as:

The Rev George Walker's Regiment		
(formerly Sir Arthur Rawdon's dragoons)	15	companies
Major Baker to be Colonel of Charlemont's Regiment	25	
Major Crofton to be Colonel of Canning's Regiment	12	
Major Mitchelburne to be Colonel of Skeffmgton's Regiment	17	
Lt-Col Whitney to be Colonel of Hamilton's Regiment	13	
Major Parker to command the Coleraine Regiment	13	
Captain Hamill to be Colonel of a regiment	14	
Captain Adam Murray to be Colonel of Horse	8	

With a total of 117 companies, each with a nominal strength of sixty men, this order of battle amounts to a total force of 7,020 soldiers with 341 officers within the walls.[2] Mackenzie also recorded the presence of 'several volunteers in town who did good service'. Among the latter were Captain Joseph Johnston, Captain William Crooke and Mr David Kennedy. (Johnston later suffered a fatal leg injury in a mortar attack.)[3] Since the force that had marched out to do battle at the fords had supposedly disposed 10,000 men, the final strength of the garrison suggests that that figure was greatly exaggerated or that casualties in the field force had been very high. The former is the more plausible explanation, although it is possible that many men, suffering an acute blow to their morale, took the opportunity to desert.

Each regiment was allotted a section of the walls to defend and to which they were to repair 'upon all alarms, without any parading, . . . into their own ground and places, without the least disorder or confusion'.[4] (The complete set of standing orders for the garrison is reproduced in Appendix Three.) It is assumed that the soldiers of Murray's Regiment, although cavalry, were assigned a dismounted role, although, as we shall see, they also took part in a number of well-planned and executed forays outside the walls in the course of which Murray demonstrated considerable qualities as a leader and a soldier. (Such forays began very early on with Mackenzie recording a sally on the evening of 20 April, the same day on which Lord Strabane had approached the city to parley and had offered Murray a colonelcy and £1000 if he would join the Jacobites; this offer was refused.)[5] His regiment was of limited use in the overall context of a siege: it was as true in the seventeenth century as it is in the twenty-first that infantry are essential to seize and hold ground; whether supported by cavalry or tanks, the infantryman has always shouldered the greater part of the burden of the battlefield. The drummers of each regiment were quartered in one house 'so that on the least notice they repair'd to the respective post of the company they belong'd to'. This allowed the drummers to beat the alarm for their own companies at which the soldiers would take up their battle stations.

Other standing orders issued by the council of war provided that all the adjutants – those officers responsible for the efficient running of each regiment – should be quartered together, with the adjutant of each regiment remaining on the main guard until his unit be relieved from its spell of duty. No drinking was permitted after 8 o'clock each evening and no candles were to be lit in case these might help the enemy in firing their cannon at night-time. The garrison's store of ammunition was to be moved 'out of the grand store and lodged in four several places' to prevent the loss of the entire supply by accidental fire 'or treachery'. A further indication of the fear of treachery is shown by the order to lodge all the keys to the gates on the main guard with none of them to be in the possession of anyone below the rank of captain, two of whom should 'attend at each gate every night'. To prevent soldiers breaking into shops and cellars, the goods of merchants who had fled the city were to be gathered into the common store and an inventory made. Finally, soldiers were forbidden to fire any unnecessary shots.[6]

The walls were also defended by some 200 artillerymen under a master gunner called Alexander Watson, who had experience as an artilleryman. However, few of Watson's men would have had gunnery experience and would therefore have needed considerable guidance. Watson's gunners manned twenty pieces of artillery of which eight were sakers, firing a six-pound round, and twelve were demi-culverins, firing rounds of between ten and twelve pounds.[7] At some stage, and it is not certain when but it must have been before the siege began since these guns are said to have fired on James and his retinue,[8] an additional battery was emplaced at St Columb's Cathedral with two cannon hoisted to the top of the tower and sited there; these guns had been brought from Culmore Fort and the task was overseen by Captains Robert and George Gregory, two brothers.[9] The original spire, which had been removed some years before, had been a wooden construction covered in lead. That lead had been retained and was later put to good use by the defenders, as we shall see. Since the cathedral stands on the highest ground of the island of Derry, the guns on the tower commanded an excellent field of fire all around the city. Thus the cathedral tower acted as a cavalier, a high block behind the bastions of a fortress that gave the gunners a clear view of the area surrounding the fortress.[10]

Outside the walls, the Jacobite army was making ready for a siege although it lacked much of the equipment considered necessary. Walker's claim that the Jacobites mustered over 20,000 men is far from true.[11] The besieging army is not likely to have been more than 10,000 strong, and at least one Williamite source supports this. It is also possible that there were no more than about 7,000 Jacobite soldiers at Derry. In the course of the next 105 days King James' generals may well have deployed some 20,000 men in total at Derry, but this would have involved a *roulement*, or rotation, of units at the city and the figure would also have included those troops deployed to protect the Jacobite lines of communication with Dublin; these were not only open to interdiction by the Inniskilling men but also traversed countryside where the rule of law had broken down. During the siege thirty-five Jacobite regiments, including ten of cavalry, would have taken their place at some time in the lines around the city. The anonymous author of *A Jacobite Narrative of the War* in Ireland also claims that, in May, there were 20,000 Jacobite troops – horse, foot and dragoons – deployed around the city, but this is an exaggerated number, probably intended to support the author's contention that the city should have been taken quickly.[12]

Against the defenders' twenty cannon, not even the strength of a single artillery regiment in modern terms, the besiegers could deploy only 'eight cannon, two of which were 18-pounders'.[13] The 18-pounders would have been culverins; although the word 'cannon' is used generically to describe artillery pieces, in strict terms 'cannon' describes a gun capable of firing a round of thirty-three pounds or greater. This lack of strength in artillery was to be one of the major problems faced by the besieging Jacobite army. Walker puts the strength of the Jacobite artillery at twelve field guns as well as three mortars, one of which was large and the other two small, whereas the Jacobite narrative claims two mortars, 'one large and the other little'.[14] However, the disparity in the two figures is so small that dispute is unnecessary; Walker's slightly higher assessment might have occurred as a result of the Jacobite artillery moving some of their guns from time to time. It is known that, except for two pieces, the Jacobite guns were dispersed widely; the other two 'were raised in one place'.[15]

What were conditions like for the soldiers of the opposing forces? Since the Jacobites had travelled north for a swift campaign, they were not best equipped for static warfare, a situation exacerbated by the comparative haste with which their army had been created. Tentage was in very short supply and, with few solid buildings around the city, most Jacobite soldiers had to improvize, constructing shelters from sods of earth on the hillsides that overlooked the city. Since the army's commissary left much to be desired, food was scarce with meat in very short supply. The basic ration was water and oatmeal from which was produced an insipid gruel although, when fires had been built, bread could be baked. The rain that had fallen on King James as he sat astride his horse on Foyle Hill on 18 April was an augury of the weather in the days and weeks to come; one French officer was to comment that it almost always rained at Derry. In their crude hillside shelters the Jacobite soldiers must have endured extremely unpleasant conditions, suffering wet and cold; their morale and, therefore, their effectiveness as a fighting force would have been much diminished.

Within the walls the conditions facing the Williamite soldiers were much better in the opening days of the siege. They had solid buildings in which to shelter although, as the weeks passed, many of the city's buildings would have lost all or part of their roofs as Jacobite mortar shells fell through them. The defenders' rations were certainly more generous than those of their enemy: a private soldier was allocated a weekly quota of a salmon and a half, two pounds of salt beef and four quarts of oatmeal, while a ration of a small amount of beer was also made, initially in lieu of pay.[16] Remembering that this was also perceived as a war for the survival of Protestantism in Ireland, it is worth noting that the inhabitants were well served with clergymen, of whom there were twenty-six in the city. Most of these, eighteen, were from the established church and the remaining eight were from 'the church of Scotland, or Presbyterian persuasion'.[17] Among the latter was John Mackenzie who wrote that

> At this time, that there might be a good understanding and harmony among the besieged, it was agreed to by Governor Baker, that the Conformists should have the Cathedral Church the one-half of the Lord's-day, during the whole time of the siege, and the Non-conformists the other half.[18]

Thus the Presbyterians were to use the cathedral from noon each Sunday, and during their assemblies they held collections for the relief of the poor, the sick and the wounded soldiers. With two sermons in the cathedral each Sunday, plus two or three other meetings at other locations in the city and the use of the cathedral every Thursday, the Presbyterian clergy were kept busy.[19] This was true also of the Church of Ireland clergy. Of all the clergymen one chronicler wrote that they all encountered the dangers of the siege – four Presbyterian ministers died during it – and

> each in his turn, performed Divine Service daily in the Cathedral. It must be acknowledged, however, that the 'raw' multitude, on some trying occasions, exhibited feelings of extreme dissatisfaction which would have been of serious consequence, had not the Clergy of both parties prudently quieted them, by preaching forbearance and obedience on account of the common cause which they had all unanimously agreed to defend.[20]

This hints of the tensions that existed between the Anglican and Presbyterian defenders. In the aftermath of the siege the strongest evidence of this tension was provided by the accounts written by George Walker and John Mackenzie which began a debate that continued even into the twentieth century. Walker confirms that the Anglican churchmen, when not in action, led prayers and gave sermons every day while 'the seven nonconforming ministers were equally careful of their people, and kept them very obedient and quiet'. This comment – that they kept their people 'very obedient and quiet' – does more than hint at tension between the two denominations: it confirms the existence of that tension and indicates that Walker had little time for Presbyterians, which is proved when he goes on to state that the state of the Presbyterians of the city was in marked contrast to the

> behaviour of their brother Mr Osborn[e] who was a spy upon the whole North, employed by my Lord Tyrconnel, and Mr Hewson, who was very troublesome, and would admit none to fight for the Protestant Religion till they had first taken the Covenant.[21]

Perhaps the strongest evidence of Walker's attitude to his Presbyterian fellow defenders is contained in his own account of the siege in which he names all the Anglican clergy of the city during the siege but claims that he did not know the names of the Presbyterian ministers.[22] One of those men whose names he wrote that 'I cannot learn' was the Reverend John Mackenzie, chaplain to Walker's own regiment. Mackenzie's subsequent account of the siege led Walker to take up his pen again to produce *A Vindication of the True Account of the Siege of Derry in Ireland* in which he maintains that he had not known the names of the Presbyterian ministers and although he 'took some pains to enquire into them could not be informed'.

However, he had since established the names of the ministers and included these in his *Vindication*. If anything, this exacerbated the hurt already felt by the Presbyterians since Walker included a Mr W. KilChrist and a Mr J. Machiny.[23] The latter was, of course, Mackenzie, whose name he must have known, and the former was Gilchrist. Not only was the misspelling 'KilChrist' insulting, and probably deliberately so, but it also verged on blasphemy.

However, all parties were exhorted to forget their denominational differences and to act 'as one in defence of the interest' of William and Mary and the Protestant religion against the enemies of both.[24] Religious belief was to play a large part in maintaining the defenders' morale over the weeks to come. Walker reflected on their situation and their prospects:

> It did beget some disorder amongst us, and confusion, when we look'd about us, and saw what we were doing; our enemies all about us and our friends running away from us; a garrison we had compos'd of a

number of poor people, fright[e]ned from their own homes, and seem'd
more fit to hide themselves, than to face an enemy; when we considered
we had no persons of any experience in war among us, and those very
persons that were sent to assist us, had so little confidence in the place,
that they no sooner saw it, but they thought fit to leave it; that we had
but few horse to sally out with, and no forage; no engineers to instruct
us in our works; no fire-works, not so much as a hand-granado to annoy
the enemy; not a gun well mounted in the whole town; that we had so
many mouths to feed, and not above ten days provision for them, in the
opinion of the former governors; that every day several left us, and gave
constant intelligence to the enemy; that they had so many opportunities
to divide us, and so often endeavour'd it, and to betray the governors;
that they were so numerous, so powerful and well appointed an army,
that in all human probability we could not think our selves in less danger, than the Israelites at the Red Sea.[25]

While much of this is accurate it should also be remembered that
it was an assessment written with hindsight, when the siege was
over and when Walker was attempting to enhance his own role in the
defence. Thus it is not entirely true to say that there were no experienced soldiers in their midst, nor that there was no one to advise on
defensive works; and neither was it accurate to claim that there was
not a well-mounted gun in the town. On the contrary, both Henry
Baker and Jonathan Mitchelburne were experienced soldiers, and there
were others, while both Baker and Mitchelburne had a good working
knowledge of defensive works – and Lundy had already done a good
job in this respect – and most of the guns were as well mounted as
might be, again thanks to Lundy. Thus, while bad, the situation was
not quite as dire as painted by Walker.

In these early days of the siege at least one Royal Navy warship
ventured close to the city following the departure of the relief fleet.
HMS *Bonadventure*,* under Captain Thomas Hobson, anchored at what
Hobson described as the 'mouth of the harbour of Londonderry' on
Thursday 25 April. In fact the ship was in ten fathoms of water off
'the Tunnes' – the Tuns.[27] This is a well-known hazard to shipping, a
dangerous sandbank feature just off the mouth of Lough Foyle; the

---

*This is the contemporary spelling used in the ship's log. Built as HMS
President in 1650, the ship was renamed *Bonadventure* in 1660 and rebuilt six
years later. It was broken up in 1711.[26]

Tuns stretch for some three miles towards Portstewart and the feature is above water at low tide.*

Next day *Bonadventure* moved inside the lough to Greencastle and Hobson's log refers to damage to another, unnamed, vessel in bad weather conditions. But the weather was not all that the ship had to contend with, for on the Sunday a sailor in the ship's boat was shot in the arm by Irish soldiers on the shore. A bone was broken and the unfortunate sailor had to have his arm amputated the following day.[28] The boat party seem to have run foul of a group of Jacobite soldiers who had travelled a considerable distance along the north-eastern shore of Lough Foyle, probably in search of plunder.

On the last day of the month two Scottish men of war sailed into the lough, but the little fleet remained on station there until 3 May when *Bonadventure* left the 'river of Derry' and later anchored off Rathlin Island. Next day the ship was 'at sea en route for Chester over Liverpool'.[29] There is no clear indication from surviving records of why *Bonadventure* and the other vessels were in Lough Foyle but they might have been following orders that had been overtaken by the events of recent days.

Since they were not Royal Navy vessels, the two Scottish men of war deserve some explanation. Their presence in Lough Foyle indicates the link between events in Ulster, especially the siege, and Scotland. This was several decades before Scotland was absorbed into the Union, and thus the country retained its own government. In 1689 this took the form of the Convention of Estates, which sat from 14 March to 24 May 1689 and which included both Jacobites and Williamites. However, James' 'sheer political folly . . . and his condescending attitude towards the convention' ensured that the Jacobite faction was kept in check by the Williamites, who also demonstrated greater political skills. A later Constitutional Settlement declared that James VII had forfeited the throne of Scotland.[30]

Scotland's government was concerned at the threat to the country's security posed by developments in Ireland, especially in Ulster which

---

*The feature may be seen from Greencastle on the Inishowen side of the lough or from the viewing point on the Bishop's Road on the County Londonderry side. The sand of the Tuns is so hard that a game of soccer has even been played on the feature. Folklore has it that the Tuns are the home of the Celtic sea god Mannanan MacLir, who also gave his name to the Isle of Man, since he was banished there by Saint Patrick. In January 1884 the McCorkell Line's ship *Nokomis* met its doom on the Tuns.

was so close to Scotland and where so many Scots had settled. (One estimate is that between 1660 and 1688 some 10,000 Scots had settled in Ulster to add to the many already there.)[31] This government decided that it would aid the Protestants of Ulster and take measures to defend the west and south-west of Scotland. Travel between Ireland and Scotland was restricted and then, on 16 April, sailings to Ireland were embargoed, lest the vessels be taken and used for an invasion of Scotland.[32] When a Jacobite spy, Francis Brady, was captured at Greenock in April he was found to be carrying letters to Scottish Jacobites from James and Melfort; those letters proposed the establishment of a Jacobite convention which was seen as a threat to the existing convention and also heightened fears of an invasion from Ireland.[33]

One of the earliest decisions of the convention was to monitor coastal activity and shipping, to which end two small vessels, *Pelican* and *Janet*, were hired in Glasgow. To command these ships Captains John Brown and William Hamilton were commissioned on 13 April. The two frigates, as they were described, were 'to cruise betwixt Scotland and Ireland' to garner intelligence, and their commanders were authorized to fight and sink any ship belonging to King James VII anywhere from Skye to Cornwall.[34] In addition to their own ships' companies, Brown and Hamilton were given a company of infantry to man the vessels.[35] They were also left to their own devices to acquire armament for the ships. It was this pair of frigates that joined Hobson's *Bonadventure* in Lough Foyle at the end of April, which suggests that the two captains had already fitted out *Janet* and *Pelican* with ordnance; this was a considerable achievement.*[36]

Meanwhile, King James' lack of decisiveness had left his commanders with no clearly defined objective. The French general Maumont was placed in overall command at Derry, with Pusignan, another Frenchman, Richard Hamilton and the Duke of Berwick, James' son, as his subordinates. Although James had left no specific orders, Berwick noted that the army's first intention was to establish a blockade to cut the city off from resupply and reinforcements. Maumont, in a letter to Louvois, wrote that he had been placed in charge of 'le siege de Dery' but was also responsible for dealing with the other rebels who had taken refuge in Enniskillen.[37] While performing this role, the Jacobite

---

*In March *Pelican* was to have sailed to Londonderry with James Hamilton under escort by HMS *Jersey* but the arrangement broke down and *Deliverance* made the journey instead.

army would be waiting for the supplies and equipment needed to conduct a proper siege. No consensus existed in the Jacobite high command, with some, such as Melfort, believing that time spent before Derry was time lost in Scotland. Melfort and his supporters argued that there should either be a proper siege or that a force should be left to blockade Derry while the main body of the army sailed for Scotland. Those arguing for a Scottish campaign were supported by Viscount Dundee in Scotland, who was urging strongly that such a strategy be followed.[38] Had this strategy been adopted, and the necessary ships been available, there was no need for the port facilities at Derry; the fleet could have embarked men and equipment in Lough Foyle below Culmore; the Williamite relief fleet, it will be remembered, had dropped anchor at Redcastle.

In the prevailing situation, the Jacobite forces began their deployment around the city. On the west bank of the Foyle infantry units were arrayed in an arc that touched the river's banks to the north and south of the city. Since the high ground within this arc, from west to north, was occupied by Jacobite troops, they dominated the area completely:

> a detachment of both horse and foot pitched their tents at Pennyburn in order to intercept supplies from Culmore to the town – guards were also placed on the opposite side of the river, and plundering parties were dispatched towards Innishowen.[39]

At this stage Culmore was still in Williamite hands; the troops at Pennyburn were fortunate in that some of them at least seem to have had tents, although this may refer only to officers. The 'plundering parties' sent into Inishowen illustrate the lack of supplies within the Jacobite army which was having to live off the land; presumably it was one such party that engaged *Bonadventure*'s ship's boat. These foragers come in for critical comment from Mackenzie, who noted that, on 20 April,

> A party of King James's horse and foot marched down to Culmore, and from thence down through the barony of Innishowen, and there robbed a great number of people, that were waiting for passage to Scotland. They placed guards on the waterside, to stop all passage from this city to Culmore by land, which debarred us of intelligence from that place.[40]

On the east side of the Foyle a strongpoint was created by the commanding officers of two Jacobite infantry regiments, Lords Bellew and

Louth. Based on Stronge's orchard, this faced the walled city and probably included the land on which Ebrington Barracks was later built as well as that occupied by the modern St Columb's Park. References to 'the guards on the opposite side of the river' and 'on the waterside' include the Stronge's orchard position as well as locations established on the high ground overlooking the city in the areas now known as the Top of the Hill and Gobnascale. The lower ground in this latter area was then covered in forest which stretched for over two miles from the present-day Craigavon Bridge almost to the village of Newbuildings. The principal Jacobite account of the war states that 'the army marched to the north and east side of Londonderry, in the county of Tyrone' and that it was 'divided into two principal bodies on the county of Tyrone's side'.[41] In fact, the bulk of Jacobite troops on the east side of the Foyle were in County Londonderry rather than Tyrone. The latter county's northern border with Londonderry lies some five miles south of the walled, city and no 'principal' part of the besieging army would have been based there.

And it was from the position in Stronge's orchard that active hostilities began on 21 April. Those within the city watched as a demi-culverin, a 12-pounder gun, was emplaced in the orchard within 500 yards of the city. Mackenzie states that the weapon was 180 perches distant east by north from the town; this was 990 yards at which distance the weapon's effectiveness would have been much reduced. The gun opened fire, becoming the first Jacobite artillery piece to do so. Some forty rounds were fired, which indicates that the bombardment lasted several hours. One account, from Joshua Gillespie, tells us that a man in the city was killed and that buildings were damaged, including the town house in the Diamond. The effect of this fire calls into question Mackenzie's ability to estimate distance. However, Mackenzie states that the bombardment 'did little harm, though it was then a little more frightful to our people than afterwards' while Walker comments that, apart from some damage to the Market House, the firing had little effect. It may be that Gillespie was confusing the effects of the single gun with the bombardment of two days later when additional weaponry had been emplaced at shorter range. However, the vulnerability of the Shipquay Street area was demonstrated effectively by this bombardment. Had the designers of the walls foreseen such an event, they would surely have included a curtain wall, to create an *enceinte*, in the area.

A besieging army should also have begun the circumvallation – the digging of an encircling entrenchment – of Londonderry. However, this was a task of almost impossible proportions for the Jacobites. To excavate the necessary trenches would have required thousands of pickaxes, spades and shovels, but such tools had not been brought with the army. Acquiring them would take time and they would probably have to be brought from Dublin. This lack of digging equipment is another indication that the Jacobites had not been expecting a prolonged siege. So, also, was the lack of ladders which would be essential in any attack on the city since many of the soldiers would be expected to escalade, or climb, the walls using ladders. Of course, these could have been manufactured locally since there was no shortage of wood from trees in the area but obtaining wood meant chopping down trees which required axes which were also in short supply. Even with the trees felled, there remained the lack of the many woodworking tools, including saws, adzes, augers and chisels, needed to turn the wood from its raw state into the components of ladders. These tools would also have to be brought from Dublin, if not from France, such would have been the quantity required.

The Jacobites were not alone in beginning active operations on the 21st. At noon that day Adam Murray led a force of 300 cavalry with a large detachment of infantry out of the city to attack the Jacobite camp at Pennyburn. Since the names of four company commanders are recorded, this force probably included four infantry companies and, therefore, some 240 men; the companies were commanded by Captains Archibald Sanderson, Beatty and Thomas Blair, as well as Lieutenant David Blair. A further force of infantry, under Lieutenant-Colonel John Cairns (actually the second-in-command of Murray's regiment) and Captain Philip Dunbar was also deployed on rising ground close to Pennyburn to cover Murray's eventual withdrawal to the city. Sitting on the route from Culmore, the Jacobites' Pennyburn camp represented one of the most serious threats to the garrison since the Jacobites there could cut off the city from receiving any supplies or reinforcements that might be landed at Culmore.[43]

Murray divided his cavalry into two squadrons, the first of which he commanded himself while the other was led by Major Bell, from County Meath. The first squadron led the attack on the Jacobites and was engaged by Jacobite cavalry, as was Bell's squadron. Captain Cochran was bringing up the rear of Murray's cavalry and 'whilst some of his men were thrown into disorder, [Cochran] with a few spirited companions, bravely encountered the enemy'.[44] It would seem from this account that some of Cochran's men were shocked enough to want to make an escape but their captain's example appears to have restored the situation since his men then fought with determination. Cochran himself was wounded badly in one leg and had his horse shot under him.[45] The Jacobites fought well, as was to be expected from their cavalry, which, on this occasion, had the overall commander at Derry at their head. Maumont's presence at Pennyburn during this battle was not planned. He had been at his headquarters, some miles away, when an alarm about Murray's attack was received together with a call for reinforcements. Maumont decided to lead those reinforcements and took with him a troop of horse, ordering a troop of dragoons to join him on the way. His decision was to prove fatal: Maumont was killed in the early moments of the clash between Jacobite and Williamite cavalry. Allegedly his death occurred in a hand-to-hand fight with Adam Murray although there is no firm evidence to prove this; Avaux reported that he fell to a musket ball in the head, along with one of his aides de camp and a brother of Lord Carlingford.[46] The Murray family possessed a sword, said to have been Maumont's, in 1788.[47]

When further Jacobite cavalry reinforcements hit the rear of his squadrons, Murray ordered a withdrawal. His force was pursued hotly by Jacobites but the latter rode into an ambush since 'In the meantime, Colonel Murray's reserve of infantry advanced down on the strand, and lining the ditches by which the enemy's troops had to return, cut off a great number of them.'[48]

Berwick, who may have been the leader of that pursuit, although a Jacobite account suggests that it was Lord Galmoy, recorded that not one man or horse of the Jacobite cavalry who survived did so without injury. Among the other Jacobite dead on this day was Major John Taaffe who was 'a younger son of the late old earl of Carlingford', Major Waggon (actually Wogan) of Sir Maurice Eustace's Regiment, Captain Fitzgerald and Quarter Master Cassore.[49]

On the defenders' side this had been a well-planned and well-executed operation with Adam Murray showing both a fine tactical sense and a good appreciation of co-operation between cavalry and infantry. It is possible that Murray might have been a soldier at some earlier stage in his life although no evidence survives to support this theory. His father had been a cavalry officer and Adam certainly proved to be both a very good officer and an inspiring leader. He had now given the defenders' morale a substantial boost while the Jacobites must have been demoralized by what had happened at Pennyburn; not only had Maumont been killed but they also lost colours to the Williamites. Maumont's decision to lead the reinforcements calls into question his judgement as a commander since his place was not in the thick of battle but to oversee all operations. Of his courage there can be no doubt and he was probably trying to raise the morale of his men. Although Murray's men had suffered fatalities as well, these would have been offset by the morale effect of their success which enhanced the reputation of their commander. Among the Williamite dead were Lieutenant McPhedris,* Cornet Brown, Mr McKee, 'one Harkness and five or six private soldiers'.[51] Only one of the cavalry troopers involved in this action is recorded for posterity: Trooper Tom Barr who features in the account from Doctor Joseph Aickin, one of the defenders, who later wrote an epic that certainly does not merit the description of poetry** called *Londerias, or a Narrative of the Siege of London-Derry.* In his execrable verse Aickin recorded that 'Tom Barr, a trooper, with one mighty blow/Cut off the head of an opposing foe'.[52] That Murray was becoming more popular in the city is shown by Walker's inclusion in his account of the siege of a story of how he himself had gone to assist Murray when the latter was hard-pressed.[53] Walker's version must be treated with scepticism. The victory was Murray's and his alone.

Two days later the Jacobites added four field guns to the demi-culverin already emplaced at Stronge's orchard, and the five guns began a bombardment. The additional weapons were sited closer to the city: both Mackenzie, who refers only to two additional guns, and Walker place them at about eighty perches (about 440 yards) from the town; this would have put the guns close to the riverbank.[54] Their fire on this occasion killed several people and caused considerable damage to buildings but the Williamite artillery 'returned the fire with spirit, and killed Lieut-Colonel O'Neill, Lieutenant Fitzpatrick, two sergeants, some private soldiers and two friars dressed in their canonicals'.[55] In addition to their overall commander the Jacobites had now lost a regimental commander – O'Neill – and two of their chaplains. They added mortars to the artillery in Stronge's orchard the following day and these fired by day and night. Their high trajectory meant that the mortars were particularly frightening; their bombs would sail high into the air to plummet down through the roofs of buildings so that no one could feel safe anywhere inside the city's walls.

---

*Macrory suggests that this name may be the modrn McFetridge.[50] It may also be the modern McFeeters.

**Macrory describes him as 'undoubtedly a spiritual ancestor of the Great McGonagall'.

While the Jacobites were emplacing their mortars in the orchard, Adam Murray was leading another foray on the western side of the Foyle. This time his objective was a set of Jacobite trenchworks at Elagh, about a mile north of Pennyburn. The infantry manning the trenches quit their positions when attacked by Murray's cavalry and were pursued by Williamite infantry, Murray having once again taken out a mixed force. However, the Williamite infantry were soon on the retreat themselves as a group of Jacobite cavalry appeared to protect their infantry. Now it was the turn of the Williamites to flee, which they did until they reached the trenches so recently taken from the Jacobites. There Murray rallied his men, both cavalry and infantry, and the two sides clashed in an engagement 'which continued till near the evening'.[56] Murray lost two men killed and another ten wounded. Jacobite losses are not known save for two: the new commander, the French general Pusignan, had been involved in the battle and had been injured seriously. Within days Pusignan had breathed his last.*[57] His death seems to have been due not so much to his wound, which might not have been serious, but from the ministrations of the Irish surgeons. The other known Jacobite fatality was Captain Maurice Fitzgerald. A further senior French officer also wounded at Pennyburn, the artillery and engineer commander Jean Bernard Louis Desjean, Marquis de Pointis,** a naval officer, refused to be treated by the Irish surgeons. This was a wise decision. A skilled surgeon did arrive from Dublin but was too late to save Pusignan, although he probably helped de Pointis.[59] Since France was far ahead of any other nation in the treatment of battlefield trauma at this time, it is safe to assume that the new surgeon was a Frenchman. The *London Gazette* subsequently published a report, said to have come from Holyhead on 1 May, of a 'second sally from Londonderry' and the news that 'M. de Pusignan and the French bombadeer were both dead of the wounds received in the former sallies'.[60] That 'bombadeer' was, of course, de Pointis, who was still very much in the land of the living.

The Jacobites had now suffered the loss of two commanders in less than a week. Such losses cannot have done any good for morale in the

---

*According to the author of *A Light to the Blind*, both Maumont and Pusignan were killed in the first battle. Mackenzie also snakes the same claim as does Ash, who refers to the latter as 'the French engineer, Lieut. General Basinian'[58].

**De Pointis had come to Ireland in January to report on the situation there for Louis XIV before the king made the final decision to support James in an Irish campaign.

Jacobite army, which was probably worsened by the knowledge that not only had de Pointis been injured but that the Duke of Berwick was also *hors de combat*, having been wounded; so too was Dominic Sheldon, an English Jacobite from an old Warwickshire family. It seemed that the Jacobite command was being culled in a very effective manner. Command of the besieging army now devolved on Richard Hamilton. Of him Avaux wrote that his 'incapacity was so great that it made his fidelity suspect'. However, comments about Hamilton by Avaux must be considered in the light of Louis XIV's opinion of the Irishman: Hamilton had dared to pay attention to a lady of the French court and his behaviour had earned him the opprobrium of the Sun King who had regarded him as being of insufficient social standing to consort with a lady of high breeding: 'an amour with one of the monarch's illegitimate daughters drew down on him the ire of Louis XIV'.[61] Thus Avaux knew that any adverse remarks about Hamilton would find an eager reader in Louis. We have another assessment of Hamilton from Macaulay, who described him as having no pretensions to being a great general although he was both a brave officer and a gentleman. However, Macaulay adds, he had never seen a siege. Although Hamilton had no direct experience of a siege, he served with French officers who knew all about siege warfare while, inside the walls, such experience was now probably limited to Baker and Mitchelburne.

Hamilton thus succeeded to the command almost by default. The euphoria of his pursuit of the Williamites across Ulster to Derry had by now evaporated in the reality of the situation for his army before the city. Indeed Hamilton's command hardly deserved the description of 'army'. One of his first tasks as commander was to report to Dublin, and his despatch made gloomy reading since he needed, urgently, all the paraphernalia of siege warfare, including heavy artillery and more men. Around Derry he deployed only six single-battalion regiments, none of which could muster its full strength of 600 men. His entire force could not have been much more than 3,000 strong, which is in stark contrast to the figure of over 20,000 put forward by Williamite writers.[62] Hamilton also bemoaned the lack of serviceability of his men's firearms with only one musket in ten fit to fire; this problem of unserviceable weaponry was a major headache for the Jacobites since Ireland's gunsmiths were all Protestant and, therefore, unlikely to do other than sabotage any Jacobite weapons brought to them for repair.

Adam Murray had demonstrated a particularly aggressive spirit during these opening days of the siege. That aggression had already cost the Jacobites dear, and it is possible that Murray was aware of his opponents' lack of strength in depth and was trying to damage further their morale. But he could not have been expecting the personal turn of events to which this would lead. The Jacobites had already recognized Murray as the defenders' outstanding military leader and the man who had caused them most difficulties through his pursuit of aggressive tactics. Hamilton knew that Murray's father lived nearby and decided to use the father to coerce the son. Some days later, at the beginning of May, he had Murray senior brought from his farm at Faughanvale to the Jacobite headquarters and then sent to the city to persuade his son to bring the rebellion to an end; otherwise Hamilton threatened that he would have the older man hanged.[63] Although Gabriel Murray (one source gives his name as John) agreed to undertake this mission, he told Hamilton that he believed that it would be fruitless since he knew his son too well to believe that he would be dissuaded from his present course even by Hamilton's threat. Both Murrays met at the city walls, where Gabriel relayed Hamilton's message to Adam but then produced a bible on which he urged his son never to yield to popish power. His task over, Murray senior returned to Hamilton's camp to meet his fate. But Hamilton's gentlemanly instincts supervened his threat and he had the old man escorted home where he remained under protection from Jacobite troops for the remainder of the campaign.[64]

That Murray senior was granted protection by the Jacobites raises a question about the threat posed by King James' army to the Protestants of north-west Ulster. Indeed, the very fact that Gabriel Murray had already been living close to the city bears scrutiny. Nor was he alone in this; there were many other Protestants living close to the city, with some of them visiting the city from time to time. Walker relates that 10,000 refugees left Derry as the siege began and that 'many more grew weary of us' as the siege wore on.[65] Although the figure of 10,000 is undoubtedly exaggerated, it begs the question: where did these people go? It seems that most of them, lacking the means to sail to Scotland or England, remained close by. This surely casts doubt on that part of the mythology of the siege that avers that the Jacobites were intent on destroying Protestantism. If this really was the case, why did they not slaughter those Protestants who were living outside the walls?

Murray and his father had scored yet another psychological blow against the Jacobites but the latter could now claim one significant success: they had taken Culmore Fort. This was a serious reverse for the defenders since the fort, at Culmore Point, dominated the narrows where the Foyle flows into Lough Foyle. Any relief fleet for the city would have to pass under the shadow of the fort, and with it in

Jacobite hands the chances of a fleet trying to force the narrows were much reduced. Culmore had been lost by the Williamites without a fight; no shots had been fired nor any blood spilt. Less than three weeks later the *London Gazette* published an account of the surrender of Culmore, suggesting that the garrison, although equipped with three cannon, had run out of fresh water.[66]

Instead of attacking the fort, the Jacobites used subterfuge to take their objective; Mitchelburne asserted that 'King James did tamper with Captain Robert [Galbraith], Captain William and Benjamin Adaire for the surrender of Kilmore'.[67] William Adair, of Ballymena, was the commander of the 300-strong garrison at Culmore but knew little of what was happening upriver in the city since communications were poor. He was convinced by the Jacobite argument that his troops had little chance against the Irish army and was promised that the conventions of siege warfare would be observed: his soldiers would be permitted to march out with all their possessions, including their swords, as well as horses and pistols in the case of the officers. Even though Berwick, who led the troops at Culmore, later wrote that his force had 'not the means of taking [Culmore fort]', Adair accepted the Jacobite version of events and handed the fort over. Ash tells us that

> Within a fortnight after the siege began, Culmore was betrayed to Gen. Hamilton by two of the Adairs, and long Galbraith the attorney, who, it is said, sold it to the enemy for a considerable sum of money. I have heard since, that one of the Adairs has lost his senses; I know not how true this may be; but certainly God Almighty will not let such treachery go unpunished.[68]

The garrison of Culmore Fort was allowed to march out but when the soldiers reached Coleraine they found a different attitude among the Jacobite soldiers there: 'they were not only disarmed but stripped to their shirts, their money all taken from them and they themselves sent a 'begging by order of Colonel Charles Moor, Governor of the Town'. A protest to Richard Hamilton brought the response that he would punish any Jacobite soldiers who could be shown to have been among the transgressors at Coleraine.[69]

It is surprising that, in spite of Culmore's importance to the overall defence of the city, some weeks passed before its loss became known to the defenders; the news seems to have been known in London before it was known in Londonderry. Even then this was only through letters found on the bodies of dead Irish officers. One wonders how an episode such as the fort's garrison marching out could not have been reported to the city. The garrison must have been ferried across the river close to Culmore if they were able to reach Coleraine without their departure being known to their overall commanders.

By now the Irish army was deployed from St Johnston 'along the country about eight miles in length and Brook Hall was ordered for the Duke of Berwick, Mr Fitz-James, and General Hamilton's quarters' [70] (Mr Fitz-James was Berwick, the title referring to his being an illegitimate son of James.) Culmore was now garrisoned by about a hundred men while two regiments of infantry were based at Pennyburn with most of the infantry being close by. About St Johnston and Carrigans in Donegal was to be found the greatest part of the Jacobite cavalry, with two regiments of horse under Galmoy and Sir Maurice Eustace of Castlemartin plus Lord Duleek's regiment of dragoons. In all there were about 7,000 Jacobites west of the Foyle and another 3,000 on the east side of the river.[71]

Before learning of the loss of Culmore, the city's garrison had had several other adventures to the south of the town while two of its officers had been lost in less than auspicious circumstances. These were commanding officers of regiments, the first of whom to go being Colonel Parker, of the Coleraine Regiment. Parker had been accused of being 'negligent in bringing off a rear-guard of foot, who were suffering severely by the enemy; for which omission, he was to answer before a court-martial'. Rather than face that court martial, Parker deserted and went over to the Jacobites, creating the suspicion that his negligence might have been due to Jacobite sympathies. Parker left the city on the night of 24–25 April.[72] Two days later, on the 27th*, Colonel Thomas Whitney, of Hamilton's Regiment, faced a court martial at which he was found guilty of charges of 'having sold flour and horses, belonging to the garrison, to a Captain Darcy, who was considered an enemy'.[73] (Darcy had been brought to the city from Scotland before the siege as a prisoner by Captain Hamilton; he had fled from England where he had been a known supporter of James II.)[74] Whitney was incarcerated in the city for the remainder of the siege. New commanding officers were appointed in place of the pair: Captain Lance took command of the Coleraine Regiment and Captain Murray took over Hamilton's.[75]

Although the Jacobite artillery had discharged the first shots of the siege on 21 April and fired a considerable bombardment on the 24th,

---

*Ash gives the date as 2 May.

they then seem to have suffered a shortage of ammunition with only some thirty rounds expended between the latter date and 4 May. An ammunition shortage is the only plausible explanation for this dearth of activity, which was hardly the artillery programme of a determined siege. Neither had the Jacobite army shown any inclination to build the entrenchments and parallels necessary to bring the artillery close enough to the walls to do serious damage* and make a breach through which a storming party might enter the city. This was probably due to a lack of the tools needed for the job. Whatever the reason, things changed in the first days of May.

The Jacobite artillery had opened fire on the 3rd, wounding two men, one of whom lost an arm and the other a leg.[77] That night a party of Jacobite soldiers approached the city walls, close to Butcher's Gate, and opened fire on the sentries. A company of Williamite soldiers under Major Fitzsimons rushed to the spot and engaged the attackers who then withdrew.[78] This may have been intended as a prelude, testing the reactions of the defenders, to the next operation carried out by the besiegers.

The only area outside the walls from which the Jacobite artillery could carry out conventional siege operations – digging parallels and moving their guns closer to the walls – was on the south side, facing Bishop's Gate. And it was there that they now began to create a parallel. Lundy had established a defensive outwork that ran between Windmill Hill and the Foyle with the windmill that gave the hill its name as the pivotal feature. (The remains of the windmill may still be seen in the grounds of Lumen Christi College, formerly St Columb's College.) On the night of 5–6 May an attack by a strong force of Jacobite troops, two regiments according to Ash, under the command of Brigadier-General Ramsey seized the windmill from the defenders. The area was held only lightly by outlying picquets who beat a hasty retreat to the protection of the ravelin at Bishop's Gate. About 2 o'clock in the morning Jacobite troops approached the ravelin and opened fire at the soldiers on the walls. This led to a general alarm as the entire garrison was ordered out to take up battle stations, but the feared escalade of the walls did not materialize.[79]

The construction of a parallel was then begun by the Jacobites. According to one Williamite account,

---

*According to the French artillery expert, Lieutenant-General Surirey de Saint-Rémy, at a range of 150 yards, slightly under the optimum 200 yards for a breaching gun, a 24-pounder firing from a well-made (stone-and-earth) position could penetrate up to 35 feet of packed earth.[76]

By the next morning, the enemy had drawn an entrenchment across the hill, near the situation of the Cassino, from the slob or bog in the west, to the river in the east, raised a battery at the Windmill, and planted guns against the City, which proved to be too small to do any great mischief.[80]

How had the Jacobites managed to dig such an entrenchment if they were so short of tools? The answer is provided by Mackenzie who tells us that 'it was old ditches that they quickly made up'.[81] Thus the entrenchment was improvised and had not required a large quantity of tools. But the Jacobites now had a new battery, or gun position, from which, according to Walker, they began a bombardment and 'endeavoured to annoy our walls; but they were too strong for the guns they used'.[82] Walker is correct in that analysis: the range of a demi-culverin, if such were deployed, would not have allowed it to cause serious damage to the walls, but there was the possibility that the besiegers might be able to bring their artillery even closer, thereby presenting a much greater danger to the walls. It was decided to attack the new Jacobite positions. (See Map 5, page 218 for Jacobite positions)

Walker asserts that he made the decision for this attack. Once again, this is probably a case of his claiming credit for the decision made by someone else. In this instance the decision was more likely that of Henry Baker, who would have recognized immediately the tactics being employed by the attackers; in any event a force of ten men from each company, suggesting a strength of about 1,000, and arrayed in two detachments was sent out to attack the Irish, 'fearing that the battery might incommode that part of the town nearest to it'.[83] Walker commanded one detachment and Jonathan Mitchelburne the other; Adam Murray was also included among the officers, presumably having command of the cavalry. Leaving the city by the Ferry Gate and Bishop's Gate the two elements united about 150 yards from the latter gate, on ground just below where the nineteenth-century city gaol, a tower of which still stands, was later built. At this point the Williamites formed a line with its left flank on the riverbank.[84]

The Williamite attack was then launched. Ramsey's men held the trench line with infantry while dragoons were posted in the hedges. As the latter were infantry who rode to battle on horseback but dismounted to fight, their deployment was probably designed to provide mobility in the event of an action. In the ensuing engagement the dragoons fell back but it seems that the Jacobite infantry withdrew, leaving the dragoons to hold the trench. This proved an impossible task and the dragoons were also forced to retreat. Many Irish soldiers were killed in the engagement, 'a desperate action on both sides, although it lasted only for half an hour', which became known as the battle of Windmill Hill. This developed into a close-quarter encounter with muskets used as clubs, a pattern of fighting for which Irish Jacobite infantry were to become noted; it seems that their opponents also favoured it. Included in the Jacobite dead, which a Jacobite source puts at 150 and a Williamite one at 200 dead with another 300 dying of wounds later, was Brigadier-General Ramsey. The Scot had attempted, without success, to rally his men. A very competent officer, Ramsey was a man the Jacobites could ill afford to lose. Also dead were Captains Fox, Barnwell and Fleming, Lieutenants Kelly and Walsh and Ensigns Kadell and Barnwell. Lord Netterville and Lieutenant-Colonel William Talbot, a son of the late Sir Henry Talbot and a cousin of Tyrconnel, were among the wounded; Netterville and Talbot were taken prisoner, as were several other officers, with Talbot dying some days later. Sir Garrett Aylmer, of Balrath in County Meath, Captain John Brown, a Mayo man, and Thomas Newcomen, described as an adjutant, were also made prisoners. Williamite losses were said 'to be considerable' but the exact number was not recorded; only one officer, Lieutenant Douglas, was noted as being killed.[85] That evening some Jacobite cavalry returned to the riverbank.[86] This was probably a reconnaissance party which withdrew on 'observing the hedges lined with infantry from the garrison'.

The injured Jacobite prisoners were brought into the city where their wounds were dressed before they were confined in the home of Thomas Moor, with 'a guard placed over them'. Otherwise, they were treated honourably 'as persons of distinction'.[87] Such treatment was accorded only to officers who might have prosperous relatives or friends prepared to pay a ransom to obtain their release. Common soldiers would never have received such treatment as their families would have had no means with which to pay a ransom.

In addition to the deaths the Jacobites also lost 'drums, pickaxes, spades, &c.' and five stands of colours to their foes.[88] The loss of colours is always a matter of shame for any unit and no less so for the Jacobites on this occasion. Taking the colours was yet another boost to the morale of the defenders. It is unlikely that these colours were regimental: they probably belonged to companies and there would have been about ten such colours per regiment. Two of the captured colours hang to this day in St Columb's Cathedral: although the silk has been replaced a number of times, the staffs are original. The colours are in plain gold silk with the *fleur de lys* of France embroidered in one corner; these suggest that French support for the Jacobites in Ireland was more of a token than a military reality. These two colours were taken by Colonel Mitchelburne who, when he later became governor of the city, presented them to the cathedral.[89]

In the aftermath of the battle a short truce was observed to allow the dead to be buried. Walker tells us that he sent a message to Hamilton to request that a Jacobite burial party, under an officer, come forward to carry out the burials. This was done by sending a drummer to the Jacobite camp. However, Walker is quite caustic about the manner in which the Jacobite dead were buried the following morning, this being done 'in a very careless manner, scarcely covering some of the bodies with earth, [while] others were cast into the ditches'. More respect was shown to Ramsey, who was buried with full military honours in the grounds of the Temple More, now the site of St Columba's Church, better known as the Long Tower.[90] His death was much felt by those who knew him and 'he was reckoned the best soldier in the army next to Col. Richard Hamilton'.[91] Three days later Colonel William Dorrington, who had landed in Ireland with James and who 'was esteemed a great soldier', arrived in the Jacobite camp. His arrival was soon known to the defenders of Derry.[92]

That truce seems to have been restricted to the area over which the battle of Windmill Hill was fought since that same day Quartermaster Mardock was shot dead on the Church bastion in what was either a negligent discharge by one of the defenders or a stray round; the Jacobites were so far from that bastion that no aimed shot could have killed Mardock, who was hit in the forehead. Elsewhere three of the garrison were killed and another eight wounded in a further skirmish at Pennyburn.[93]

The siege was less than three weeks old but the attackers had already lost three senior officers, suffered two humiliating defeats, at Pennyburn and Windmill Hill, and lost several stands of colours. Their sole success to date had been the capture of Culmore Fort, although this was a significant gain that gave them control of the seaward approach to the city. In contrast, Williamite morale had been increased by the clashes at Pennyburn and on Windmill Hill while the loss of Culmore had not yet percolated through to them. Confidence within the walls was high, largely thanks to the leadership of Adam Murray. And the defending troops had even been issued with leather to make shoes. Meanwhile, Baker was conscious of the possibility of enemies within the walls who might 'work mines in cellars near the walls' and, with William Mackey, a trusted citizen, searched every cellar close to the walls on the pretext of examining provisions. No evidence of sabotage was found.[94]

A third sally by the defenders towards Pennyburn was not as successful as the earlier two. This, involving a thousand troops, was made early on 11 May and it was hoped to catch the enemy still asleep. Some Jacobite gunners were on full alert, however, and opened fire with two artillery pieces. Although no Williamites were killed, the element of surprise was lost which compelled the attackers to withdraw.[95]

The situation in north-west Ulster had become a matter of increasing concern in London. On 18 April, the day on which King James rode up to Bishop's Gate, Captain, later Colonel, Jacob Richards, an engineer officer in King William's army, and Irish by birth, left London with orders to travel to Chester, where he learned that the first relief fleet had quit Lough Foyle.[96] This latest news was not known to the editor of the *London Gazette* who included a report from Chester, dated 13 April, indicating that

> The *Swallow* frigate with the regiments under command of Colonel Cunningham set sail out of this river on Wednesday last for Londonderry; Where it's not doubted, they are by this time arrived.[97]

From Chester, Richards went to Liverpool where the news that the relief fleet had not only arrived at Londonderry but had subsequently returned was confirmed. There he also met 'one Stevens, a messenger from King William, with orders to go to Londonderry and to make his report of that place'.* Stevens left for Ireland on the 30th. It soon became clear that preparations were in hand to send another relief force. Richards had orders from the Duke of Schomberg, commander of William's new expeditionary force for Ireland, on 2 May to 'embark with some regiments to relieve Londonderry, which we hear is now invested with the Irish Catholics, on whom the town has made several sallies and have killed many of them'.[98] This was obviously a reference to the first battles at Pennyburn, news of which seems to have travelled extremely quickly as already noted.

Over the next few days the preparations continued, with four regiments assigned to the relief force, arrangements made for provisions and bakers and brewers kept busy. Major-General Percy Kirke also

---

*This was John Stevens, a king's messenger.

arrived to take command of the force, which included Cunningham's and Richards' regiments; these were now under the command of Colonels George St George and Steuart respectively.[99] Percy Kirke already had a formidable, and unpleasant, reputation. A veteran of Tangier, of which he had been governor for two years, he had played a major role in the suppression of the Duke of Monmouth's rebellion in 1685, and his regiment had earned the ironic soubriquet 'Kirke's lambs' for its brutality; the regiment's badge was the paschal lamb, apparently part of the arms of Charles II's queen, Catherine of Braganza.[100] That regiment, the Queen's* also known as the 1st Tangerines, had served twenty-two years in 'that lawless but hard-fighting garrison, during which time it escorted its colonel, the notorious Percy Kirke, in his embassy into the interior of Morocco'. Note the use of the adjective 'notorious' to describe Kirke, who was also said to be 'ruthless'.[101] A measure of his ruthlessness may be gained from the fact that he had served on the continent with the Duke of Monmouth's Regiment while that unit was in French pay, but had no compunction in fighting against Monmouth in the latter's rebellion. This was to be the man responsible for the relief of Derry.

Stevens returned to Liverpool on 8 May to report that the Protestants of Londonderry continued to hold out and had gained some victories over the Irish; they had also killed a French general and 'several English men of quality' and Berwick was reported as wounded, perhaps dead. Kirke called a council of war and ordered Captain Richards to sail for Londonderry to advise 'the Protestants of the measures taken here for their relief and also order what I should find necessary for the fortifying of Londonderry'.[102]

Following the setback at Windmill Hill, the Jacobite command seems to have suspended siege artillery operations in that area and turned the artillery to creating terror within the walls. This proved highly successful, as evidenced by the various accounts of the siege. Living within the city walls that summer must have been a terrifying experience for the remaining citizens and the refugees. This would have been especially so after the end of May when the Jacobites had received additional mortars, weapons that were much more effective for striking terror into the hearts of civilians. (The word mortar comes from

---

*Amalgamations in the second half of the twentieth century mean that this, the senior English infantry regiment of the Army, is now part of the Princess of Wales's Royal Regiment.

a German word, *meerthier*, meaning sea monster, which goes some way to explaining the weapon's origin: when Mohammed II was confronted by an enemy fleet during the siege of Constantinople in 1451 he proposed a new weapon that could throw its shot to a great height before plunging down though the decks of the enemy ships. Thus was the mortar born, and although it was not then accurate enough for its first intended purpose it was soon recognized as an ideal weapon for siege warfare and its use spread throughout Europe.)[103]

The trajectory of conventional artillery at this time was quite low, and so only those guns emplaced in Stronge's orchard would have been able easily to fire into the city. In doing so they caused considerable damage and some deaths. They were supported by mortar fire, both by day and night, and this proved both extremely effective and terrifying: on 25 April a mortar round killed an old lady, Mrs Susannah Holding, when a shell struck a house belonging to a Mr Long; this was one of eighteen fired into the city during the night. (Walker described Mrs Holding as 'an old woman in a garret' whereas Ash writes that she was an eighty-year-old gentlewoman.) Three other persons also died that day from cannon fire. On the last day of April a cannonball wounded two members of an infantry company marching up Shipquay Street while one of Colonel Mitchelburne's soldiers was killed whilst on parade outside the walls in the old cow market. This soldier died because he remained standing whereas his companions dropped to the ground to save themselves.[104]

Since it was now recognized that the town house in the Diamond was in danger from such fire, 'the upper part of Shipquay-street was barricadoed to protect it from the enemy's cannon, stationed in Stronge's Orchard'. This curtain wall, creating an *enceinte*, was built with 'timber, stones and dung' between Coningham's and Boyd's corners.[105] Even that precaution, arguably overdue, did not prevent a round from demolishing the town clock. In retribution a Williamite gun, firing across the river from the ramparts, knocked one of the Jacobite cannon from its carriage and killed the gunner.[106]

Following their success at Windmill Hill, the defenders spent some days strengthening their forward positions. Lundy's original line of outposts was improved to become a defensive line with redoubts across Windmill Hill from the low ground in the west to the river in the east; a second arm at a right angle to this provided cover from the west and the bog.[107] The new fortifications were intended to protect the soldiers manning them from cannon fire from the other side of the river and to provide a base for sorties from the city. At first it was decided that the line would be garrisoned by the city's regiments in turn but this plan was superseded when suspicions were expressed about one of the commanding officers. Fearing that an entire regiment might defect with disastrous consequences, the plan was changed to create an ad hoc defensive unit made up from detachments of each regiment in the garrison.[108]

Those who manned this line of outposts had to be on constant alert as was shown when, on 10 May, Colonel Blair's detachment was 'nearly surprised by a large body of the enemy's troops'. Blair was holding that part of the line on the right flank which adjoined the boggy terrain. His troops were posted in the ditches on low-lying ground as the enemy cavalry approached and they did not notice the horsemen. However, Adam Murray, watching from the city walls, saw what was about to happen and immediately mounted his horse, galloped through Butcher's Gate, down Bog Street and on to Blair's position where he warned the latter of his danger. Blair was thus able to withdraw his men with no loss although one officer, Captain Ricaby, received a bullet wound in his arm. Murray returned unhurt although he had to pass Jacobite infantry who had taken up position in the hedges.[109]

On the day after this engagement a force marched out of the city to attack the Jacobite camp at Pennyburn. By now, however, some Jacobite artillery had been deployed there and these guns opened up on the attacking Williamites. In the face of heavy fire the attempt was abandoned and the force returned to the comparative safety of the walls. On the 12th a number of sorties were made against 'strolling parties of the enemy'. Some Jacobite soldiers and officers in those parties were shot, while, that night, some cavalry scouts from the garrison were attacked on the edge of the bog opposite the Royal Bastion. There was a spirited exchange of fire in which a Jacobite officer was said to have been killed.[110]

Both sides maintained artillery fire over the next three days during which a boy lost his leg to a cannon ball in Pump Street, close to the city centre; the round then rebounded and struck the cathedral, lodging in the wall.[111] At the same time the Jacobite army moved its main headquarters from St Johnston to Ballougry Hill, some two miles from the city. A second grand division encamped at Pennyburn and a third at Stronge's orchard, from which entrenchments now extended along the ridge on the east side of the river. Some effort at circumvallation was being made and the Jacobite army was closing in on the city, in spite of their setback at Windmill Hill. It was noted that the enemy had 'taken possession of several strong positions, so as to intercept all communications between the town and the country'.[112] To make matters worse, the water supply within the walls had become polluted and undrinkable, forcing rationing of water. Drinking water had now to be drawn from wells outside the walls, including St Columb's well, which is still in existence, on the verge of the bog.[113]

Small actions continued to be the principal story around the city, with a Williamite sergeant and four Jacobite soldiers killed between 16 and 19 May.[114] But not only was water in short supply, forage for the horses was also running very low. This imperilled Murray's Regiment by threatening the horses with starvation. In an effort to alleviate the situation a foraging party was sent out towards Creggan on 18 May. (This is not the modern housing estate of that name, which is actually built on the townlands of Edenballymore and Ballymagowan, but a townland to the north-west of the city beyond the Rosemount area.) Three officers, Captains Cunningham, Noble and Sanderson, commanded the party, which, on the outward journey, drove the Jacobites from a small fort. However, on the return trip the party was intercepted by a Jacobite cavalry detachment commanded by Lord Galmoy (Piers Butler). In the ensuing action, seventeen Williamites were taken prisoner, including Captain Cunningham. There followed an incident that must have caused considerable revulsion in the Williamite ranks. Proposals were made for an exchange of prisoners but these were refused by the Jacobites after which Cunningham and his companions 'were treacherously and barbarously butchered'. Some of the defenders believed that Galmoy was among the Jacobite wounded but this proved false. Cunningham's body was subsequently brought to the city where he was buried with full military honours on the 20th.[115]

This incident was unusual in the conduct of the conflict at Derry thus far. Those Jacobites taken prisoner at the battle of Windmill Hill were treated with dignity and accommodated within the city and the Williamites might have expected this to be reciprocated. However, the incident was almost inevitable given the involvement of Galmoy, a man who had already gained a reputation for barbarity in Fermanagh. There Galmoy had negotiated with the defenders of Enniskillen to exchange Captain Woolston Dixie, of the Enniskillen garrison, for Captain Brian Maguire, a Jacobite officer held prisoner in Enniskillen. Although Maguire was released, Galmoy had Dixie and another Williamite officer, Edward Carleton, hanged from a signpost in Belturbet. This was bad enough but the bodies were then decapitated and, allegedly, used by Galmoy's soldiers in a grisly game of football in the local market place. Galmoy's explanation for hanging Dixie, the eldest son of the Dean of Kilmore, was that a commission from William to raise troops was found on him for which offence he was tried by court martial, found guilty and sentenced to death.[116] However, it is entirely likely that Galmoy knew of the commission and intended to court martial and execute Dixie while he was conducting the negotiations for the exchange. This would have made his behaviour much more reprehensible to the Enniskillen defenders. His behaviour at Creggan did not even have the patina of the due process of military justice about it that he could claim for the Dixie hanging. The behaviour of Galmoy and the murders of his prisoners can only have inspired fear and loathing in the defenders of the city.

Siege warfare includes periods when little seems to happen even though people such as engineers and pioneers, or labourers, may be kept busy. As one chronicler of the siege commented, 'Nothing considered very important in the way of warfare' occurred between 21 and 26 May, although he goes on to note that five Jacobites were killed.[117] The circumstances of these deaths are not described but it may be assumed that they perished as a result of some form of military action. Here is a parallel to Remarque's comment that on the day the central character in his story was killed the official communiqués noted that it was 'all quiet on the Western front'.

These days of quiet were marked by particular religious observance, the Presbyterians holding a solemn fast with sermons 'preached accordingly' while the Anglicans also held a fast and they, too, had 'appropriate sermons'.[118] One wonders if these fasts and sermons were inspired in any way by the fate of Captain Cunningham and his men.

Far from the besieged living together in a state of harmony, there were tensions. As we have already noted, there was an underlying tension between Anglican and Dissenter but there was also tension between some of the most experienced soldiers of the garrison. Henry Baker, the governor, and Jonathan Mitchelburne, the commanding officer of one of the regiments in the city, had 'some sharp words' which led to a scuffle between the two. According to Mackenzie, this arose from suspicions about Mitchelburne that were entertained by Baker and the garrison in early May. The governor decided to confine Mitchelburne to his chamber but the latter struck out with his sword when he was apprehended. In the ensuing clash he was wounded, just above the left ankle, by Baker. The dispute is not mentioned at all by Walker while Ash dismisses it summarily although Mackenzie provides a little more detail but comments that the grounds of the suspicion 'were too tedious to relate'. There is, however, an account from Mitchelburne himself, who recorded that he had been instructed by Baker to oversee the issue of a tobacco ration to the garrison but that he, Mitchelburne, decided to provide only a half ration to the companies of Baker's Regiment since these were only at half strength. This seems sensible but some of the soldiers complained to Baker, who described Mitchelburne as a 'rascal' and ordered him to be confined.[119] Following the contretemps between the pair, Mitchelburne was placed under house arrest but Baker seems to have thought better of his original suspicions as, when he was taken ill subsequently and confined to his quarters, he nominated Mitchelburne, now recovered from his wound, to act as governor in his place. Macrory suggests that the original suspicion arose from one of those rumours that 'so easily arise when men are cooped up behind walls and surrounded by an enemy'.[120] In this case it was not a rumour but a grievance without substance. But Macrory is certainly correct when he asserts that Mitchelburne's record was such that his loyalty to the defenders' cause was not in doubt.[121]

But Mitchelburne was not the only prominent member of the garrison on whom suspicion fell at this time. George Walker also found himself being investigated for his behaviour. Naturally, this is not mentioned in his own account of the siege, which may also explain why he did not mention the suspicions about Mitchelburne. The Reverend John Mackenzie, Presbyterian chaplain to Walker's own regiment, enlightens us about this episode, however:

> About the end of May, most of the officers having been for some time suspicious of Governor Walker, drew up several articles against him, some of which were to the effect following, according to the account I had of them from the memories of some of the officers then present.[122]

The first complaint against Walker was that, about 18 April, he, and others, had a secret meeting at which they decided to seek terms from King James and sent a messenger to the Jacobite camp to this effect. Next on the list of complaints came Walker's involvement in the later escape of this messenger who, on his return to the city, had been confined on suspicion of dealing with the Jacobites. Then it was said that, at the end of April, while defending troops were outside the walls, Walker and others conspired 'to shut the gates upon them, to facilitate a surrender'. He was also accused of stealing or embezzling the stores, of offering to betray the town for £500 in hand and a pension of £700 a year from King James, which offer was approved by James, and of abusing officers who went to the stores. Mackenzie also notes that there was another complaint against Walker, 'relating to personal vices, [but which] I shall not mention'.[123]

Over a hundred officers of the garrison signed a resolution asking that Walker be prosecuted and that he be removed from 'all trust either in the stores or in the army'. This led to a proposal, to which Baker gave his assent, that the stores and garrison be henceforth administered by a council of fourteen with Baker as its president. No decisions were to be made without the council being consulted, which was likely to lead to an extremely unwieldy conduct of the city's defence. This proved to be the case, as the council's meetings were interrupted frequently by bombs and, although the council remained the ruling authority until the end of the siege, it seems that Baker was able to conduct affairs effectively without having to call meetings.[124]

This period of relative calm ended about midnight on the 27th when there was another engagement close to the windmill. This followed a double sally by the defenders with about 150 moving out from the windmill towards Ballougry and another party of equal strength making for Pennyburn. These detachments were commanded by Lieutenant Green and Ensign Dunbar although it is unclear who commanded which. However, the party that 'went the way of Ballougry did nothing' but the second party engaged with Jacobite troops near a fort that the latter had erected. As a result of this encounter two Williamites were killed and four wounded. Although they had 'shot briskly' at the enemy, no effect was claimed for their efforts. Ash notes that the defenders' artillery later killed a Jacobite captain and wounded two men.[125]

Subsequently the garrison's guns on the Double Bastion fired on a troop of Jacobite dragoons who were making their way towards Pennyburn and claimed to have killed three of them, an incident which Ash confirms and for which he notes that Governor Baker gave the gunners half a cob (a loaf of bread). Whether in retaliation or not, the Jacobites fired eighteen shells into the city that night, prompting an order to move 107 barrels of gunpowder from the cathedral into dry wells where they were safer.[126] Some Jacobite reinforcements appeared with two regiments of horse and foot that arrived from Strabane. These stopped to rest near Captain Stuart's house, on the east bank of the Foyle, but were persuaded to move on when five cannon fired at them from the Church Bastion.[127]

The morale of the defenders was lifted on the 31st when it was learned that Jacobite despatches to Dublin, captured from a messenger the previous day, claimed that their losses thus far totalled almost 3,000 men.[128] Yet another skirmish took place close to the windmill although no casualties were noted, and a shell, presumably from a mortar, burst near the city's main magazine, on the site of Docwra's fort, previously O'Doherty's fort.[129] (This is the site of the modern Tower Museum which incorporates a 1980s' reconstruction of the fort.)

The artillery continued to fire both cannon and mortars, and a number of the rounds fired by the Jacobites are recorded together with their results or lack thereof. A large shell weighing nineteen pounds struck the cathedral but did little damage, whereas two men lost their legs to another round that fell on a cabin at the rear of the bishop's house. In both cases the rounds are probably mortar bombs, which is borne out by the statement that they were 'thrown into the town at night'.[130] Additional works had been carried out on the defences with new gun platforms built at the end of May on which six more guns were placed.[131] There is, however, no explanation of where these extra guns came from; it is probable that they had been in the city all along but had hitherto not been emplaced.

By the end of May the situation of the besieged was worsening. Until then they had been able to keep some cattle, but forage was running out and the cattle began to die. Provisions for the garrison and the inhabitants were also becoming scarce and expensive although a rationing system was in place. Mackenzie commented that 'where they could find a horse-a-grazing, near the Wind-Mill, they would kill and eat him'. Although there was a stock of oats, shelling – grain husks – and malt in the town, there was no way of milling these and they remained unusable for the time being.[132]

And still the Jacobite artillery pounded the city: on 3 June there was a heavy bombardment that damaged many houses and left 'streets furrowed' while three civilians, two men and a woman, were killed. One of the garrison, Major Graham, died from injuries he received while leaning over Ship Quay Gate where he was hit in the belly. That night another fifteen shells landed inside the city causing considerable damage to buildings and killing many, including seven soldiers of Colonel Lance's Regiment who had been sitting in the house belonging to a Mr Harper in Shipquay Street.[133]

This bombardment followed the arrival of what Berwick described as 'six pieces de gros canon' which, it is reasonable to assume, were specialist siege guns. These had come overland from Dublin* rather than being transported by water which was the preferred way of transporting such heavy weapons (and one of the reasons why France, The Netherlands and Russia have so many canals). However, they did not represent the entire additional complement of artillery that had been intended for the Jacobite army at Derry. The French commander of the Jacobite artillery and engineers, the Marquis de Pointis, a naval officer, had travelled south to Kinsale during May 'to aid the bringing over of arms, but all in vain for the heavy battering guns became unserviceable'.[134] It is not clear how these guns became unserviceable but this meant that the defenders of the city were spared the full weight of the siege artillery that their foes had hoped to deploy against them.

Meanwhile de Pointis had also been busy building a boom across the Foyle. The site chosen was almost that of the modern Foyle Bridge, to the north of the city, but de Pointis' first effort was little removed from a farce. He chose to have the boom made from oak of which there was a plentiful supply, but this boom was so heavy that it sank below the surface and was soon broken by the force of the tides.[135] It was back to the design board for the Frenchman, who contrived a second boom, made from squared fir beams and articulated so that it could rise and fall with the tides – the Foyle is tidal as far as Strabane – and this appeared to be more successful. The ends of the beams were socketed, albeit roughly, and metal hooks were fitted to allow them to be linked together with cables, while a thick rope, about five or six inches in diameter, was fastened along the length of the boom, 'like a rod in curtain rails', to steady it; this rope was underwater to make cutting it more difficult.[136] This new boom certainly floated, and its deterrent value was increased by the construction of artillery positions on the river banks at either end of the boom; these were supported by infantry posts designed to enfilade the boom. A feature of the design was that the boom 'lay not directly athwart the flow of the Foyle but with its western end retracted to allow for the thrust of the flood and perhaps with calculation that boom, bank, following wind and incoming tide would provide a fatal pocket for any challenging vessel'.[137] The principal defensive positions on either end of the boom were described as forts, that on the west bank being Charles Fort and its opposite number being Grange Fort. A third, small, fort was also built on the west bank. This was New Fort with a battery of two small guns.[138]

---

*See Appendix Seven for a description of the overland move of an artillery train and for a description of a siege gun.

In length the boom measured some 200 yards and was 'about five or six feet across'. On the west bank of the river it was held fast to a rock by a frame designed by de Pointis' engineers, whereas the eastern end was secured by a great mound of rock and stones. Its designer was pleased with his work and reported this satisfaction to the French naval minister, Seignelay.[139] Moreover, he told Seignelay that he intended to build a second boom which could be completed in two days. 'With that it is admitted we shall be secure.'[140] This was not built, nor is its proposed location known, but it would seem logical to have placed it closer to the city. Pointis was also concerned about his health, telling Seignelay that he had 'got the fever again and the exertion I have given myself has apparently caused some bone splinters to become loose'.[141] A much more effective obstruction to any relief fleet could have been achieved by sinking vessels in the channel. The Foyle is a shallow river and scuttling a ship, or ships, in the narrows close to Culmore would have denied access to the city for any vessels. That this was not done is believed to have been due to the intervention of James, who forbade the use of 'a device which might have rendered the port unusable for an incalculable period'.[142] Thus James made yet another in the litany of errors that lost him his kingdoms.

Pointis finally had his boom in place on 4 June, the day on which another battle occurred at Windmill Hill. This was a major encounter and was much more serious than the first battle almost a month earlier. Its genesis lay in that earlier defeat for the Jacobites, which was described as 'a great vexation to the army, through the loss of so many persons of worth'.[143] Hamilton thus resolved to avenge the defeat. Once again the battle began with a Jacobite advance, using both cavalry and infantry against the defensive line between bog and river. In the van of the attack, on the Jacobite left flank, were two columns of grenadiers advancing on the trenches between the windmill and the bog. These men, drawn from all the grenadier, or right flank, companies of the army were led by Captain John Plunkett, youngest son of Nicholas Plunkett, of County Dublin. Cavalry and dragoons commanded by Lieutenant-Colonels Edmund Butler and McDonald were on the right flank, along the river. Butler was Lord Mountgarrett's second son. These advanced along the river strand, the tide being out, in the face of a heavy fire from the defending Williamite infantry. As the first clash occurred here, a strong party of Jacobite infantry, the 'greatest part of the foot', attacked the defensive positions between the windmill and the river.[144]

As the Jacobite cavalry and dragoons closed on the defenders' trenches, the infantry there left their positions 'and received them with such determined bravery, that the enemy soon got into confusion and retired'.[145] At first the Williamites fired at the soldiers but their rounds failed to penetrate the buff, or leather, coats worn by the horsemen. This is described as armour by Walker with subsequent writers accepting this as meaning metal breastplates, but such armour had gone out of fashion and very few would have been wearing it still. Ash, a soldier himself, correctly identifies the cavalrymen as being 'all clad in buff'. The leather coat, however, offered protection against small-arms fire at all but very close range and gave the effect of armour without the weight of metal. Thus it was that only when their officers ordered them to fire at the horses did the defenders achieve success.[146] The attack was broken, and Edmund Butler was among those captured, being taken prisoner by Captain John Gladstanes. Butler had attempted to rally his men.

> the said lieutenant-colonel Butler, being extraordinarily well mounted, resolved to show the way, if possible. At which, clapping spurs to his charger, he flies over but was immediately taken prisoner. Cornet Purcell, of Thurles in the county of Tipperary, followed, but his horse was killed, and he leaped back in his armour, and so saved himself. A private man and an old gentleman, Edward Butler, of Tinnahinch, in the county of Carlow, attempted and gained the ditch, but he and his horse were both slain.[147]

At the same time the infantry, headed by 'the line of colonels, their pikes* in hand', attacking in the centre of the Jacobite line also met determined resistance with the defending soldiers keeping up a steady fire. This was described by one Williamite writer as 'successive, or what is called file-firing'. Walker presents a more accurate description, noting that the defenders had placed themselves in three ranks so that one rank was always able to 'march up and relieve the other, and discharge successively upon the enemy'. This suggests that the defenders had been given some effective training since the battle of the fords. The Jacobite infantry had advanced using bundles of rods, or fascines, described as bundles of faggots, to act as body armour and deflect musket balls which worked well enough until they reached the earth bank behind which the defenders were ensconced.[148] This was much higher than had been appreciated and, in the absence of

---

*These were not the long pikes carried by pikemen but a short pole on which was a pear-shaped metal head, the badge of office of a commanding officer.

scaling ladders, presented an insurmountable obstacle to the attackers. The attack broke down into mayhem, but the question remains: if the defenders' fire was so effective, how did the Jacobites reach the line at all? Analysis of this encounter indicates that the Williamites prevailed because they had the protection of an earth wall, about twelve feet high, and the ranks of soldiers were able to load, move up to the wall and then fall back to allow the next rank to take over. There is a certain similarity to the situation of Jacobite infantry at Aughrim two years later when they fought well with the protection of earth banks but were unable to react effectively when attacked from the flank by Williamite cavalry. A Jacobite account of the infantry attack in the centre is probably the most accurate available:

> Notwithstanding this great check . . . they went on boldly, and attempted to mount the entrenchment; but their endeavours proved all in vain, by reason the [earth] was so high that they had need of ladders to carry it suddenly. Otherwise a small delay would slaughter them all, by reason that the rebels were very numerous withinside, and, being wholly covered, could not be lessened by the fire of the assailants; for what harm could the assailants do when they could not lay sight on their foes?[149]

The only element of the Jacobite attack that met with any degree of success was that by the grenadiers on the left flank. Here the defensive line was hinged back at a right angle to cover the approach from the bog to the west of the walls, and it was from the west that the grenadiers attacked. These were men drawn from all the infantry regiments in the Jacobite army. Each regiment had a grenadier company, also known as the right flank company, which included the tallest and strongest men in the regiment. Their task was to throw grenades, small bombs about the size of a cricket ball, which were pitched overarm, thus necessitating a special hat, similar to an old-fashioned sleeping cap, without a brim that would interfere with the act of throwing. A mustering of grenadier companies such as this was an indication of a determined attack; the Jacobites were hoping to break into the city.

At first the Irish grenadiers made good progress. Possibly intimidated by the size of these men, the defenders abandoned their trenches and fled, pursued by the Jacobites. However, not every Williamite fled; a small boy remained and pelted the Irish soldiers with stones.[150] One Williamite account suggests that the grenadier attack was 'gallantly repulsed' by the defenders in the trenches, but this is not true. In fact, Henry Baker, watching the developing battle from the walls, ordered troops to sally out of the city and engage the grenadiers. It was this deployment that forced the grenadiers to retreat. They had also lost their commander, Captain Plunkett, who 'received at the first fire his mortal wound, and being carried off to his tent, he died within an hour later'.[151]

The entire Irish attack had been thrown into confusion, and Hamilton's men were now compelled to retreat. Walker claims that some 400 Irish soldiers were killed, whereas Captain Ash puts the figure at sixty with over a hundred wounded or taken prisoner.[152] Included in the latter were Butler, as we have seen, Captain McDonnell, Cornets McDonaghy, Watson and Eustace and a number of French officers. Both Watson and Eustace had been wounded and died soon after being captured.[153] A Jacobite writer estimates his army's losses at 'at least two hundred men killed'. These dead included Lieutenant-Colonel Roger Farrel, Captain Barnewal, of Archerstown, County Meath, Captain Patrick Barnewal, of Kilbrue, County Meath, Captain Richard Grains, Queen's County, Captain Richard Fleming, Staholmock, County Meath, and Captain William Talbot of Wexford.[154] Williamite losses were said to be not more than twelve dead, with one source saying that only six died; a Jacobite source says that the Jacobites did 'no damage to the defendants'. Among the Williamite dead, however, was Captain Maxwell, who lost an arm to a cannon ball although he did not die until some time later.[155]

In spite of all the effort that had been put into the attack, the Jacobites had failed once more, prompting the comment: 'You see here, as you have seen all along, that the tradesmen of Londonderry have more skill in their defence than the great officers of the Irish army in their attacks.' When King James learned of this disaster he ordered Marshal Conrad de Rosen north once more with orders to reduce the city.[156]

As for the garrison, they could see that yet another Jacobite attack had been repulsed, which must have raised their spirits considerably. They also enjoyed another bonus: the dead Jacobite horses were dragged into the city to add to the store of food for those inside the walls.

Notes

1: Simpson, op cit, p. 115
2: Ibid; Walker, op cit, p. 29–30; Mackenzie, op cit, pp. 34–5
3: Mackenzie, op cit, p. 41

4: Walker, op cit, p. 30

5: Mackenzie, op cit, p. 38

6: Quoted in full in Milligan, op cit, pp. 163–4

7: Milligan, op cit, p. 165

8: Walker, op cit, p. 14. He describes all the heavier weapons as culverins.

9: Milligan, op cit, p. 165

10: Hughes, op cit, p. 70

11: Walker, op cit, p. 64; Simpson, op cit, p. 111

12: Gilbert, op cit, p. 65

13: Ibid

14: Walker, op cit, pp. 34–5; Gilbert, op cit, p. 65

15: Gilbert, op cit, p. 65

16: Milligan, op cit, p. 163

17: Simpson, op cit, pp. 115–6

18: Mackenzie, op cit, p. 40

19: Ibid

20: Simpson, op cit, p. 115

21: Walker, op cit, p. 31

22: Ibid, pp. 95–6

23: Dwyer, *The Siege of Londonderry in 1689*, p. 83

24: Walker, op cit, p. 31

25: Ibid, pp. 31–2

26: Colledge & Warlow, *Ships of The Royal Navy*, pp. 44 & 275

27: NA Kew, ADM52/9, Captain's log of HMS *Bonadventure*

28: Ibid

29: Ibid

30: Kelly, *The Sieges of Derry*, p. 54

31: Quoted in ibid, p. 53

32: Kelly, op cit, p. 57

33: Ibid, p. 58

34: Ibid, p. 60

35: Powley, op cit, p. 241

36: Ibid, p. 63

37: *Franco-Irish Correspondence*, pp. 89–90: letter and report, dated 29 April, from Maumont to Louvois. The date is from the Gregorian calendar then in use on the continent rather than the Julian calendar still in use in Britain and Ireland.

38: NA Scotland, GD26/8/15. A letter, dated 17 May 1689, from James to Dundee assuring the latter of support 'as soon as the siege of Derry is over'.

39: Simpson, op cit, p. 116

40: Mackenzie, op cit, p. 38

41: Gilbert, op cit, p. 63
42: Simpson, op cit, pp. 117–8; Walker, op cit, p. 34; Mackenzie, op cit, p. 39
43: Simpson, op cit, p. 117–8; Walker, op cit, pp. 34–5; Mackenzie, op cit, pp. 39–40
44: Simpson, p. 118
45: Ibid
46: Ibid; Gilbert, op cit, pp. 68–9; Mackenzie, op cit, pp. 39–40; Milligan, op cit, pp. 175–6; Avaux, p. 117
47: Simpson, op cit, p. 118n
48: Ibid, p. 118
49: Ibid; Gilbert, op cit, p. 68; Walker, op cit, p. 89
50: Mackenzie, op cit, p. 39; Walker, op cit, p. 34
51: Macrory, op cit, p. 232
52: Aickin, *Londerias*
53: Walker, op cit, p. 35
54: Mackenzie, op cit, p. 40; Walker, op cit, p. 35
55: Simpson, op cit, p. 118
56: Ibid, p. 119
57: Gilbert, op cit, p. 68 (he claims that Pusignan was killed in the same action as Maumont); Walker (p. 89) and Mackenzie (p. 40) also believed Pusignan to have died in the first action.
58: Ash, op cit, p. 63
59: Avaux, op cit, p. 136–7 comments that Pusignan would not have died had the army had a competent surgeon.
60: *London Gazette*, 23–27 May 1689
61: Young, op cit, p. 265
62: See Milligan, op cit, p. 369, note 17
63: Witherow, *Derry and Enniskillen*, p. 133; Aickin, *Londerias*
64: Ibid
65: Walker, op cit, p. 30
66: *London Gazette*, 13–16 May 1689
67: Mitchelburne, op cit
68: Ash, op cit, p. 84. In his inimitably refreshing manner, Ash again includes this information in his diary long after it had occurred; in this case the entry is made for 1 July although he emphasizes that the fort fell within a fortnight of the siege starting.
69: Witherow, op cit, p. 127
70: *Derriana*, p. 23
71: Ibid
72: Mackenzie, op cit, p. 40; Simpson, op cit, p. 119
73: Mackenzie, op cit, p. 41

74: Ibid
75: Ibid
76: Quoted in Chandler, *The Art of War in the Age of Marlborough*, p. 183
77: Ash, op cit, p. 64; Simpson, op cit, p. 120
78: Simpson, op cit, p. 120
79: Ibid, p. 121; Mackenzie, op cit, p. 42; Walker, op cit, pp. 36–7; Ash, op cit, p. 65.
80: Simpson, op cit, p. 121
81: Mackenzie, op cit, p. 42
82: Walker, op cit, p. 36
83: Ibid, p. 37
84: Ibid, p. 37; Mackenzie, op cit, p. 42; Ash, op cit, pp. 65–6; Mitchelburne, op cit; *Londerias*
85: Simpson, op cit, pp. 121–2; Walker, op cit, pp. 37–8; Mackenzie, op cit, p. 42; Ash, op cit, p. 66; Mitchelburne, op cit; *Londerias*
86: Simpson, op cit, p. 122
87: Ash, op cit, p. 66; Simpson, op cit, p. 122n
88: Simpson, op cit, p. 121
89: St Columb's Cathedral
90: Walker, op cit, p. 38; Ash, op cit, p. 66
91: Ash, op cit, p. 67
92: Ibid
93: Ibid
94: Mackenzie, op cit, p. 41
95: Simpson, op cit, p. 123; Ash, op cit, p. 67
96: Witherow, *Two Diaries of Derry in 1689: Richards' Diary of the Fleet* (Hereafter Witherow: *Richards'*), p. 1
97: *London Gazette*, 18 – 22 April 1689
98: Witherow: *Richards*, op cit, pp. 1–2
99: Ibid, p. 2
100: Chicester & Burges-Short, *Records and Badges of the British Army*, 1900, p. 196
101: Ibid
102: Witherow: *Richards*, op cit, p. 2
103: Hogg, *The Illustrated Encyclopedia of Artillery*, p. 18
104: Walker, op cit, pp. 35–6; Ash, op cit, pp. 63–4; Simpson, op cit, pp. 119–120
105: Simpson, op cit, p. 120; Ash, op cit, p. 64
106: Simpson, op cit, p. 120; Walker, op cit, p. 36
107: Simpson, op cit, pp. 122–3; Mackenzie, p. 42
108: Mackenzie, op cit, p. 42; Simpson, op cit, p. 123

109: Simpson, op cit, p. 123; Mackenzie, p. 42
110: Simpson, op cit, p. 123; Mackenzie, op cit, p. 43; Ash, op cit, p. 67
111: Ash, op cit, p. 68; Simpson, op cit, p. 123
112: Simpson, op cit, pp. 123–4; Walker, op cit, p. 40; Mackenzie, pp. 42–3
113: Walker, op cit, p. 40: Simpson, op cit, p. 124
114: Ash, op cit, p. 68
115: Mackenzie, op cit, p. 43; Simpson, op cit, p. 124
116: Witherow, *Derry and Enniskillen*, op cit, pp. 236–7; *Derriana*, op cit, p. 7
117: Simpson, op cit, p. 124
118: Ibid; Mackenzie, op cit, p. 43
119: Mackenzie, op cit, p. 41; Ash, op cit, p. 68; Mitchelburne, op cit
120: Macrory, op cit, p. 243
121: Ibid
122: Mackenzie, op cit, p. 45
123: Ibid
124: Ibid
125: Ash, op cit, pp. 69–70; Simpson, op cit, p. 124; Mackenzie, op cit, pp. 42–3
126: Ash, op cit, p. 71; Simpson, op cit, p. 124
127: Ash, op cit, p. 69
128: Simpson, op cit, p. 125; Ash, op cit, p. 71
129: Simpson, op cit, p. 125
130: Ibid; Ash, op cit, pp. 71–2
131: Simpson, op cit, p. 125
132: Mackenzie, op cit, pp. 46–7
133: Simpson, op cit, p. 125; Walker, op cit, p. 42; Mackenzie, op cit, p. 46. Simpson provides the detail included in this paragraph while the other diarists note the effects of these and other bombardments at this time.
134: NA Kew, State Papers Ireland, de Pointis to Seignelay; Powley, op cit, p. 218
135: Mackenzie, op cit, p. 46; Powley, op cit, p. 219
136: NA Kew, State Papers Ireland, de Pointis to Seignelay
137: Powley, op cit, p. 220
138: Ibid
139: Ibid, p. 220; NA Kew, State Papers Ireland, de Pointis to Seignelay
140: NA Kew, State Papers Ireland, de Pointis to Seignelay
141: Ibid
142: Powley, op cit, p. 220
143: Gilbert, op cit, p. 76
144: Ibid
145: Simpson, op cit, pp. 125–6; Walker, op cit, pp. 41–2; Ash, op cit, pp. 73–5
146: Ash, op cit, p. 74

147: Gilbert, op cit, p. 77
148: Ibid; Simpson, op cit, p. 126; Mackenzie, op cit, p. 43
149: Gilbert, op cit, p. 77
150: Ash, op cit, p. 74
151: Gilbert, op cit, pp. 76–7; Mackenzie, op cit, pp. 43–4; Simpson, op cit, p. 127
152: Walker, op cit, p. 42; Ash, op cit, p. 74
153: Simpson, op cit, p. 126; Ash, op cit, p. 74; Walker, op cit, p. 42 & p. 90
154: Gilbert, op cit, p. 77
155: Simpson, op cit, pp. 126–7; Walker, op cit, p. 42; Ash, op cit, p. 75
156: Gilbert, op cit, pp. 77–9

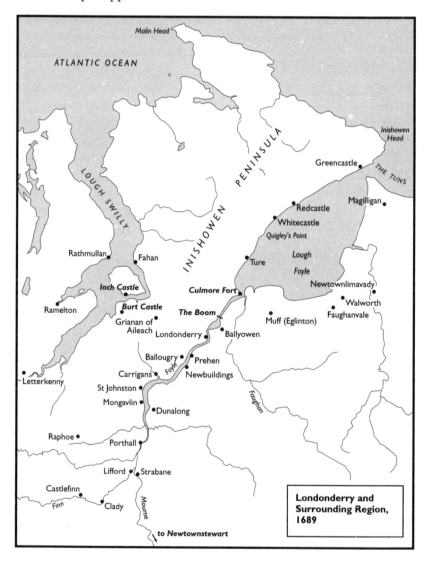

Londonderry and Surrounding Region, 1689

CHAPTER SIX

Give Signal to The Fight

There was considerable frustration in the Jacobite army following the defeat at Windmill Hill. It seemed that this army could not execute any plan successfully. Its major achievement to date, the taking of Culmore Fort, had been achieved by psychological means, tactics that offered no opportunity of breaching the walls of the stubborn city that lay before it. Losses were mounting with the worst being those of such officers as Maumont, Pusignan and Ramsey. Living conditions for the majority of soldiers could not have been good, with wet weather adding to the toll of disease in the ranks; there is a comment in Ash's journal for 17 May that there were 'great rains in the afternoon'.[1] That intercepted report of up to 3,000 casualties must have included many men who had succumbed to illness. Dysentery would have been the main problem, but typhus and other ailments would also have been found by the doctors. Such were the results of living in unhygienic conditions for an extended period.

Frustration often leads to anger and this was probably the reason for a heightened tempo from the Jacobite mortar batteries in Stronge's orchard that night. This increased rate of fire continued over the following days. During the night of 4–5 June three dozen mortar bombs were fired into the town, each, it was said, containing seventeen pounds of powder. (These are described as shells since the bombs were hollow to contain the explosive charge of blackpowder. On exploding, the casings of the shells shattered and pieces of the casings acted as a form of shrapnel.) The death toll from this bombardment included twenty-eight soldiers, four of whom were officers. Among the buildings struck was the home of Councillor Cairnes (Kems in Simpson's *Annals of Derry*), in which two people died and several others were wounded. The town house was also hit by a shell that fell through the roof and landed within 'a few yards of a vault, in which were deposited several barrels of gunpowder'.[2] This was a fortunate near miss for the defenders; a sympathetic explosion of the barrels of powder would probably have destroyed the town house.

The mortarmen kept up their bombardment the following night, when twenty-six bombs were fired into the city. These were larger shells, said to be 'of enormous size', but some failed to burst since their fuses had burned out in flight.[3] Those burning fuses made it possible to observe the flight path of each bomb, especially during the hours of darkness, and so take avoiding action. (In daylight it was possible to watch a mortar or cannon round throughout its flight; its initial speed was no more than 200mph which diminished as the flight progressed.) This seems to have been the practice adopted by many citizens who abandoned living indoors and took to lying in the streets.[4] In this is an augury of civilian life under air attack in the twentieth century. Nonetheless, the bombs continued to kill, with Major Breme and Surgeon Lindsay among the dead. Lindsay's loss was felt especially as he had been 'most useful to the sick and wounded'; he had been the surgeon to Walker's Regiment. Also killed was Henry Thompson, one of the city burgesses, as well as fourteen men, all of whom perished by the same shell which, in addition, caused two barrels of gunpowder to explode. Yet another round took seven lives, and a fourth bomb killed three people. Nor was there any let up over the next two nights when 'constant cannonading was kept up against the town, which committed great havoc'.[5] About this time the Jacobite artillery seems to have added an additional mortar to their inventory. This was much larger than the other mortars and, according to Walker, fired a bomb of some '273 pound weight' with which the Jacobites ploughed up streets and knocked down houses in the city.[6] This further encouraged the inhabitants to abandon their homes for the relative safety of the walls and the more remote parts of the town, presumably out of range of the mortars in Stronge's orchard. (In mid-June these were redeployed to the west bank of the river and were then able to threaten a larger part of the city.) Sadly some of the sick could not be moved and perished when their houses were destroyed. With mortars firing at night and cannon during the day, there was little opportunity for rest for anyone inside the walls

The movement of the inhabitants from the shelter of buildings to lie in the streets and 'about the walls' did no good for the general health of the population who 'contracted colds' that, 'together with the want of nutritious food and rest, brought on the worst kinds of fever, with dysentery, of which many died'.[7] Conditions in the city would have been rife for an epidemic of dysentery of which there are two forms. One, known as bacillary dysentery, is caused by infection from a bacterium of the *Shigella* family and is also known as *Shigellosis* while the other is amoebic dysentery. Either could have afflicted the people of Derry. The former is spread by flies in areas of poor sanitation or by infected individuals failing to wash their hands after defecating and before handling food. Either strain causes diarrhoea which can lead to dehydration. In turn, this can be fatal in individuals with low resistance and must have accounted for many deaths in the city. With a shortage of potable water the problem of dehydration would have been exacerbated, while having to move so often and not being able to have proper rest caused many to tire 'into faintness and diseases'. Typhus would also have presented a great danger: caused by *rickett-siae*, a micro organism similar to bacteria, the most common type was epidemic typhus which was spread between humans by body lice; it was prevalent at times of famine, in war situations and in the wake of natural disasters. Conditions in the city would have been ideal for typhus. For the civilians within the walls the mortaring was making the siege very personal, and their fears of the treatment they would receive in the event of a Jacobite victory must have been heightened.

But now the Jacobite army's attention was diverted to the north of the city and Lough Foyle. What appeared to be the advance guard of a relief fleet had sailed into the lough to anchor off Redcastle on 1 June. Among the ships in the flotilla was the frigate HMS *Greyhound* commanded by Captain Thomas Gwillam, and on board *Greyhound* was Major-General Percy Kirke's chief engineer, Captain Jacob Richards. The latter kept notes of his experiences on this expedition and later produced an account from those notes. (Although a naval captain outranks an army captain, the naval rank equating to lieutenant-colonel in the army, Richards' overall role was that of expedition commander and, as such, Captain Gwillam generally deferred to him.) Richards includes a transcript of the orders he received from Kirke at Liverpool on 10 May.

> It being thought fit and found requisite for their Majesties' Service, that you and the four French officers, with the gunners and the miners, should immediately embark and repair to Londonderry in Ireland provided it be still in the Protestants' hands; to accomplish which you are to follow these instructions:
> 1. To go no farther than within cannon shot of Culmore Fort, where you are to stay till you have such intelligence as may advise you in what condition Londonderry is in; whether any batteries be raised to hinder the passing of ships, or whether any other means are made use

of, as the choking the channel or chaining it over. Of all which you are to be well satisfied before you pass the said Fort of Culmore.

2. If you find that there is no passing without evident danger of losing yourselves or ship, you are not to attempt it, but lie bye somewhere in safety either in Lough Foyle or on the coast, so that you may from time to time be able to observe and learn what the enemies do; and then cause the ketch sent with you to return to me with an account of your proceedings, for which this shall be your sufficient warrant.

Richards had left Liverpool on 12 May aboard the merchant ketch *Edward and James* which carried a detachment of forty soldiers commanded by an ensign. He later transferred to HMS *Greyhound* which was also accompanied by the *Kingfisher*, the ketch referred to in Kirke's orders; the frigate had sailed on the 13th. With Richards were four French officers, Messieurs Dompiere, de la Barte,* Mainvilliers and Sundini, who had travelled from London with him. These were probably Huguenot officers who had fled religious persecution in their homeland. The ships spent over two weeks making for the entrance to Lough Foyle. Off the north coast of Ireland, on 29 May, they met a squadron under Captain George Rooke in HMS *Deptford*; the other ships of this squadron were *Antelope, Portland, Dartmouth* and *Henrietta*. Rooke, soon to be Admiral Sir George and destined to be one of the Royal Navy's outstanding commanders, had been patrolling Irish waters but had put into Greenock in Scotland to have repairs carried out to *Deptford* which had sustained damage in the Battle of Bantry Bay on 1 May. In Greenock he had learned about the relief fleet and had sent *Dartmouth* to meet the ships and order them to join him off Cape Kintyre. When the relief ships rendezvoused with him, Rooke promised to 'attempt whatever be advisable with safety to their Majesties' ships for the relief of Londonderry which [was] agreed on by all to be in great distress'. He told them that Captain Leigh in HMS *Portland* was off Lough Foyle and 'would assist us in going up'. And so, as we have noted, *Greyhound*, *Kingfisher* and the *Edward* and *James* sailed into the lough on 1 June.

---

*de la Barte may really be Jean de Bodt, a French engineer and Huguenot refugee to The Netherlands who accompanied William of Orange to England and is known to have served under Richards in Ireland during the winter of 1690–1. Also with Richards in Ireland during that winter was Johann von Bodt, who was born in Paris, and whose father came from Mecklenburg.[8]

Although the ships were able to sail from Greencastle up the lough to Redcastle, weather conditions then kept them at anchor until the following Friday, the 7th, when Richards decided that he had to make for Derry. Without a wind to fill the sails, the crews were forced to resort to manpower and the ships were kedged and warped as the tide flowed in from the Atlantic. This was a slow process that produced much sweat from the sailors as each ship either ran out and secured a hawser to a fixed point after which the seamen hauled on the lines to draw their ships forward or dropped a kedge anchor which was used in a similar fashion. By the time the tide turned the fleet was within three miles of Culmore Point. Richards then ordered the vessels to drop anchor.

By now the ships had been spotted by lookouts in the cathedral tower. Contact had to be made with the vessels, but, since the Jacobites held Culmore Fort, this could be done only by boat. But the city now had no boats. One would have to be built. The task fell on several soldiers under the direction of Lieutenant Crookshanks,* one of the apprentice boys who had shut the city gates and an officer of one of the companies raised by David Cairnes, but it was soon clear that neither the building party, nor Crookshanks for that matter, knew much about boats. Although they managed to knock together a large rowing boat with sixteen oars, eight to either side, they had placed the oars too close together. This did not become obvious to them until the boat had been launched and its crew attempted to set off downriver when it was found that the rowers were obstructing each other. The crew struggled to return to their starting point. This was unfortunate as the Jacobite artillerymen in Stronge's orchard had spotted the boat as soon as it entered the water and opened fire on it. No rounds had struck it but the crew must have wondered if they might be so lucky a second time. Adjustments were made and the voyage recommenced. Once again the guns across the river opened fire, but fortune continued to favour the Derrymen as every round missed. However, the adjustments to the oars had not been as effective as they might have been; they were still too close together and the crewmen were hard pressed to make any progress.[10]

On board *Greyhound* Richards was anxious to receive any information at all about the situation in the city. Some news was coming to him but only in dribs and drabs, and he had no proof of its accuracy.

---

*Crookshanks was later a burgess of Londonderry and sheriff of the city in 1692.

Three Protestant gentlemen, who had not taken refuge in the city but remained at their homes close to the lough shore where they enjoyed protections from Hamilton, were among a group that came aboard the ship. This trio, Gage, Hamilton and Newton, appeared to have some information about the boom. Such intelligence was critical to Richards, but the three men could not agree on the exact nature of the boom and nor could the remainder of the party. Richards still had no idea of the scale and structure of de Pointis' work. 'Some said it was a chain only, others several cables floated up with timbers, and others said it was a chain, cables and timbers, linked together.'

Further intelligence came from two other local residents, also presumably living under guarantees of safety from Richard Hamilton. The first of these was an elderly man, described as a Scot, who signalled from the shore and was brought aboard Richards' ship. Then a woman also signalled from the shore. This latter incident was just before nightfall, which is quite late at that time of year in these latitudes, and a boat was sent to collect the woman and bring her out to the ship. The lady and the crew of the ship's boat came close to being captured when a party of Jacobite dragoons arrived on the scene; the boat was fired on as it made for the *Swallow*. Neither the old Scot nor the woman had information of any military value. Richards noted that they both told him that 'our friends in Derry had sallied out and killed several officers and two or three hundred Irish'. Since Richards had earlier heard cannonfire from the direction of the city, he assumed that this was also part of the engagement that the two informants were telling him about. He does not seem to have queried how they could have had such up-to-date information about events in and around the city. What they were telling him about was the battle at Windmill Hill three days earlier, whereas the 'great firings' that he had heard were probably the gunners in Stronge's orchard trying to hit Crookshanks' makeshift boat.

The pair also claimed that the Jacobites had abandoned Culmore, but Richards did not believe this as he had seen Jacobite soldiers knocking down a house near the fort. This had been only at 4.00pm that day when Richards was observing the fort through his telescope. A consultation with the French officers led to a decision to take *Greyhound* closer to Culmore. Once a favourable wind blew up, Richards would ask Gwillam to sail his ship to within 'cannon shot of the . . . fort' as specified by Kirke. Whether an exact distance was intended by this instruction we do not know, but it does seem as if Richards was to sail into what the modern United States Navy would describe as 'harm's way', although the order may also be interpreted as instructing Richards not to hazard the ship. He would be taking the ship into the firezone of the Jacobite artillery at Culmore, and there would be risk to Gwillam's ship although a broadside from *Greyhound*, probably about six cannon,* would have more destructive power than the enemy artillery. However, the Jacobites would also be able to pour musketry into *Greyhound* if she came too close to the shore.

' Once darkness fell Richards was able to observe a number of large fires burning along the shore. One of these was the house that he had earlier watched Jacobite soldiers demolish; he now described it as being 'all in flames'. Since the weather remained wet, even though it was now early June, these fires might have been lit by Jacobite soldiers to dry out their clothing as well as to provide heat and a cooking facility. There are only a few hours of darkness at this time of year and it was not long before dawn broke. The new day brought with it a 'handsome gale' from the north-west, which was exactly what Richards wanted to close on Culmore. Orders were issued to the crew to make the ship ready for action, and the gun decks were cleared of their partitions to reduce the risk of injury from splinters; kit was bundled into hammocks to provide protection from musketfire for the quarterdeck; and the crew took up their action stations.

Greyhound sailed at 8 o'clock and was within range of Culmore later in the morning. The anchor was dropped and there was silence all around. No fire came from the gun positions on shore, but Richards could see activity in the enemy positions. Watching through his telescope he learned the reason for the lack of response from the Jacobite guns: they had not been positioned to deal with a threat from the lough. This was either incompetence or a dereliction of duty on the part of the garrison whose prime role was to stop any Williamite vessel entering the river at Culmore. Now the Jacobites were struggling to move a cannon, one of only two that Richards could see, from its normal position to one from which it could be trained on the ship.

The duel was very uneven: *Greyhound* 's broadside against one Jacobite gun, which was probably no heavier than a demi-culverin and might even have been a saker – a 6- to 7¼-pounder. In spite of the smoke and fury of the exchange, little damage was wrought, although Richards believed that he saw a Jacobite gun split; this could happen as

---

*As a sixth-rater, *Greyhound* would have carried fewer than thirty guns. From the navy estimates of 1690 we know that she had only sixteen guns and a crew of seventy-five.[11]

a result of overcharging a weapon with powder, from sustained firing or simply from a manufacturing defect. As the firing continued over the next forty-five minutes, Richards took the opportunity of climbing to the maintop, the platform atop the ship's main mast, to check the boom, the reason for his foray to Culmore. What he saw of the boom was enough to convince him that *Greyhound* would not be able to break it and sail up the river to Derry.

However, Jacob Richards also saw something that convinced him that there was a more immediate danger to the ship. He had spotted movement to the west, past Culmore. Closer examination revealed at least one team of horses dragging another artillery piece towards the fort. He descended to the deck and issued orders to weigh anchor and set sail to rejoin the other ships, from where he could send *Kingfisher* with a messenger to Kirke with the information he now had about the boom. But it seemed as if fate was taking a hand against Richards and his expedition. As *Greyhound*'s anchor was hauled out of the water, the wind not only dropped but also changed direction, 'two points to the northward'. *Greyhound* was blown onto the shore across from Culmore. At this point the river is very narrow as it empties into the lough and the ship was at the mercy of the Jacobites, lying as it now was less than a quarter of a mile from them.

Although *Greyhound*'s crew made an attempt to haul their ship out of its predicament by kedging, the tide was receding and the vessel soon grounded. Her bow was facing seaward, but the falling water level meant that *Greyhound* was no longer floating as she should but was leaning towards the far bank. This meant that her starboard guns were not so much facing the Jacobites at Culmore as the air above the Jacobites. By now the latter had deployed a number of pieces, which Richards estimated at eleven, into positions where they could fire on the ship from either bank of the Foyle. He writes that these weapons included 24-pounders, 8-pounders and 3-pounders. If there were any of the heavier guns mentioned present, they must have been from the six pieces of heavy artillery that had arrived at Derry only days before. Guns of this size might have been English or French weapons while 8-pounders would have been French.*

The artillery was not the sole threat to the ship, as the Jacobites had a number of camps close enough to Culmore to be able to alert

---

*English artillery had developed the sequence 3-, 6-, 12- and 24-pounder guns as did that of Austria, Denmark, Prussia and Russia. France and Spain used the sequence 4-, 8-, 12-, 16- and 24-pounders.[12]

several units to march to the fort to deal with the Williamite ship. Richards now had a large body of infantry, estimated at 'three or four battalions', facing his ship, and, although the range was too great for accurate musket fire, the Jacobite musketeers could still cause much harm if any balls found their marks in sailors of *Greyhound*. Some help was soon at hand for *Greyhound* as Richards had already sent a message indicating his predicament to the *Edward* and *James* and seeking assistance. In response, the forty soldiers on the latter were brought up to *Greyhound* in a small boat and boarded the vessel to add their firepower to that of the sailors who had been keeping up fire with about 120 small arms.

From about midday the battle intensified, with both sides firing all that they could at their opponents. Of course, the crew of *Greyhound* and their soldier reinforcements could use only muskets, but the Jacobites were able to use both artillery and muskets. The Jacobite artillery holed *Greyhound* below the waterline no fewer than seventeen times while putting another fifty rounds through the ship above the waterline. Although several men were wounded badly by splinters – one of the greatest dangers in a contemporary naval engagement – only two were killed, one a soldier in Richards' party and the other a crewman. Among the injured was Captain Gwillam, who 'was wounded in several places'. While this fighting was underway, efforts had been made to lighten *Greyhound* so that when the tide came in again it might be possible to float the ship off the mud that was holding her and make way out into the lough and relative safety. To achieve such a reduction, most of the ship's guns and many barrels of provisions were dumped overboard.

The tide was right for floating the ship off by about 7.00pm but there was so much water in *Greyhound* that she could not right herself. Captain Boyce, who had come on board to take command with Gwillam out of action, spoke to the warrant officers, who considered the situation hopeless, and they decided that *Greyhound* would have to be abandoned. The wounded, who now included Boyce who had been 'shot in the belly', would be taken off to safety and the ship would then be set alight. With the evacuation process underway, a skeleton crew was preparing to burn *Greyhound* when fate seemed to turn in the ship's favour: the wind changed round from north to south, the skeleton crew loosed the sails, *Greyhound* caught the wind, righted herself and began slowly to sail away from Culmore and the Jacobite guns. The danger had not passed completely since the ship was still leaking like a colander and listing so heavily that the crew feared that she might sink at any time. To save their vessel they ran her ashore again so that they might careen her, repair the holes both below and above the waterline, and make her seaworthy once more. That task had been completed by 9 o'clock next morning, and *Greyhound*'s masts had been hauled back into place 'and her rigging spliced'. Richards was pleased that the ship had been saved but not quite so pleased to learn that he had lost his money, instruments and clothing, worth some £300 or more. Some of these had been destroyed by enemy fire; the rest had been plundered by the sailors who had also looted their own captain's belongings.

HMS *Greyhound* was now despatched across the North Channel to Greenock in Scotland for a complete refit since her hull was still 'very leaky'. She left Lough Foyle on 9 June 'in a great and breaking sea which so much worked [her] that she was in great danger of foundering'. However, the frigate did make safe harbour and Richards came back to Ireland on board HMS *Portland*, meeting Kirke's fleet off Inishowen on the 11th. Kirke was on board HMS *Swallow* to which Richards transferred to make his report to the overall commander. That report included Richards' assessment of the boom, although his diary does not record Kirke's reaction to that information. When we consider the course of Kirke's subsequent actions, it would seem that the general was in awe of that particular piece of French engineering and that his mind exaggerated the threat it represented to any vessels trying to force their way upriver to relieve the city. Whatever the physical strength of the boom, it now gave the Jacobites a further psychological victory and sentenced those within the walls to an even lengthier period of hardship. Hamilton seems to have considered that *Greyhound*'s apparent decision not 'to pass beyond Culmore had a military significance', while de Pointis wrote to Seignelay that he doubted if the Williamites planned to bring their ships into the river.[13] Fatefully, this persuaded Hamilton to cancel the Frenchman's plan for a second boom.

Strangely, one Williamite account of the *Greyhound* episode dismisses it in few words.

> Three ships come up to Culmore, and fired at the Castle, which was, at that time, in possession of the enemy; one of them having run aground, was, for a short time, greatly exposed to their shot, but having at length got safely off, was obliged to return down the river.[14]

The chronicler was more interested in recording the bombardment of the town which continued on 8 June 'by which many lost their lives'.

However, there was no firing from the Jacobite artillery the follow-ing day as this was the feast of Saint Columb, the city's patron. Thus the city was spared bombardment on two days since the 10th was a Sunday and it had been Jacobite practice not to fire their artillery on Sundays. But, against this respite, the inhabitants had to balance the news that the few surviving horses in the city were to be slaughtered for meat. The garrison was reduced to 6,185 effective men with each soldier's ration now reduced to a pound of tallow, a pound of meal and a half-pound of horse flesh per day.[15]

This reduction in rations could not have done much for morale, and the bombardment by the Jacobites continued, claiming a further seven lives between 13 and 15 June, these men being killed by cannon rather than mortar fire.[16] But, on the evening of the 15th, came news of the sighting of a fleet of thirty ships in Lough Foyle,

> which we believed came from England for our relief, but we could not propose any method to get intelligence from them, and we did fear it was impossible they could get to us, and the enemy now began to watch us more narrowly.[17]

Thus Kirke makes his first appearance to the garrison and people of the besieged city. But he had arrived in Liverpool on 5 May, so why did it take so long to reach the Foyle? His critics might argue that this pro-vides circumstantial evidence of Kirke's ambivalence about the expe-dition, and that would be supported by Lord Shrewsbury's despatch to him on 13 May in which the Secretary of State expressed the king's concern that Kirke was 'still on this side of the water' when he had been appointed to lead forces for the speedy relief of Londonderry.[18] But it was not so easy for Kirke, or anyone else for that matter, to act as promptly as William and Shrewsbury desired. The relief fleet's departure from the Dee and the Mersey depended on the winds, which proved contrary between 5 May and the 22nd. Thus the fleet did not weigh anchor until the 23rd and even then was forced to turn back the following morning. It finally departed for Ireland on 30 May.[19] Even today the maritime traveller will notice the many navigational buoys in the Mersey estuary which attest to the navigational complexity of those waters.

The Jacobites had cut off any possibility of landward communication between the fleet and the city, and there was no one within the walls with sufficient knowledge of naval signalling to send a clear message to the ships. Thus Walker noted that in spite of efforts from both sides 'very little information' was passed between them.[20]

This communication problem inspired a return to basics by Kirke, who sent a messenger called Roche, an Irishman, who made his way to the Waterside before swimming across the Foyle to reach the city. Roche's story is worth some detail. When Kirke realized that he would have to use a messenger to contact the garrison, he issued a call for volunteers, with an offer of 3,000 guineas to anyone who succeeded in reaching the city. Roche was still recovering from wounds received in the Battle of Bantry Bay when he learned of Kirke's call with its very attractive reward. However, he was not fit enough to make the journey, and so two other volunteers set off to try to earn the reward. The pair were put ashore but one returned to the fleet a day or two later, having got no farther than a Jacobite camp where he had been forced to turn back. The two men had become separated in the darkness, and the one who returned said that he had overheard Irish soldiers 'talking of a spy the Papists had taken and hanged this morning, which he thinks to be his companion that was sent with him'.[21] There is one shadow of doubt about this story which lies in the fact that most of the Jacobite army would have been Gaelic-speaking, although it is conceivable that the messenger did overhear a conversation in English, or that he himself was a Gaelic-speaking Irishman.

With the first attempt to reach the city a failure and he now feeling that he was in better physical condition, Roche volunteered to be Kirke's emissary to Derry. One other volunteer came forward, James Cromie, who, although he could not swim, knew the countryside and could guide Roche to the city. Walker tells us that Cromie was a Scot but his possessing local knowledge indicates that he lived near Derry and may have been a locally-domiciled man but originally from Scotland. The two were dropped off by boat at a place that Roche called Faughan but which Sir Patrick Macrory believes was at the mouth of the Faughan river which flows into Lough Foyle. Since this would have meant that the boat landed within sight of Culmore Fort, just across the lough, and where there were many Jacobite patrols, it is more likely that the landing spot was some distance away. Roche and Cromie walked through the darkness, avoiding Jacobite patrols, through the enemy lines and, at about midnight, reached a fish house some three miles from the city. The building was abandoned, and it was from there that Roche entered the cold waters of the Foyle to swim to Derry, presumably with the help of an incoming tide.[22]

Roche's account states that he came ashore at Derry at about 4 o'clock that morning, by which time it would have been daylight. What at first appeared as a welcoming committee, complete with restorative spirit, turned into judge, jury and would-be executioners as the Williamites prepared to hang Roche as a spy. Somehow he was able to argue for a stay of execution while he proved his credentials. This he could do, he claimed, by making a pre-arranged signal from the tower of St Columb's Cathedral to the fleet, to which the latter would respond. The signal would be 'the discharge of four guns from the tower at 12 o'clock at noon'. When the fleet responded to this signal Roche was transformed immediately from villain to hero in the eyes of the Williamites and then gave the garrison 'an account of the ships, men, provisions and arms in them for our relief'. He also told them of the number of ships and men with provisions and arms that were available for their relief and of 'the great concern of the Major General for us, and his care and desire to get with his ships up to the town'. In addition, Roche passed over a letter from Kirke which assured them that help would soon be with them but advised them to 'husband their food, an admonition more alarming to them than all the menaces of the enemy'.[23]

Roche had arranged to return to the fleet with a rendezvous arranged for that night. Thus, with a letter from Walker in a bladder tied to his hair, he slipped into the river again and swam back to the fish house where he had left Cromie. According to his own story, lodged in the House of Lords' Library, Roche was able to swim to that exact spot, which is a considerable achievement of navigation in itself, but, once there, found three troops of Jacobite dragoons waiting for him instead of Cromie. He took to his heels and ran, stark naked, through three miles of woodland before jumping from a height of thirty feet into the river. En route he had received a number of injuries, as well as many cuts and grazes from brambles, and was hit by bullets when he entered the water. These rounds caused wounds to a hand, a shoulder and his chest. Realizing that Cromie had been captured, he swam back to Derry.[24] This story of considerable heroism is somewhat diminished by Ash's version which notes that Roche 'attempted to go back . . . but seeing the enemy on the shore opposite to him, he desisted and returned to us, where he yet continues'.[25]

Among the questionable aspects of Roche's version are the distance he ran with dragoons in pursuit and the height from which he jumped into the river. In the area in which this adventure allegedly occurred there is no ground that matches his description. However, when Roche later approached the government for his reward his story was accepted, if not in every detail, and he was commissioned as a captain in the army, awarded a grant of tolls and, some time afterwards, was given land in County Waterford.[26] Of Kirke's promised reward of 3,000 guineas there is no further mention.

What of his companion in this venture? Cromie was captured by the Jacobites and taken to the camp at Stronge's orchard where, according to Walker, he became a traitor. However, that is Walker's version, and Cromie might in fact have further assisted the Williamites. His captors hung out a white flag of truce and two Williamites, Lieutenant Colonels Fortescue and Blair, crossed the river to parley with Lord Louth and Sir Neil O'Neill in Stronge's orchard. The two men were told that they were mistaken if they thought Kirke was going to relieve the city and that they might learn more from Cromie. When asked why his story differed so much from that of Roche, Cromie told Blair that he was a prisoner in enemy hands while Roche was in the city. This convinced Fortescue and Blair that the Jacobites were, again, attempting a subterfuge, but Walker continued to consider Cromie to be guilty of treachery.[27]

As arranged, a boat had been sent to collect Roche and Cromie. When it was about fifty yards or less from the shore, the crew rested their oars and were shortly hailed from the riverbank. The lieutenant in charge of the boat asked for the password, but the figure on the shore claimed to have forgotten it. When the lieutenant asked the man if he knew the name of the ship, he replied that he had also forgotten that but asked that the boat should come in closer. Asked where his companion was, he said he 'had not seen him since he went into Derry'. The lieutenant then invited the man to wade out to the boat and he would take him on board but made it plain that the boat was coming in no closer. At that the man disappeared and several musketeers opened fire on the boat crew who began rowing for their ship. No one was hurt but it appeared that both messengers had been captured. Kirke, therefore, remained unaware of the true situation within the walls. Since the Jacobite ambush party did not know the password, it seems reasonable to assume that Cromie had not become a traitor.[28]

The appearance of the relief fleet had caused consternation in the Jacobite lines. John Mackenzie noted this and commented that the enemy were 'pulling down tents (as we heard) in order to be decamping; and many of their soldiers (as the country people informed us) changed their red coats and ran away'. But, whatever the degree of panic in Jacobite ranks, it was not long before they had recovered and were soon engaged in work intended to make it impossible for the relief fleet to reach the city.[29]

Before any of Kirke's ships could reach Derry they would have to break the boom as well as endure fire from artillery on either bank of the river, to which would be added small-arms fire from the infantry. Hamilton's men now improved their positions along the river. From the ships, Richards could see that the Jacobites had been working for some days 'on this side the Otter Bank, and have now raised several timbers, as if they would frame a wooden fort such as that was in the water at Tangier'. He was also able to see the boom. On a lighter, if not more positive, note, he recorded that three fat cows swam by his ship which put out its longboat to catch them; they were believed to have fallen from the ferry at Culmore. There were, however, no fat cows for George Walker in the city who wrote that the Jacobites

> now begin to watch us more narrowly. They raise great batteries [gun positions] opposite to the ships, and line both sides of the river with great numbers of fire locks [muskets] They draw down their guns to Charles-Fort, a place of some strength upon the narrow part of the river, where the ships were to pass.[31]

This was at the boom, and Walker confesses that this increased fortification of the approaches to the city not only troubled those within the walls but left them with little hope.[32]

Roche and Cromie had failed to bring information back to the fleet, which had been the main objective of their expedition to the city. The former was now in the city where he made efforts to signal to the fleet from the tower of the cathedral. His method was to use flag signals and, on 29 June, these were seen from the fleet, but the latter had no idea what was meant: a larger flag than usual had been flying from the tower and this was 'lowered and hoisted four times' and two guns were fired. Opinions on the ships were divided about the meaning of this flag: some thought that it was a Jacobite flag taken in a sally the previous night, while others considered it to be a symbol of bravado and a mark of the garrison's last success against the Jacobites. No one on the fleet would have known that there had been a determined attempt by the Jacobites to take the city the previous night; they believed that the sounds of firing that they had heard had been the defenders sallying out.

Observation from the ships to the city would have been very difficult and, although the city had the advantage of height, especially from the cathedral tower, weather conditions reduced visibility. On 28 June there was 'much wind and rain' in a day when Richards described the weather as 'very thick', and two days later he was recording similar conditions. Since Roche's signalling had no effect another attempt to send a messenger was made. A man called McGimpsey, whose first name is not recorded, approached Adam Murray and volunteered to swim down the Foyle with a despatch for Kirke. He carried in a bladder three letters in one of which the garrison's commanders implored Kirke to bring relief as they could not hold out for more than another six or seven days before being compelled to surrender. McGimpsey took to the water from the Ship Quay two hours before midnight on 26 June, the bladder around his neck and weighted with musket balls so that he might cut the string that held it to his body and allow it to sink in the event of interception.[33]

The unfortunate but courageous McGimpsey was not to be seen alive again. He drowned in the river, possibly by hitting the boom, which the defenders thought to be broken, and had no time to cut the string. His body was washed ashore, as the Foyle almost always gives up its dead, and was found by the Jacobites who hanged the corpse from a gallows and called across to the garrison that they had captured and hanged the messenger. But the Jacobites had the letters from the garrison, and these, with that counsel of despair from senior officers in the city,* must have been a source of great satisfaction to them.[34] In fact, that satisfaction was soon transmitted by letter to King James by Marshal Conrad de Rosen, who had just arrived back at the city. George Walker notes that it was about 24 June, 'or thereabouts, [that] Conrad de Rosen, Marshal General of the Irish forces, is received into the enemies camp', although Mackenzie puts his return some four days earlier.[35] What is unquestioned is that the siege now began to take on a different complexion.

Conrad de Rosen had brought reinforcements from Dublin for the Jacobite army and had decided on a plan to use those reinforcements to bring about a speedy surrender of the recalcitrant garrison and townspeople. On 26 June one of the senior Irish officers, Colonel Gordon O'Neill** sought a conference with some of the garrison's commanders. Colonel Lance and Lieutenant-Colonel Campbell went

---

*The letter was apparently written and signed by Murray, Lieutenant-Colonel Cairnes and Captain Gladstanes. Neither Walker nor Mitchelburne's signature appeared on it.
**Son of Sir Phelim O'Neill, leader of the 1641 rebellion, and Lady Strabane.

out to meet with O'Neill who informed them that King James had told Rosen that

> if the city would surrender, all those who chose to go to their respective dwellings, should have liberty to do so, and any losses they should sustain, should be made up to them by reprisals; and those who would enter his army and take the oath of allegiance to him, should be entertained without distinction of religion; and those who wished to go to England or Scotland, should have free liberty. These were the conditions, which he said should be performed by King James tomorrow.[36]

An answer was to be given to O'Neill that night and it seems that it was at this time that McGimpsey left the city on his doomed expedition to reach Kirke's force in the lough. But it was not until the next day that Lance and Campbell returned to meet O'Neill with the garrison's answer, 'which it seems was not agreeable'.[37] That night ten mortar bombs fell into the city, one of which fell on a house in Bishop's Street, the home of Joseph Gallaugher. Two barrels of powder were stored in the house and these were detonated by the bomb, as a result of which fourteen died. Ash noted that his own quarters received a hit from a mortar bomb which 'fell upon the lanthorn . . . knocked down the dormant, then fell into the street' but without doing any harm. By now the mortars were firing from the west side of the city, and areas that had been considered relatively safe were no longer so.[38]

Walker claimed that Rosen, having found that the besieging army had made no progress in the siege,

> expressed himself with great fury against us, and swore by the belly of God, he would demolish our town and bury us in its ashes, putting all to the sword, without consideration of age or sex, and would study the most exquisite torments to lengthen the misery and pain of all he found obstinate.

This rather fanciful piece of prose suggests that Walker had detailed information from the Jacobite camp about Rosen's state of mind. He then goes to state that no one was to be allowed to mention the idea of surrender 'upon pain of death', telling his readers that he, the governor, made an order to this effect. As with much of Walker's writings this stands in contrast to the preceding words that indicate that no one would consider surrender since they had the strength of God to protect them.[39]

Further contradiction is included in the information that people were deserting the city on a daily basis and providing information to the enemy. As a result, the stores of ammunition in the city had to be moved frequently. But there was precious little ammunition left in the magazines, and the garrison had to improvize with their own locally-produced shot. This was made from 'balls of brick, cast over with lead, to the weight of our iron ball'. Lead from damaged buildings provided some of the raw material for these 'Derrymade' rounds but the principal source was the lead covering that had been removed from the wooden spire of the cathedral. Although Walker wrote that the Williamite gunners were not 'great artists', they were 'very industrious' and 'scarce spent a shot without doing some remarkable execution'.[40] Once again this is an implausible boast.

Having received a rebuff to his overtures for a surrender, Rosen now began preparations for a determined attack on the city. Three mortars and several guns were emplaced south of the city 'against the Windmill side of the town' (this was the redeployment of the mortars mentioned above), while two culverins were brought into position opposite Butcher's Gate.[41] These were, as we have seen, either 17- or 20-pounders but more likely the latter as they were French weapons. Although not the ideal weapons for battering a wall, two culverins could be fairly effective where there was already a weakness, and the weakness in this case was provided by the opening in the wall that was Butcher's Gate. Rosen also deployed his sappers and miners, with the former excavating a sap towards the half bastion at the gate. This, Walker describes thus: 'He runs a line out of Bog Street up within ten perches [fifty-five yards] of the half bastion of that gate, in order to prepare matters for laying and springing a mine.' (There is no record of the line becoming a tunnel, although that is probable and would have been standard practice; it would certainly have had to be subterranean by the time it reached the half bastion.) In addition, the Jacobites pushed closer to the Williamite outworks, which was intended both to cause problems in relieving the garrisons of those outworks and prevent the besieged from drawing water from St Columb's well.[42]

Walker is ignorant of what was really happening here. Rosen was carrying out all the preliminaries to an assault. While his guns were pounding the walls to create a breach, his sappers were digging their line closer and closer so that the miners could place a petard, or mine, under that part of the wall already weakened by the artillery fire. Then, when the engineer officer in charge decided that the time was right, the petard would be detonated and the leading assault party, the forlorn hope, would make for the breach thereby created. To protect the wall, the defenders built a blind,* a wall of gabions or large wicker baskets filled with soil, to absorb the shot from the culverins while attempts were made to countermine the Jacobite sap.

This was a period of great activity and probably the most intense spell of operations during the entire siege. It was also the period when the city stood in most danger of being taken by the Jacobites. Rosen was applying all the skills of a commander experienced in siege warfare with all the resources available to him, and he must have been confident of success. Jacobite soldiers were posted in strength along the sap and were poised to seize any Williamite outworks where the defenders might slacken their watch.[43]

Active in the Williamite ranks was Colonel Jonathan Mitchelburne who had some experience of siege warfare; although Walker claims the credit for some of the defence's tactics, especially the blind, there can be no doubt that an experienced soldier, and not Walker, was directing operations. One Williamite account, usually favourable to Walker, describes Mitchelburne's reaction to this Jacobite activity:

> Unremitting vigilance and exertion on the part of the enemy were directed to the mining of the gunner's bastion,** and for the object of approaching close to the walls if possible. Their designs having been perceived by Colonel Mitchelburne, that officer ordered a blind or screen to be erected before Butcher's-gate, under the superintendence of Captain Schomberg, that the gate might not be demolished by the enemy's guns, as well as to enable the troops of the garrison to prevent the enemy from sapping the bastion.[44]

However, some idea of the intensity of those few days is given by Walker's account.

> The enemy fired continually from their trenches and we make them due returns with sufficient damage to them; for few days passed, but some of the choice and most forward of their men fell by our arms and firing.[45]

---

*The term blind meant that the enemy were deprived of a view of their target and that the target was protected. The second sense of the word survives in modern French and Italian where, for example, an armoured car is 'une voiture blindee' or an 'autoblinda'.

**The halfbastion beside Butcher's Gate was known as the Hangman's Bastion; the Gunner's Bastion was farther along the wall. It seems more likely that the writer was referring to the Hangman's Bastion.

Some scepticism should be exercised when reading this comment since the Williamite guns on the walls would not have been able to depress sufficiently to engage the forward Jacobite positions while the soldiers there would have ensured that they remained out of effective range of musketeers on the walls. It is unlikely that many Jacobites were injured during this phase while Rosen's artillery continued to pound at the half bastion.

The assault was launched on the night of 28 June, according to both Ash and Mackenzie, but Walker dates it two days later.[46] In the Jacobite van was Lord Clancarty's Regiment, which had joined the besieging force only recently; it may have been among the reinforcements to accompany Conrad de Rosen on his journey from Dublin. Lord Clancarty, Donough Macarthy, was a young nobleman, nephew to Lord Mountcashel and, as is so often the case with young officers, intent on achieving glory. Avaux, the French ambassador, had written scathingly of him to his master, saying that the Irishman was both a 'young madcap and a little dissolute'. But a young madcap was perhaps the best type of leader to conduct an assault such as that being launched on this June night. Furthermore, it seems that Clancarty might have felt himself destined to achieve success: Walker notes that the Irish 'had a prophecy among them, that a Clancarty should knock at the gates of Derry'. In fact, the attack was led by Lieutenant-Colonel Skelton, under whose overall command Clancarty's Regiment was operating.[47]

That night the Jacobite mortarmen fired twenty bombs into the city, killing a man, two women and a child 'and afterward Alex Poke's wife,* her mother and brother'.[48] Then, at 10 o'clock, the defenders were hit by the leading elements of Clancarty's force, which reached the half bastion. En route, the Williamite line, or counter sap, was seized and miners were able to reach a low cellar beneath the bastion. Ash notes that the attackers 'came over the bog, opposite Butcher's Gate, and with ease possessed themselves of our works, there being but few to oppose them'.[49] It seems that the attackers had achieved the vital element of surprise. The leading Jacobites were now so close to the walls that the defenders above could not engage them. To anyone with an inkling of what siege warfare entailed, this was a prelude to a mine being blown beneath the already weakened half bastion, after which a forlorn hope would fight its way through the breach into the city. That would be followed by a larger party of Jacobite troops, with

---

*Alex Poke is probably Alex Pogue.

DIEU ET MON DROIT

J. ACOBUS II.ds
D.G. Angliæ Scotiæ Fran: et Hiber. REX.
Fidei Defensor. etc.

Vaer sculp.   *Sam.l Lowndes es*

1. King James II. Britain's last Roman Catholic monarch, it was the popular belief that he wished to impose his own religious beliefs on his people that led to James' downfall. In March 1689 he came to Ireland in an attempt to regain his lost thrones but his failure to provide firm leadership and demonstrate clear strategic thinking doomed his efforts. (St Columb's Cathedral)

2. King William III. Son-in-law and nephew to James II, William Henry Nassau, Prince of Orange, was the choice of those who wished to depose their monarch and he led the last successful invasion of Britain, landing at Torbay in Devon on 5 November 1688. The two kings met only once in battle in Ireland – at the Boyne in July 1690. (St Columb's Cathedral)

3. King Louis XIV. The Sun King, he supported James in his expedition to Ireland but only to divert William's attention from the continent. French support for James' cause fell far short of what was needed to bring about a Jacobite restoration. (Tony Crowe)

4. Richard Talbot, Earl of Tyrconnel. King James' Lord Deputy in Ireland, Tyrconnel, known to Protestants as 'Lying Dick', initiated a policy of replacing Protestants with Catholics in the government and army of Ireland and thus ensured that Ireland's Protestants would have no sympathy with King James. (St Columb's Cathedral)

5. James FitzJames, Duke of Berwick. Illegitimate son of James II and Arabella Churchill, sister of John Churchill, first Duke of Marlborough, Berwick was one of the greatest cavalry commanders of his era, although he gained notoriety for his scorched-earth policy in Ireland, which he first demonstrated during the siege. Before serving under his father in Ireland, he had already fought in Hungary and later went on to become a Marshal of France, leading a French army to victory at Almanza in 1707. Granted French citizenship, he was created Duc de Fitz-James by Louis XIV and Duque de Liria y Xérica by King Philip V of Spain. (Tony Crowe)

6. David Cairns (or Cairnes). A lawyer and one of the prime movers in the defence of the city, he travelled to London to raise funds for the defence. Cairns had been elected a burgess of the city in 1680 and was the uncle of William Cairnes, one of the apprentices who shut the gates of the city against the Earl of Antrim's troops. (Tony Crowe)

7. Henry Baker. A soldier and veteran of Tangier who commanded one of the defending regiments in Londonderry, he was elected governor of the city in succession to Colonel Robert Lundy; George Walker was elected as his assistant. Baker fell ill and died on 30 June, the seventy-fourth day of the siege, and was succeeded by Jonathan Mitchelburne. (Tony Crowe)

8. Jonathan Mitchelburne. Another soldier, Tangier veteran and commander of what had been Skeffington's Regiment, Mitchelburne was nominated by Baker to be his successor. After the siege he settled near the city and left money in his will for the flying of the crimson siege flag – 'Mitchelburne's bloody flag' – from the spire of St Columb's Cathedral on the anniversaries of the shutting of the gates and the relief of the city. (Tony Crowe)

9. Lord Mountjoy. William Stewart from Ramelton in County Donegal was the commanding officer of the garrison regiment in Londonderry which was ordered by Tyrconnel to march to Dublin, leaving the garrison role to Antrim's Regiment, against which the gates were shut. Mountjoy had also been Master-General of the Ordnance in Ireland. He was subsequently sent on a diplomatic mission to France where he was imprisoned in the Bastille. Shortly after his release, he was killed in action, at the Battle of Steenkirk, in 1692. (St Columb's Cathedral)

10. George Walker. Assistant governor to both Henry Baker and Jonathan Mitchelburne, Walker wrote the first published account of the siege in which he gave himself a leading role and made little mention of the many doubts that existed about his integrity. (St Columb's Cathedral)

11. John Harvey. The keeper of the city's stores during the siege, Harvey was later City Chamberlain. He died in 1737 at the age of 81. (Tony Crowe)

I Short Sculp

EZEKIEL HOPKINS
EPISCOPUS DERENSIS.

12. Ezekiel Hopkins, Bishop of Derry. When Antrim's Regiment arrived on the east bank of the Foyle, Hopkins was a leading advocate of allowing the soldiers to enter the city. His argument was that they were the king's soldiers and that, since the king was God's anointed, refusing them entry would be an act of disobedience to the Almighty. Hopkins subsequently left the city. He was succeeded as Bishop of Derry by the Reverend George Walker, who was killed at the Boyne in July 1690 before he could return to the city. (St Columb's Cathedral; photo: Ian Bartlett)

Colonel Murray rallying the defenders

13. Adam Murray rallying the defenders. The son of a farming family from County Londonderry who rose to military prominence during the siege, Murray was one of the most energetic leaders of the defence. He commanded a cavalry regiment and showed great tactical skill as a soldier as well as leading a 'commando' operation behind Jacobite lines in which he was wounded. (Tim Webster)

14. The locks and keys of the four original gates. When they were built the walls had only four gates, each of which took the shape of a small fortress. These are the locks of those four gates together with the keys which the thirteen apprentices seized to shut the gates against Antrim's 'Redshanks'. (St Columb's Cathedral; photo: Ian Bartlett)

15. Cannonballs and musket rounds. A selection of cannonballs of varying weights with some musket balls that were fired during the siege. (St Columb's Cathedral; photo: Ian Bartlett)

16. Derrymade cannonball. An example of the rounds produced by using the lead that had covered the original wooden spire, which had been removed from St Columb's Cathedral, combined with brick dust. On this ball the damage of impact has exposed part of the inside of the round, which is a pinkish hue. (St Columb's Cathedral; photo: Ian Bartlett)

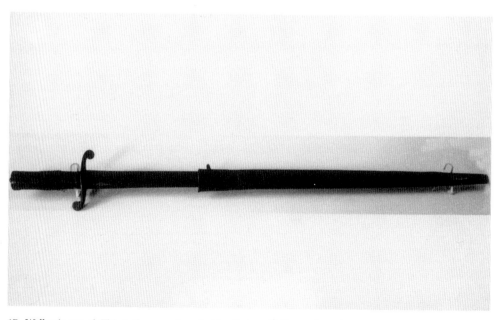

17. Walker's sword. This is the sword carried by George Walker in his role as the commanding officer of one of the defending regiments during the siege. Walker's Regiment had previously been Sir Arthur Rawdon's Dragoons. (St Columb's Cathedral; photo: Ian Bartlett)

19. French flags taken at Windmill Hill. During the first battle at Windmill Hill, the Jacobite attackers were beaten off and a number of their company colours captured. Two of these were later presented to St Columb's Cathedral by Jonathan Mitchelburne and were hung in the Cathedral. Although the fabric has been replaced the staffs are original and the new fabric shows the pattern of the original colours with the fleur-de-lys of France embroidered in the upper left quadrant. This suggests that the colours were presented to the Irish unit by the French. (St Columb's Cathedral; photo: Ian Bartlett)

18. Adam Murray's sword, believed to have been taken from a French general during one of the early engagements of the siege, at Pennyburn, to the north of the city. (St Columb's Cathedral; photo: Ian Bartlett)

20. St Columb's Cathedral in 1689. A contemporary illustration of the Cathedral as it appeared at the time of the siege. The tower was used as a battery, or gun platform, on which were mounted two cannon taken from Culmore Fort. From the tower the defenders enjoyed an excellent view of Jacobite positions around the city. (St Columb's cathedral)

Left and opposite above:
21 & 22. The shutting of the gates, December 1688. This was the act of rebellion against King James II that led to the beginning of the siege five months later. Plate 21 shows the apprentice boys shutting Ferryquay Gate against Antrim's soldiers (St Columb's Cathedral) while plate 22 is a modern depiction by Tim Webster showing Antrim's reconnaissance party outside Ferryquay Gate as it is closed against them.

Ferryquay Gate is shut against the Earl of Antrim's Redshanks

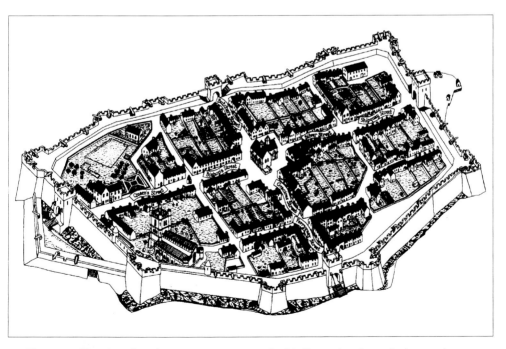

23. The city walls in 1689. Based on a contemporary work, this illustration shows the layout of the walls during the siege. The ravelin built on Governor Robert Lundy's orders is on the left, at the south wall of the city. (Tim Webster)

24. Culmore Fort. Situated at Culmore Point, where the Foyle flows into Lough Foyle, the fort should have played a vital part in the city's defences but was taken early in the siege by a clever ruse on the part of the Jacobites. (St Columb's Cathedral; photo: Ian Bartlett)

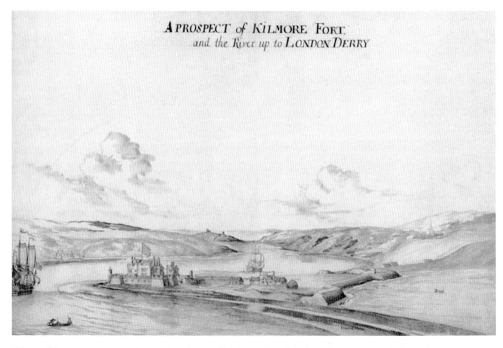

25. As this contemporary illustration shows, Culmore Fort dominated the approach from the sea via Lough Foyle to the city. (St Columb's Cathedral; photo: Ian Bartlett)

26. Clady bridge. The first major actions of the siege were fought on the Tyrone/Donegal border. This is the bridge at Clady, built on the site of the original which was destroyed by the defenders to impede the Jacobite advance. However, Jacobite cavalry were able to charge across the Finn, which is both narrow and shallow, to force the Williamites to retreat. (Private photo)

27. Mongavlin Castle: A Jacobite headquarters was established at the small castle at Mongavlin on the west bank of the Foyle south of St Johnston in County Donegal. (Private photo, courtesy Mr Roy Craig)

28. Cavanacor House: Having decided to leave the conduct of the siege in the hands of his generals, James II left for Dublin but stopped to dine *alfresco* at Cavanacor House near Ballindrait. This Protestant property was given a protection by the king and was the sole substantial Protestant-owned house to survive the ire of the Jacobites when they were forced eventually to abandon the siege. (Private photo, courtesy Cavanacor House)

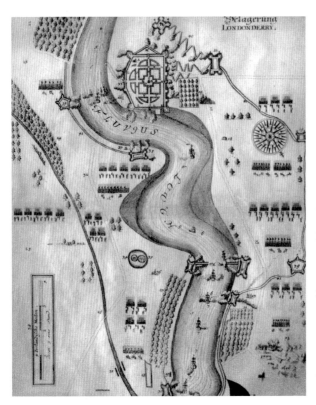

29. Under siege: A contemporary German print. The grid layout of the city and Lundy's ravelin are shown clearly, as well as Jacobite positions close by. It will be noted that the orientation of the plan is reversed with North being to the bottom where the 'narrows' and the boom may be seen. (St Columb's Cathedral)

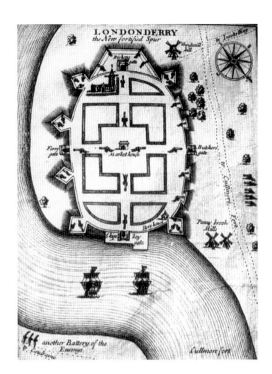

30. Another contemporary print, showing the city and the Jacobite position in Stronge's orchard. This is much simpler than plate 29 and shows Windmill Hill closer to the walls than in reality while Pennyburn is shown as Pennybrook. Once again the orientation is reversed. (St Columb's Cathedral)

31. A Jacobite view of the besieged city from the Dutch artist Romeyn de Hooghe. Although the terrain and the layout of the city owe more to the artist's imagination than to reality, the military detail of the battery in the foreground is accurate with the detachments manning the mortar and the field piece protected by gabions. Also accurate is the detail of the infantry soldiers who may be seen in the panorama. (St Columb's Cathedral)

32. A typical infantry soldier of the period, armed with a musket, a sword and carrying a bandolier of twelve charges for his musket. He wears a wide-brimmed felt hat which was usually turned up at one side and a long frock coat with deep cuffs that could be pulled down over his hands. Those soldiers of the Jacobite army who had been issued with uniforms wore red coats as did many of their Williamite foes. Collars and cuffs were usually in the facing colours of the soldier's regiment. (Tim Webster)

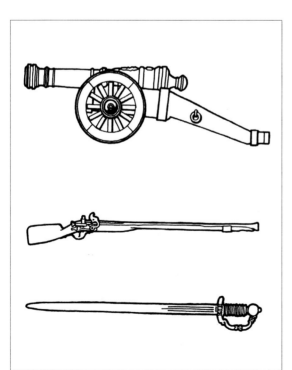

33. Some typical weaponry of the siege. The artillery piece is a demi-culverin on a field carriage as used by the Jacobite army while the firelock musket and sword would have been common to both armies, although the older matchlock musket was also still in use. (Tim Webster)

Roaring Meg *Walked on here us morning. It is the old city Wall.*

Londond[e]

34. Roaring Meg: The most famous of the defenders' artillery pieces, this gun, named on account of its loud boom when discharged, was presented to the city by the Fishmongers' Company in 1642. As with all the defenders' artillery, 'Roaring Meg' sat on a garrison, or naval, carriage. Sadly, in the recent refurbishment of the city's cannon, the local council have seen fit to finish some as field pieces, a completely inaccurate representation. (Ian Bartlett)

35. The Windmill. The first major engagement after the close investment of the city was fought at Windmill Hill. The remains of the windmill still stand in the grounds of Lumen Christi College. (Private photo, courtesy Lumen Christi College)

36. During the first battle at Windmill Hill, the Jacobite Brigadier-General Ramsey was killed. He was buried with full military honours in the grounds of the Temple More, now St Columba's, or Long Tower, Church. His grave is not marked but may be in this section of the churchyard which is overlooked by the city walls: the double bastion and the spire of St Columb's Cathedral can be seen clearly in the background. (Private photo)

37. The Battle of Windmill Hill. This impression compresses the area, bringing the windmill much closer to the walls. It shows Bishop's Gate, the ravelin and the defensive palisades to good effect. (Tim Webster)

38. Having decided that the boom and the Jacobite defences along the narrows presented too grave a danger to the fleet and that the defenders were not in immediate peril, Major-General Percy Kirke took his relief fleet around the coast of Inishowen into Lough Swilly to anchor off Inch island where he established a camp. This is Inch from the nearby Grianan of Aileach. The two causeways and the flat land in the middle ground date from the late-nineteenth century. To the right may be seen Lough Swilly and the fleet's course in from the Atlantic. (Private photo)

39. Burt Castle, once a stronghold of the O'Dohertys, is close to Inch and features in contemporary accounts, although it seems to be confused with Inch Castle, which is on the island. Burt Castle stands on high ground overlooking the lough and surrounding area as may be seen from this photograph. (Private photo)

40. Although the Jacobite forces had established a close investment of the city, strenuous and heroic efforts were made by the defenders to maintain communications with their counterparts at Enniskillen and elsewhere. In one such effort, Adam Murray led a small 'commando' party by boat into County Tyrone. This illustration shows a small boat leaving from the shadow of the city walls. (Tim Webster)

41. An offer of surrender terms was made to the defenders in early-July. Those terms were contained in a note fired into the city in this mortar shell which stands in the vestibule of St Columb's Cathedral. A 12-inch (30 cm) ruler provides an indication of the size of the hollow round. (St Columb's Cathedral; photo: Ian Bartlett)

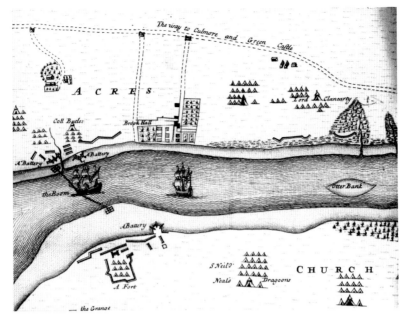

42. At the end of July, three merchant ships and a Royal Navy warship were despatched to make the run upriver to the city. While the warship, HMS *Dartmouth*, drew the fire of the guns at Culmore Fort, two of the merchantmen, the *Mountjoy* and the *Phoenix*, entered the narrows and made for the boom. This contemporary illustration shows the two ships, with *Mountjoy* leading, sailing upriver. (St Columb's Cathedral)

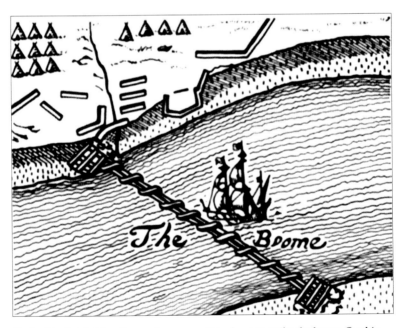

43. In this detail, *Mountjoy* can be seen as it is about to strike the boom. On this occasion, the boom held and it was not until sailors from HMS *Swallow*, manning that ship's longboat, attacked the boom with an axe that the construction gave way and the merchant ships were able to make for the city. It was at this time that *Mountjoy's* captain, Michael Browning, was killed. (St Columb's Cathedral)

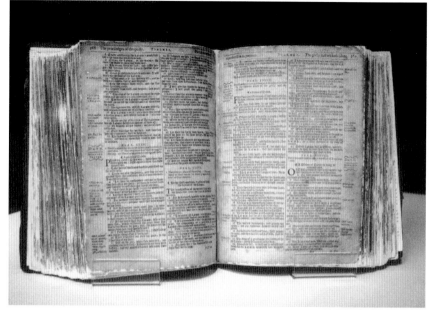

44. Walker's bible: With the siege at an end, Walker preached from the Psalms to the congregation in the Cathedral. His bible, open at the pages from which he drew his inspiration, is preserved in the Chapterhouse of the Cathedral. (St Columb's Cathedral; photo: Ian Bartlett)

45. This stained-glass window in St Columb's Cathedral commemorates the relief of the city and shows Mitchelburne's bloody flag of defiance with Walker pointing to the relief ships as they make their way to the city's quay. (St Columb's Cathedral; photo: Ian Bartlett)

46. *Phoenix* was the first to arrive at the Ship Quay, followed closely by *Mountjoy* and both ships began discharging their cargoes almost as soon as they tied up. Enemy fire was directed at the work parties and gabions were used to protect them. The arrival of supplies and the imminent arrival of reinforcements meant the end of the siege and the Jacobite commanders were forced to admit defeat and withdraw from the city. (Tim Webster)

47. Captain Michael Browning, a native of the city, who died as the relief ships sought to break the boom, is commemorated by this tablet on the city walls, overlooking Shipquay Place and across from the city's Guildhall. (Ian Bartlett)

48. Browning is also commemorated in St Columb's Cathedral where his mortal remains rest alongside those of Henry Baker, governor of the city from April 1689 until his death on 30 June. (St Columb's Cathedral; photo: Ian Bartlett)

49. In the Cathedral grounds the many who died in the 105 days of the siege are commemorated by the mass grave known as the Heroes' Mound. The Mound has been refurbished recently by the Associated Clubs of the Apprentice Boys of Derry, who maintain it in conjunction with the Cathedral authorities. (St Columb's Cathedral; photo: Ian Bartlett)

50. The most controversial figure of the siege was Colonel Robert Lundy who was the city's military governor in the months leading up to the siege. In May 1686, Lundy's daughter Aromintho was baptised in St Columb's Cathedral. This is the record in the Cathedral register of baptisms which reads: 'Aromintho, daughter of Colonel Robert *Lunday* and Martha his wife'. Martha Lundy was the daughter of the Very Reverend Rowland Davies, Dean of Ross. (St Columb's Cathedral; photo: Ian Bartlett)

51. Letter from the Lord Deputy, the Earl of Tyrconnel, to the Earl of Antrim telling him to have his regiment ready, at an hour's notice, to march on Derry. Dated 18 December 1688, the letter was written at Dublin Castle after the shutting of the gates on Antrim's Regiment. (St Columb's Cathedral; photo: Ian Bartlett)

52. The undertaking from Jonathan Mitchelburne, as Governor of the city, that James Stronge of Gobnascale within the liberties of Londonderry would be repaid £1,000 that he had provided towards the costs of the defence of the city. This debt was never repaid by the government and the original of this document was destroyed when James Stronge's descendant Sir Norman Stronge and his son James were murdered by republican terrorists in their home at Tynan Abbey, County Armagh in 1981 which was then destroyed by arson. (Tony Crowe) grenadiers to the fore, and the defenders would soon be fighting for their lives.

One of Skelton's men, who was on horseback, rode close to the gate and called for fire to burn it. But at least two of the defending officers had kept cool heads and their immediate actions were to save the day for the defenders. Captains Noble and Dunbar assembled a small group of defenders, no more than sixty to eighty at first, and led them out of the city through Bishop's Gate; they were soon followed by other troops. The first group of defenders to sally out made their way under cover of the walls without attracting the attention of the Jacobites. Waiting until they were close to their enemies, they opened fire. This took Skelton and Clancarty's men by surprise and forced them to fall back. In doing so they came into the field of fire of the men on the walls and, as the sally party was reinforced, the Jacobites were caught in fire from several directions. Soon there was no option but to retreat and rejoin the main body of the attacking force which was still some distance away.[50] This withdrawal was carried out and yet another Jacobite plan had been thwarted.

The French commissary, Fumeron, sent an account of the attack to Louvois in which he claimed that the assault was led by French officers with the Marquis d'Anglure at their head. According to Fumeron, Anglure reached the city gate, 'accompanied by several French officers', who, he stated, had exposed themselves to risk on many occasions to give an example to the Irish troops. For his efforts, Anglure was wounded in the arm, 'but lightly', although another French officer, Captain Paget, was among the dead, who also included about fifteen soldiers.[51]

Not recognizing the serious threat that the attack had presented to the city, Walker finds the episode almost funny and wrote scathingly that Clancarty had made the assault because he believed in the prophecy that a member of his clan would knock at the gates of Derry.

> the credulity and superstition of his country, with the vanity of so brave an attempt, and some good liquor, easily warmed him to this bold undertaking; but we see how little value is to be put on Irish prophesies, or courage so supported.[52]

More recently, Sir Patrick Macrory, in his eminently readable book on the siege, describes the attack as 'an almost farcical interlude provided by Donough Macarthy, my Lord Clancarty'.[53] Far from being in the realms of farce, this attack – and it was Skelton's rather than Clancarty's – represented what was arguably the most serious attempt by the Jacobites to bring the siege to an end. Various elements of siege warfare may be seen in the preparations for and the execution of the attack: the offer of surrender followed by the bombardment of a chosen part of the wall to create a breach; the driving of a sap to enable miners to approach the walls to place a petard; the placing of that petard; and the presence of a forlorn hope. Why Macrory should refer to the assault as he does is a mystery since he had a reputation as a military historian, but it may be that his knowledge of siege warfare was limited; his description of the attack follows Walker's account so closely as to suggest that he accepted at face value that version of the action.

Walker claims that about a hundred of Clancarty's best men were left dead while the miners were abandoned in the cellar and several officers and men who had been wounded later died of those wounds. Contrast this with Ash who puts the Jacobite death toll at twenty-five or thirty with 'as we may well conjecture, twice the number wounded'. Mackenzie agrees with Ash's total of Jacobite dead. Ash also recorded that he had 'never heard so many shots fired in so short a time'. He noted the Williamite casualty list at one dead and three wounded. Two Jacobite prisoners were taken, and it may be assumed that these were the unfortunate miners, left to their fate when the attack was repulsed.[54] Whose version, Walker's or Ash's, is the more credible? Since Walker wrote his for immediate publication and to ensure his own place in history, in which he was eminently successful, his account is not always reliable. On the other hand, Ash kept a journal that was not intended for publication and which did not see the light of day until two generations later when his granddaughter first had it published. Ash was also a soldier and his observations show the eye of a soldier. On balance, Ash is a much more reliable witness to this battle.

Why did Rosen decide to attack on this side of the walls? Even the casual visitor to the city today, walking around the walls, would see that this was a far from ideal location for an attack as the approaching troops would be advancing uphill under the view and fire of the defenders. Although Rosen has not left us an account of the siege, it is possible to work out his thinking when he returned to the city. He knew that the obvious place to attack was in the area between the Royal and Church bastions where it was possible to conduct conventional siege artillery operations, using a series of parallels to bring the guns progressively closer to the walls. But the defenders had already made this same analysis – Lundy had done so for them before the siege even began – and the defences in that area had been strengthened significantly with the ravelin and the outworks at Windmill Hill. Two attempts to break in through those outworks had failed, and Rosen had no reason to expect that a third would succeed since the defenders would be expecting yet another attack. Nor was there much time left to the Jacobites: Kirke's relief force might decide to move towards the city at any time but would be unlikely to do so if the city was in Jacobite hands. This left Rosen with one option, an assault up the slope towards the west face of the walls, a dangerous operation, a calculated risk, but one that offered a small element of surprise since the defenders would be least expecting attack from that quarter. And so he put his plan into effect, deploying the two culverins, digging the sap and creating an assault group that included some of his freshest soldiers. Had this attack succeeded, then the city would have fallen, but the quick reaction of some of the defending officers, especially Noble and Dunbar, ensured that, once again, a Jacobite attack came to naught.

Contrary to the opinions expressed by both Walker and Macrory, this battle saw one of the finest demonstrations of courage on either side during the siege. It also showed the use of initiative by both Jacobite and Williamite soldiers, the quick reaction by officers of the latter being especially noteworthy. However, comments such as those made by both Walker and Macrory demean the courage and military skills of those who fought on that June night. Walker's assessment – that this was a simple case of chasing off drunken and superstitious Irish – and Macrory's – that this was an 'almost farcical interlude' – detract from the achievements of the defenders as much as they do from the courage and enterprise of the attackers. Walker was engaged in a propaganda exercise, mostly for personal aggrandisement, and one can understand, to some extent, his attitude. Macrory's comment is less easy to understand. Here is a man with a reputation as a military historian showing not the slightest understanding of what was happening and accepting Walker's version as the full truth. Propaganda that seeks to demean an enemy in this fashion can often be self-defeating. During the Second World War, British propaganda sought to demean the Italian forces by depicting them as cowardly. It therefore came as something of a shock to Allied servicemen to find themselves being trounced by Italians, as was 1st Essex Regiment at Gallabat in Abyssinia. And it should be remembered that it was the doughty courage of Italian soldiers, fighting without hope of escape, that allowed Rommel to extricate so many of his German troops from El Alamein. Both Walker and Macrory treat the Jacobites in like fashion but in so doing take away from the achievements of the defenders of the city.

Foiled in this direct attack, Conrad de Rosen had an alternative plan. He would ensure that whatever provisions remained in the city would be consumed more speedily, thus forcing the garrison to surrender or starve to death. A Jacobite account of the siege notes that

> When he approached to Londonderry, he seized on three or four hundred Protestants, men and women, relations and friends to the people within the town, whom he brought as prisoners, and, at his arrival about the beginning of July, sent them to the gates of the fortress, in order that they might enter the place (from which they egressed at the commencement of the siege), and live there among their own.[55]

This is not entirely accurate, for the rounding-up of Protestants did not occur until after the failure of the assault on the half bastion. There are also variations between witnesses in the number of hostages that Rosen took. Ash says that there were about 200, whereas Walker tells us that there 'were some thousands of them'.[56] Once again Walker is probably exaggerating for his own ends. Rosen's action was intended to ensure that the garrison would run out of provisions quickly if the hostages were allowed into the city. But they would also serve the marshal's purpose even if they were kept outside the walls since he believed that the sight of them starving would hasten the surrender of the city. One Williamite account states that only women and children were included in the ranks of those marched to the walls; there were no men lest these should join the garrison.[57] Whether the latter is entirely accurate is not clear; Mackenzie wrote that the group did include men. Furthermore, a fratricidal tragedy was averted only narrowly and, in Mackenzie's view, by the hand of God:

> When they first appeared, we took them for a body of the enemy, and the guns were discharged at them; but the shot (being directed by an unerring hand) touched none of our friends, but, as we afterwards heard, killed some of those merciless soldiers that were pushing them on.[58]

That Rosen was able to initiate this plan highlights one of the anomalies of this siege: that so many had been allowed to leave the city and live nearby under the protection of the Jacobite army and with guarantees of safety from General Hamilton. But should Hamilton have allowed them out at all? Had they been kept inside the walls, the city might well have been forced to come to terms before this point. An effective and early circumvallation of the city might have prevented their departure.

Hamilton's chivalrous behaviour may well have cost the Jacobite army the prize they sought: the surrender of Londonderry.

> there is a difference between soldiers defending a place for their king against another prince or state (as to matter of obstinacy in holding out), and between rebellious citizens maintaining their town against their own king, into whose hands they dread to fall. The first think it enough to do their duty according to the usual manner of garrisons. The latter are apt to go beyond all mean, so sometimes they will choose to see their wives and children perish before their eyes, rather than give themselves up to the power of their sovereign lord and master. As for the particular rebels of the city of Londonderry, this plot of Rosen gave them a greater conturbation than anything which had happened to them since the dawn of that beleaguer; for, though hitherto they have remained so resolute in the defence of the town against their king, that in their nourriture they are wonderfully suffered, yet now they are extremely moved at the dismal condition of their flesh and blood a-perishing before their gates.[59]

Those within the walls were shocked at Rosen's plan. They seem to have expected the chivalry of Hamilton to continue and not to have contemplated the pragmatic approach taken by the Livonian. Now they faced a dilemma: to bring these unfortunates inside the walls and thereby increase the problems of the city, placing a greater drain on food stores and increasing the incidence of disease, since the newcomers might be more likely to succumb to the illnesses prevalent in the city, or keep them, their own kin, outside the walls and watch them starve to death. 'It was dismal to us to hear their cries,' wrote Mackenzie, but the hostages appealed to the garrison 'not to surrender out of pity to them'.[60]

It was not long before the garrison found that their commanders could match Jacobite ruthlessness with Williamite ruthlessness. The sight of the hostages not only 'did move great compassion in us' but also caused great anger.[61] A reprisal was planned and a gallows, the work of five carpenters, was erected in full sight of the Jacobite camp.[62] This was to signal to the Jacobites that, if the hostages were not allowed to return to their homes, the garrison would hang those Jacobite prisoners held within the walls. So far, the latter had been treated well, but now a message was sent to the besiegers to send priests to prepare the Jacobite prisoners for death. Walker comments, 'but none came'. This provided the opportunity to accuse the Jacobites of 'breach of promises' – although what promises they were in breach of is not clear: was it a breach of the guarantees of safety, or a failure to send priests to administer the last rites? – while the Jacobite prisoners allegedly declared that they 'could not blame us to put them to death, seeing their people exercised such severity and cruelty upon our poor friends, that were under their protections'.[63]

The Jacobite prisoners now sought permission to write to Hamilton. This was given, and a messenger was sent out to deliver their appeal, for such it was. Walker retained a copy. The prisoners wrote:

> My Lord,
> Upon the hard dealing the protected (as well as other Protestants) have met withal in being sent under the walls, you have so incensed the Governor and others of this garrison that we are all condemned by a court martial to [die] tomorrow, unless these poor people be withdrawn. We have made application to Marshal General de Rosen; but having received no answer, we make it our request to you (as knowing you are a person that does not delight in shedding innocent blood) that you will represent our [condition] to the [Marshal] General. The lives of 20 prisoners [lie at stake, and therefore require your diligence and care. We are all willing to die (with our swords in our hands) for His Majesty: but to suffer like malefactors is hard, nor can we lay our blood to the charge of the garrison, the Governor and the rest having used and treated us with all civility imaginable.[64]

The letter was signed by Netterville, Butler, Aylmer, MacDonnel and Darcy in the name of all the prisoners, although it was noted that Netterville's name was 'writ by another hand' since he had lost the fingers of his right hand.[65] A Jacobite commentator described it as 'a lamentable request' but suggests that it was made to Rosen rather than to Hamilton.[66]

Hamilton's reply did not hold out much hope for the Jacobite prisoners.

> What these poor people are like to suffer, they may thank themselves for, being their own fault; which they may prevent by accepting the conditions have been offered them; and if you suffer in this it cannot be helped, but shall be revenged on many thousands of those people (as well innocent as others) within or without that city.[67]

It would appear from this letter that some of Rosen's steel had entered Hamilton's soul and that he was prepared to accept the marshal general's plan. But neither side had the heart to go through with its threats. Although the Jacobite prisoners were paraded on the walls by the gallows where they were to be executed, the threatened date passed without any hangings. In the meantime, Hamilton thought better of his original response and, on 4 July, ordered that the hostages be allowed to return to their homes. It was believed that 'some feeble persons of the town went along with them undiscovered'.[68]

Another plan had failed. It seems that Hamilton may have sent a despatch to King James in Dublin and that the latter's response brought about Hamilton's change of heart. James referred to Conrad de Rosen as a 'bloody Muscovite' because of his plan which did not sit well with James' desire to win the hearts and minds of his Protestant people.

During this time Henry Baker, the senior governor of the city, died. He had been ailing for some time and his passing was 'justly lamented by the garrison, in whose affections his prudent and resolute conduct had given a great interest'.[69] Walker praised him, writing that his death was 'a sensible loss to us, and [he was] generally lamented, being a valiant person; in all his actions among us [he] showed the greatest honour, courage and conduct'.[70] Baker was interred in one of the vaults of the cathedral, and his pallbearers included Walker and Mitchelburne, who succeeded him as governor, Colonels Lance, Campsey and Munroe and Lieutenant-Colonel Campbell. The eulogy was given by the Reverend Seth Whittle, whom Ash calls White.[71]

The men of the Jacobite army were also suffering. On 30 June Fumeron wrote that

> The troops are very tired and many fall ill. They have been on campaign for four months, without tents and in a country without cover, where it rains almost all the time and where the nights are extremely cold.[72]

Rosen, who must have been both frustrated and angry that his plans had gone awry, now concluded that starving out the garrison was the only sure road to success for his tired army. He ordered 'some entrenchments to be cast up for the better preservation of the army' while they sat out the remainder of the siege.[73] No relief could get through, he believed, while his troops held the fort at Culmore and the batteries that protected the boom. It was only a matter of time before the city fell. Although Captain Gregory with some workmen had built a horse-powered mill at the Free School with which to grind malt, this had made little difference to the food problem.[74] Walker supports

Rosen's analysis since he notes that, by now, the townspeople and the garrison were reduced 'to feed upon horse flesh, dogs, cats, rats and mice, greaves of a year old, tallow and starch, of which they had good quantities, as also salted and dried hides'. In spite of this, he says, they were determined to hold out and 'unanimously resolved to eat the Irish, and then one another, rather than surrender to any but their own King William and Queen Mary'.[75]

Mitchelburne noted that the dogs fed on the bodies in the graveyards and that the citizens fed on the dogs: 'We have an excellent way of dressing them, seasoned with pepper and salt, and baking the flesh with decayed wine we get in merchants' cellars'.[76] But, as the bombardment continued, the resolution of the defenders was being tried to the extreme. They did have one opportunity to show defiance when, according to Walker, a 'dead shell' among the bombs thrown into the town on or about 1 July was found to contain a letter addressed to the soldiers of the garrison. Details of Hamilton's surrender proposals were included in the belief, wrote Walker, that the garrison's officers had not acquainted the soldiers with these, but the men of the garrison would 'not entertain the least thought of surrendering, and it would cost a man's life to speak of it, it was so much abhorred'.[77] The shell containing those proposals may be seen today in the vestibule of St Columb's Cathedral.

Notes

Information for that section of this chapter dealing with Captain Jacob Richards' expedition to the Foyle in HMS *Greyhound* is gleaned from Witherow's *Two Diaries of Derry in 1689* and is, accordingly, not annotated.

 1: Ash, op cit, p. 68
 2: Simpson, op cit, p. 127; Ash, op cit, p. 75
 3: Simpson, op cit, p. 127; Walker, op cit, pp. 42–3; Ash, op cit, pp. 75–6
 4: Simpson, op cit, p. 127; Walker, op cit, p. 43
 5: Simpson, op cit, p. 127; Walker, op cit, pp. 42–3; Mackenzie, op cit, p. 46
 6: Walker, op cit, pp. 42–3
 7: Walker, op cit, p. 43; Simpson, op cit, p. 127
 8: Loeber, *Engineers in Ireland, 1600–1730*, IS, vol xiii, p. 44 (von Bodt) and p. 231 (de Bodt)
 9: Young, *Fighters of Derry*, p. 172
10: Mackenzie, op cit, p. 47
11: HLRO, *HoCJ*, 9 Oct 1690

12: See Chandler, op cit, p. 180 for a table showing the English and French field artillery in general use from 1688 to 1730.

13: NA Kew, State Papers Ireland, de Pointis to Seignelay

14: Simpson, op cit, p. 127; see also Walker, op cit, p. 43

15: Simpson, op cit, p. 128

16: Ibid

17: Walker, op cit, p. 43

18 Powley, op cit, p. 154

19: Ibid, p. 224

20: Walker, op cit, pp. 43–4

21: Macrory, op cit, pp. 268–70; see also Gebler, *The Siege of Derry*, pp. 237–41

22: Ibid

23: Ibid; Walker, op cit, pp. 44–5; Mackenzie, op cit, p. 48; Ash, op cit, p. 80

24: See Macrory, pp. 268–70 and Gebler, pp. 237–41

25: Ash, op cit, p. 80

26: HLRO, *HoCJ*, 17 May 1701

27: Walker, op cit, p. 45; Simpson, op cit, p. 132; Ash, p. 80; Mackenzie, op cit, p. 48

28: See Macrory, pp. 268–70 and Gebler, pp 237–41

29: Mackenzie, op cit, p. 46. Walker does not record any panic in the Jacobite ranks but notes that the Irish army intensified its defences along the river.

30: Walker, op cit, p. 44. Macaulay wrote that the river was 'fringed with forts and batteries which no vessel could pass without great peril.' He then describes the boom and not only states that 'several boats of stones were sunk' but that 'a row of stakes' was driven into the riverbed. (*History of England*, Vol. III, pp. 59–60)

31: Ibid

32: Ibid

33: Mackenzie, op cit, pp. 48–9

34: Ibid, p. 49; Simpson, op cit, p. 132

35: Walker, op cit, p. 48; Mackenzie, op cit, p. 49

36: Ash, op cit, p. 80

37: Ibid, p. 81

38: Ibid

39: Walker, op cit, pp. 48–9

40: Ibid, p. 49

41: Ibid

42: Ibid, pp. 49–50

43: Ibid, p. 50

44: Simpson, op cit, pp. 132–3

45: Walker, op cit, p. 50

46: Ash, op cit, pp. 81–2; Mackenzie, op cit, p. 49; Walker, op cit, pp. 50–1

47: Walker, op cit, pp. 81–2; Mackenzie, op cit, p. 49; Ash, op cit, pp. 80–1; Simpson, op cit, pp. 134–5

48: Simpson, op cit, p. 134; Ash, op cit, p. 81. Simpson notes that Poke was a gunner who had taken part in an operation along the river under Adam Murray's command. Young suggests that the name may have been Pogue rather than Poke (*Fighters of Derry*, p. 178.)

49: Ash, op cit, pp. 81–2

50: Ibid; Walker, op cit, pp. 50–1; Mackenzie, op cit, p. 49; Simpson, op cit, pp. 134–5

51: *Franco-Irish Correspondence*, pp. 140–1

52: Walker, op cit, p. 51

53: Macrory, op cit, p. 277

54: Walker, op cit, p. 51; Ash, op cit, p. 82; Mackenzie, op cit, p. 49

55: Gilbert, op cit, p. 79

56: Ash, op cit, p. 84; Walker, op cit, p. 54

57: Mitchelburne, op cit

58: Mackenzie, op cit, p. 51

59: Gilbert, op cit, pp. 79–80

60: Mackenzie, op cit, p. 51

61: Ibid

62: Ibid; Mitchelburne, op cit; Walker, op cit, p. 54

63: Walker, op cit, pp. 54–5

64: Ibid, p. 55

65: Ibid; Mackenzie, op cit, p. 51

66: Gilbert, op cit, p. 80

67: Walker, op cit, p. 56; Mackenzie, op cit, p. 51

68: Walker, op cit, p. 56; Mackenzie, op cit, p. 51; Simpson, op cit, p. 140; Gilbert, op cit, p. 80

69: Mackenzie, op cit, p. 49

70: Walker, op cit, p. 51

71: Simpson, op cit, p. 135; Ash, op cit, pp. 82–3

72: *Franco-Irish Correspondence*, p. 141

73: Gilbert, op cit, p. 80

74: Mackenzie, op cit, p. 47

75: Walker, op cit, p. 52

76: Mitchelburne, op cit

77: Walker, op cit, p. 53

CHAPTER SEVEN

Expectation in The Air

Kirke's fleet continued to lie in the lough and the people and garrison of the beleaguered city wondered when the ships would ever make the run upriver to bring relief at last. With little information from inside the city, Kirke faced a dilemma: should he risk his vessels by sailing upriver to the city or wait until he had more information on what was happening there? First of all he sought to obtain more intelligence through reconnaissance. By now HMS *Dartmouth* had joined the ships in the lough and, on 15 June, Kirke asked Captain John Leake to make a reconnaissance. Leake 'sailed within a large mile of Culmore' with his ship grounding for about an hour on its way up Lough Foyle.[1] Discussion in the fleet now turned to such critical matters as pilotage – these were not men who were familiar with the waters of the Foyle – and breaking the boom. Depth soundings were also taken in the lough; at high tide there was only 17.5 feet clearance.[2] Kirke called a council of war, or court martial, on the 19th, which was attended by the army commanders, Colonels Steuart, Sir John Hanmer, Thomas St John and William Wolseley, with Richards and the four French engineers present as well as Majors Henry Rowe, Zachariah Tiffin and William Carville and the ships' captains, Wolfranc Cornwall, of HMS *Swallow*, John Leake, of HMS *Dartmouth*, Thomas Gwillam, of HMS *Greyhound*, William Sanderson of the *Henrietta* and Edward Boyce of the *Kingfisher*. Kirke presided at the court martial. The subsequent report of the proceedings read

> That by all we can see or hear it is positively believed that there is a boom cross the river a little above Brookhall at a place called Charles's Fort, where one end of this boom is fixed, the other extending to the opposite point. The boom is said to consist of a chain and several cables, floated also with timbers, at each end of which are redoubts with heavy cannon. The sides of the river are entrenched and lined with musketeers. Besides this obstacle in the river, several intimations have also been given of

boats sunk, stockadoes drove with great iron spikes, but in what manner we could never perfectly learn, but it's certain that they neither want boats, timbers etc to effect any thing of this kind.

The accident that happened on Saturday the 8th instant to the *Greyhound* frigate is evident proof that they are in a capacity to bring down cannon anywhere they should be opposed; so that, should anything be attempted in going up this straight channel and miscarry therein by several accidents as may happen, or the shifting of a wind, striking ashore, or damages received by their great guns and there is very little reason or hopes left to think to set off. And if no other opposition should be then the boom, which, if not broke by our attempt the breadth of this river is so narrow as that the ship will certainly run ashore. This loss, though great to his Majesty, would be of much more and of greater consequence in the leaving the enemy possessors of so many great guns with our stores of war and victuals, which, if they had, they would certainly make a more formal attack upon the town of Londonderry, which to this time they have not attempted. We suppose for no other reason, than for want of artillery enough, besides the miscarriage would so dishearten the town and encourage the enemy as to be of extreme consequence. Besides since the *Greyhound* and the rest of the fleet's being here, we have never received any intelligence from Londonderry, which gives us great reason and some assurance that they are not extremely pressed by the enemy or want of ammunition or provisions of mouth.

All this being considered it's the opinion of us now sitting at this council, that it will be more prudent and for his Majesty's service, to stay here, till a greater force join us so that we may be a sufficient number to make a descent and force the enemy to raise the siege by which means the town should have sent us advice of every particular relating to this affair by which we may safely take other measures.[3]

The names of those in attendance, signed on the original document, include 'all the Sea-captains whose opinions and advice would have been central to the deliberations, since it was by naval action alone that the relief fleet could overcome the Jacobite defences of the river and reach the city. Cornwall had already been to the Foyle; it was he who had, in *Swallow*, escorted the original relief force commanded by Cunningham and Richards in April, while we have seen that Gwillam had been there more recently and still bore the wounds to prove it. John Leake had also proved himself an outstanding officer of great bravery, as he had demonstrated at Bantry Bay; he would eventually achieve the rank of admiral. It was the opinion of Edward B Powley, a respected naval historian, that none of these sea captains held 'so strongly' the view that the boom could probably be broken 'as to consider it a matter of professional importance that the opinion, if he held it, should go on record'.[4] The weight of their experience has to be considered when judging Kirke and his apparent procrastination; his decision was based on their professional opinions.

The day after this meeting Kirke went aboard HMS *Dartmouth*, which was the advance ship of the fleet, and the vessel from which Richards was maintaining continuous observation. Kirke climbed to the maintop with Richards from where

> we could easily discern the rippling of the Boom, and sometimes see part of it just heave upon the face of the water; along which were several boats lying stern and stem with the Boom, as if they floated it up.

Kirke was able to see the city as well as the Jacobite dispositions. The latter were now showing no signs of the concern that the first appearance of the ships had caused. His observations did not change Kirke's view of the problems presented by the boom, nor did it make him alter his earlier conclusion that the city was not hard pressed by the besiegers; he was also able to check his earlier estimates of Jacobite strength.

Those inside the city's walls might not have been pleased to learn of Kirke's council of war and its deliberations, nor of his further conclusions based on the evidence of his own eyes from *Dartmouth*'s maintop. They would have been even less pleased to learn that Kirke entertained Jacobite officers on board HMS *Swallow* a few days later on 27 June. This followed a message to Kirke from Lord George Howard who had asked the major-general for a safe passage to visit him. Kirke issued the 'passport' and Howard and another gentleman came on board 'and they were very civilly received by the Major-General'. This appears to have been a most convivial meeting at which the two Jacobite visitors were entertained to a meal that brought forth the comment that 'they had not such a meal's meat [since] the Lord knows when'. Kirke and Howard were obviously friends, and the occasion was sufficiently relaxed for the Jacobites to express their exasperation at the French officers in their army, of whose 'insolencies' they complained, saying that they 'were almost weary of being under their command'. From them, Kirke learned that Rosen, rather than Hamilton, was now commanding the Jacobite forces in the area. Howard and his companion returned ashore that evening, having enjoyed their day, been well fed and having supplied Kirke with some useful intelligence on his enemies.

The ships of the fleet did not remain constantly at anchor in the one spot; Richards records that, on 29 June, his vessel 'watered at Greencastle' which is some distance away at the mouth of Lough Foyle. While the ship was taking on fresh water, 'under the cannon of the *Antelope*', a yacht arrived from Scotland. This was the *Ferret*,* commanded by Captain Sanders, who brought a letter for Kirke from the Duke of Hamilton, telling the major-general that Edinburgh Castle had surrendered, the Jacobites in Scotland had been routed and their principal leaders taken prisoner.

On 1 July Richards visited Kirke, who showed him a letter he had received the previous morning. This missive told Kirke that 'nothing of any notice had happened between Londonderry and the Irish camp' for the past three or four days. However, a postscript included news of an attack on the city by Jacobite troops on Tuesday 25 June. In fact, this was Skelton's, or Clancarty's, attack which had occurred on the Friday, 28 June. The writer of the letter lived in a house, described as the parson's, above Whitecastle, close to where *Swallow* lay at anchor. The scribe and his wife had devised a code to let Kirke know that they had information for him. When the pair, the lady wearing a white mantle, were seen walking back and forth along the beach before returning to their home, that would be a sign that a letter had been concealed under 'a certain stone' and this would be retrieved under cover of darkness by someone from the ship.

Richards includes an interesting note about Lord Dungan sending Kirke 'a very fine and large salmon' at 4 o'clock that afternoon (1 July). Dungan was the commanding officer of one of the Jacobite dragoon regiments, and the salmon might well have been a gift in appreciation of the meal given to Howard and his companion four days earlier. Equally, it might simply have been a gift from one soldier to another. However, Kirke's friendship with Jacobite officers emphasizes an often neglected fact about the conflict in Ireland: that it was a civil war, the type of conflict in which brother can be pitched against brother and friend against friend. In such circumstances it is not surprising that there were some who believed that Kirke was

---

*By one of those coincidences that litter history the name HMS *Ferret* was chosen for the Royal Navy's base at Londonderry during the Second World War, when the city played a major role in the Battle of the Atlantic.

sympathetic to the Jacobite cause and that his apparent prevaricating was quite deliberate. Of those inside the city who wrote accounts of the siege, only the Reverend John Mackenzie is critical of Kirke, suggesting that Kirke and Walker had conspired to create their own version of the siege; it is notable that Mackenzie gives the garrison, inspired by the Almighty, rather than Kirke the credit for relieving the city.[5]

Further accusations against Kirke were made by Sir James Caldwell, one of the defenders of Enniskillen, who listed thirty charges against the general, including 'corruption, incompetence, irreligion, and a total lack of appreciation or understanding for those who had carried on the struggle for King William in Ireland both before and during the siege'. In two queries against Kirke, Caldwell is quite clear in his allegations of treachery, asking 'whether several officers of the late King James's army did not wrong Major General Kirke when they often times declared that they expected no injury from him who they knew to be one of their own friends and that at length he would appear to be so'. In support of his claim, Caldwell states that the witnesses were 'the whole soldiers of Londonderry'. He also asks if Kirke did not have a pardon from James in July 1689 'for not relieving Londonderry and holding other correspondence with the enemy and whether it was not a common discourse among the enemy that the said Major General Kirke was their friend'.[6]

Caldwell's charges seem never to have been made at an official level but they merit some reflection. Was Kirke guilty of treachery at Derry? There is no doubt that he maintained friends in the Jacobite officer corps, but this can be seen as a legacy of their having served together in the past. The argument can equally be made that such friendships allowed Kirke to garner useful information on the Jacobites' situation while impressing upon them the strength of his own force. His seemingly lackadaisical approach may also be seen as the product of his believing that the garrison was in no great distress. The lack of communication between relief force and defenders has already been noted and it seems plausible that the signals being made from the cathedral were considered to be signs of rejoicing. However, since Kirke had already changed sides, from James to William, it is reasonable to assume that he might have done so again, had the circumstances been right. He continued to correspond with James in exile, and it seems that Kirke was determined to be a survivor, as he had always been, irrespective of the sufferings of anyone else. A pragmatic individual, Kirke was, at best, a man who looked out for himself and, at worst, a man who would have changed sides again, abandoning Derry and its garrison, had it suited him.

At noon on 2 July a Mr Hagason signed from the northern, or Inishowen, shore that he wished to speak with Captain Withers of the *Swallow*. Withers went ashore and spent about an hour with Hagason and others, returning with news that there had been another sally by the people of Derry the previous night, during which they had cut off some 300 Jacobites. From this it seems that Hagason might have been a Jacobite officer who seems to have been on familiar terms with Withers. There were also complaints about lack of provisions, and it seemed that Hagason and his friends were tired of the siege 'for there was nothing but hunger and slaughter in it'. One recent writer on the siege suggests that Hagason was a Williamite and that he was relaying information from the garrison but the description of the sally would suggest otherwise.[7]

Later that day, after dinner, Kirke called a council of war which was attended by all his field officers* and the sea captains. This was to discuss sending some 500 or 600 men to Inch, an island in Lough Swilly, to create a diversion. The proposal followed a reconnaissance to Inch carried out by Captain Thomas Hobson in HMS *Bonadventure* when he learned from Protestants on the island that a Jacobite quartermaster was there to gather provisions for the Irish army. Inch was, and is, a fertile island, and was described as 'abounding in all sorts of grain'. Hobson sent his lieutenant ashore with one of the Protestant gentlemen who took the sailor to the house where the Jacobite quartermaster was based. The naval officer relieved the quartermaster of his papers and a sum of £5 which he had on his person, presumably to pay for whatever he collected from the island. Having done so, the lieutenant went back to his boat but, having been admonished by the local man for not making the Jacobite officer a prisoner, returned to the house, only to find that the quartermaster had mounted his horse and made off. He was said to have had a considerable sum of money with him. For failing to make the man prisoner, the naval lieutenant was criticized severely, and Richards commented that 'it is thought he will be dismissed'. Nonetheless, the papers he had taken provided some good intelligence for Kirke.

The papers were letters from the general officers of the Irish camp, pressing the said quarter master to send provisions with what expedition he

---

*The rank of major and above.

could, for they and their horses came near starved, with intimations that he should take great care to preserve all sorts of provisions, for their dependence was wholly on that island.

Combined with the information from Howard and his dining companion, that from Hagason and other sources, this indicated that the Jacobite army was in a poor state. Furthermore, since Inch was so valuable to the Jacobites for supplies, it made sense to deprive them of that source of supply by occupying the island. This had the further advantage of providing a rallying point for local Protestants, some of whom asserted that several hundred of their number would 'fly to us and take up arms'. It would also allow sailors and soldiers to have some liberty from the crowded conditions of their ships and, as had already been suggested to Kirke, the island would provide a location for a hospital. And thus began the Williamite expedition to Inch.

In a direct line, Inch is only a little more than six miles from the walls of Derry. An old road, part of which has been there for centuries, probably since the days when the local centre of power was the Grianan of Aileach overlooking the island, runs almost in a straight line from the city to the island. A body of men would have had to march no more than eight miles to reach the city from the island, although this would have meant marching over high ground; but this rises to less than 500 feet. The direct route would have presented no problems, especially at this time of year. Alternatively, an approach could also have been made via the flat land where once the Foyle and Swilly waters had commingled to cut off Inishowen, the island of Eoghan. Using this route the distance would have been increased but by no more than another mile or two. Thus Williamite soldiers on Inch represented a very real danger to the Jacobites about Derry who now had to be wary of an attack from behind.

The expedition to Inch gave Richards the opportunity to practise his profession. Having landed on Inch strand near Burt castle* on 10 July, with an escort of an ensign and twenty men, he soon identified a suitable site for a redoubt facing the mainland. But their intention to begin work on this was interrupted by the appearance of some Jacobite horsemen which prompted Richards to send for reinforcements. These

---

*Although Burt castle sits on a small hill on the mainland and is clearly visible from the lough there is another castle on the south west corner of Inch, less than two miles from Burt, and it is probably this castle to which Richards refers.

arrived in the form of some men of Kirke's regiment under Captain Collier, who drove off an attack by the Jacobites, although Richards thought that the latter might have suspected an ambush and did not therefore press any harder on the Williamites.

Earlier, Richards had sent for field pieces as well as men and tools from Colonel Steuart but these had not arrived. He now learned why. The day before some Protestants from the west bank of Lough Swilly had signalled the fleet and a boat had been sent to fetch them. They brought news of a 'great herd of cattle' at Tully near Rathmullan and some troops had been sent ashore to round up these animals, about 200 in number, and bring them to Inch.[8] This had meant deploying all the boats in the fleet to ferry the cattle from Rathmullan, and thus none had been available to carry guns, men and equipment to Richards at the site for the redoubt. But Richards was soon in a much happier state, being joined by Colonel St John with about 200 men. The latter had observed what was happening and had marched to support Richards. It had been the sight of this body of men in the distance that had prompted the Jacobite horsemen to retire.

Later that afternoon Steuart arrived in Captain Rooke's barge, bringing with him tools and four field pieces. Steuart thought that the entrenchment staked out by Richards was too large, a view in which St John concurred; the latter considered himself to be an engineer, according to Richards. Work on the first of two redoubts was begun and continued until midnight when the working party retired to the far side of the island. Richards went back on board *Greyhound* for the night. Work continued the next day on the second redoubt with four field pieces emplaced to deter the Jacobites, but these were later removed and the working party was taken back to the far side of the island. That evening, at 6 o'clock, the building began again and the soldiers laboured until an hour past midnight. Returning to *Greyhound*, Richards learned from 'a man who told us he had been in the Irish camp' that the Jacobites planned to attack the works with a force of horse and foot at the next morning tide. Today Inch is joined to the mainland by two embankments, whereas, at this time, it was necessary to row across or wait until low tide when the water separating island and mainland was fordable.

Richards became so exasperated with the would-be engineers' interference, especially when St John had an outwork constructed that was effectively isolated and could provide no support to the rest of the works, that he 'troubled [him]self no farther with the works, of which I am sure any one that pretends to be an engineer ought to be ashamed'.

Eventually, by 14 July, the defensive works were completed and eight guns were emplaced in their batteries; these included six 3-pounders, possibly minions,* and two 6-pounders, or sakers. These enabled the small garrison of Inch to discourage the Jacobites while the defences were being completed.

And it was also on 14 July that HMS *Bonadventure* sailed into the Swilly to drop anchor at Inch. Its commander, Captain Thomas Hobson, had taken supplies of powder and ball to the garrison of Enniskillen. Hobson's destination at that time had been Killybegs in County Donegal, or Killy Bay as he described it in his log, since Enniskillen is an inland town.[9] On his return journey Hobson was accompanied by several men from Enniskillen who had a proposal to put to Kirke, which explains why Hobson returned first to Greencastle on Lough Foyle before sailing into the Swilly. The Enniskilleners promised that they would relieve Derry by taking a force there that would cause the Jacobites to 'raise their camp'. However, they lacked sufficient arms and so wanted 1,500 guns from Kirke as well as some officers to lead their force. Into the field they could put about 8,000 foot and 1,200 good cavalry while they also had enough small horses to raise a dragoon regiment, although weapons would be needed for these troops. (Kirke would report to London that the Enniskillen garrison had formed twenty-six companies of infantry, seventeen troops of cavalry and two troops of dragoons, all of whom were ready to come under the major-general's orders.)[10] When he had heard this proposal, Kirke ordered Rooke, who was commanding the squadron, to join him with *Portland* and *Bonadventure*. Thus Kirke was expected to arrive at Inch very soon. Even so, when news was received at the camp on Inch that the boom was broken 'in several pieces' and that the Jacobites had withdrawn their large guns from the riverbank, a messenger was sent over the neck of Inishowen to take the news to Kirke in Lough Foyle.

That messenger returned early next morning to say that the fleet had weighed anchor, left Lough Foyle and was at sea. But there was other news: the Duke of Berwick had left Derry to deal with the defenders of Enniskillen,[11] and a fleet had been seen off Carrickfergus. This latter story came from the Irish camp where it was believed to be a French fleet coming with 20,000 men and 'a vast sum of money'. Cash was a vital necessity for King James who had issued a debased coinage,

---

*One of the smallest of contemporary artillery pieces, this fired a round weighing 3.75 pounds; only the faucon, or falcon, with a round weighing 2.125 pounds and the fauconet, or falconet, with its 1.125 round, were smaller.

known as brass money.[12] Richards comments that a 'small piece of copper not the value of half a farthing* goes for sixpence'. These pieces of intelligence were as yet rumours with no firm evidence to substantiate them. On the other hand, there was no doubting the fact that the Williamite force at Inch had been strengthened by some 500 to 600 'good lusty men able to bear arms'. These new recruits had been formed into companies under local commanders but attached to the regular regiments, each of which now had eighteen companies and a grenadier company in its order of battle. Nor was there a shortage of fresh meat for the garrison at Inch since hundreds of cattle had been sent over from Rathmullan in the past week.

No serious threat to Inch was posed by the Jacobites although there was a further rumour concerning Berwick: having been trounced on the road to Enniskillen he was now going to return to Derry whence he would march on Rathmullan. In fact, a Jacobite force of about 1,500 horse and foot did march on Rathmullan, which was held by no more than 120 Williamites under Captains Echlin and Cunningham. A Williamite account puts the strength of Berwick's force at 2,000 horse and dragoons. When the Jacobites made their first foray against Rathmullan, a small ketch anchored offshore 'fired among the horse and killed a cornet and 3 troopers with its first shot'. This caused the cavalry to draw off with the foot soldiers following. The same account claims that forty Jacobites were killed together with ten of their horses while a colonel was wounded desperately. Since the Williamite officers had had barricades raised, the Jacobites failed to get into Rathmullan in spite of a determined attack. The retreating Jacobites left their dead; Williamite casualties were said to be no more than one officer – Captain Cunningham** – and two or three soldiers dead.[13] However, it was obvious that the Jacobites would attack again and that they had the advantage of numbers, and so Echlin was ordered to evacuate Rathmullan. This was completed that night although about a hundred cattle had to be left behind since there was not enough time to get them away. At least some Jacobites would feast on fresh meat over the next day or so. A deserter from the Irish army later confirmed that Berwick had led the attack on Rathmullan and claimed to have killed about 200 men.

---

*The lowest-value coin, worth a quarter (fourthing) of an old penny and removed from circulation in the 1950s.

**His rank is given as lieutenant in the London Gazette of 1–5 August, which carried the report of the action.

Kirke arrived off Inch late on the 19th and, early the following morning, came ashore, having ordered the disembarkation of all his command. He inspected the defence works, with which he seemed satisfied, and brought some news for the Inch garrison: more troops were being assembled to sail for Ireland through Chester, Liverpool and Whitehaven but three French warships had captured the *James* of Derry, a small ship that Kirke had sent to Scotland to buy wine and other supplies for the fleet. A Royal Navy squadron, commanded by Rooke in HMS *Deptford*, had sailed in pursuit of the French; Rooke's other ships were *Bonadventure*, *Portland* and *Dartmouth* under Captains Hobson, Leigh and Leake. When his men had disembarked, and ammunition and provisions had been stored in the magazine that Richards had had built, Kirke ordered two vessels to sail for Enniskillen with 500 fusils* and some officers to take command of the Enniskillen garrison; the latter included Wolseley, who was to command a regiment of horse, and Major Tiffin, who was to take command of an infantry regiment.[14]

Later that afternoon, about 5 o'clock, Kirke received a letter from Walker in Derry. According to the latter, the boom had been broken and the guns covering it had been 'drawn away'. This brought about a flurry of activity with Kirke ordering that three ships be loaded with provisions and each manned by forty musketeers. The loading operation was carried out as surreptitiously as possible so as not to attract the attention of the Jacobites and, later that night, Kirke went back aboard the *Swallow* and sailed with the other three ships for 'Derry Lough, with resolution to relieve that place or lie by it'. This report, albeit from Walker on this occasion, seems to have been the second time that the same rumour had reached Inch.[15] Although there was no truth in it, this rumour was to have a profound effect on events: it set in train the actions that would lead to the raising of the siege and the relief of Derry.

Inch was a hubbub of activity over the next few days as accommodation in the form of huts was built for the soldiers. There was also news that the Jacobites intended to attack the island. Richards wrote that attacks were expected from three points and then detailed two of those: by Captain Tristram Sweetman's and by Burt Castle, 'at which two places it is very narrow but not fordable'. At both locations the

---

*A fusil, pronounced fusee, was a lighter flintlock musket used by special service troops whose role was to defend the artillery. These soldiers became known as fusiliers.

guard was strengthened (which seems to confirm that Richards 'Burt Castle' was in fact the castle on Inch) and a ship was also posted to deter any attackers. None came, although some firing was heard at midnight from the north-west of the island; this was thought to come from a group led by Lieutenant Hart, who had been sent out into Inishowen with a foraging party of thirty men. Later it was thought to be the advanced guard at Captain Sweetman's but it turned out to be fire from one of the ships which had spotted light from Rathmullan as the Jacobites tried to fire the village; several rounds were fired by the ship to deter them.

There is no clear indication from Richards as to the third possible direction of attack but it is more than likely that this was across the neck of water between the island and the mainland which, on the 23rd, was dry from side to side. Certainly Richards notes that on that day 'we draw all our forces to our fortifications on the strand, to be ready to receive our enemies that have so often threatened us'. Lieutenant Hart returned with some provisions from his wife's relations in Inishowen but without the horses, cattle and corn he had been sent for, so Captain Echlin was sent with fifty men to complete the task. He arrived too late. Jacobite dragoons had that morning escorted about a hundred horse-loads of corn from the area and Echlin was left with what remained, about a hundred bushels*.

Fires from villages on Inishowen that evening suggested that the Jacobites were retreating from the peninsula while there was further rumour that Berwick was on the move towards Enniskillen again. Next morning, 24 July, Jacobite troops, both cavalry and infantry, appeared on the hills facing Inch and looked to be preparing to attack. The strand was dry and the Williamites made ready to meet an attack but it seemed that the Jacobites feared a possible attack from Inch since they withdrew as soon as the tide came in and the strand was no longer fordable, suggesting that their deployment had been defensive rather than offensive. There were also reports that Kirke's ships had got into Derry but Richards thought this improbable due to the winds having been contrary over recent days.

While Kirke had not reached Derry he had made contact with the *James*, the ship that had been taken by the French. This vessel had been recovered and had sailed into Lough Swilly to drop anchor off Inch on the morning of the 25th. Its captain brought a letter from Kirke to

---

*Bushel = a measure of capacity, equivalent to about eight gallons or about 36.37 litres.

Colonel Steuart which the latter showed to Richards to seek his opinion. Richards' view was that if Kirke's orders, as expressed in the letter, were followed, it would lead to disaster for the Williamites on the island since it would 'ruin our interest here, expose some thousands of souls to the mercy of a cruel enemy, and unavoidably lose the island'. It was a view with which Steuart agreed and he called a council of war of all the field officers and captains of the regiments present to solicit their opinions.

What had Kirke suggested? He had expressed concern that the island would not be tenable if the Jacobites deployed artillery against it, and proposed to recall all his regular soldiers to the ships, there not being enough cover for them on Inch, leaving the local men to provide the garrison. He reasoned that the shipborne men would be able to move quickly to defend any part of the island that was threatened. Dispositions for a detachment to be left on Inch were also detailed, while the letter had contained the news that Rooke had retaken the ships captured by the French but that adverse winds had prevented Kirke's ships entering Lough Foyle; however, he hoped to enter the lough on the next tide.

Steuart's council of war decided to maintain their positions on Inch, and Richards was asked to draft a reply to Kirke. In his letter Richards pointed out that the Jacobites could not bring heavy cannon into action against Inch as these 'cannot well be brought over the strand' while artillery on the opposite shore would present no danger due to the distance. Furthermore, all the troops were now under cover on the island and withdrawing them to the ships would make it almost impossible to oppose any assault by the enemy. He added that Jacobite intelligence about Inch was good and that a move such as that proposed by Kirke would be known to them very quickly and would probably lead to an attack. The Jacobites would have every opportunity to 'possess themselves of this Island, into which there is, since our arrival here, fled about 12,000 souls, who can expect no mercy at so cruel an enemy's hands'. He related how the Jacobites had burned Rathmullan and murdered the few Protestants left there and how they had done the same on Inishowen 'over against Capt. [Tristram] Sweetman's house, as far as over against the *Fisher* ketch, which is nigh two miles that the Irish have put in flames'. Berwick was later to gain notoriety for employing the scorched-earth tactic but it appears that he may have begun using it in Donegal. Richards argued that the refugees on Inch would be safe as long as the garrison remained and that the Jacobites would not attack while Derry held out since they had already 'neglected so many fair opportunities when our numbers were much less'.

Having despatched the letter to Kirke, Richards and Steuart continued to improve the defences of Inch. They had refused to obey an order from their commander, a serious offence in military law, but they had provided sufficient justification for their decisions, so that no action was taken against them. As the events at Derry played out to their conclusion, the two men would be vindicated in their decision. Over the next few days there would be more rumours reaching the garrison at Inch and it would be difficult to separate fact from fancy. Berwick crops up again in those reports, staving off the threat from Enniskillen; it seems that the Jacobites at Derry were now in constant worry about an attack from Enniskillen. By the end of the month the Jacobite army was being estimated at not much more than 4,000 infantry and 1,000 cavalry before Derry, while Berwick at Castlefinn had about 2,000 cavalry and dragoons.

The Williamite force at Inch now threatened the Jacobites investing Derry since it could deploy within a few hours to strike the rear of the Jacobite lines. By now in London it was learned that the presence of Kirke's men on Inch had caused the Duke of Berwick to be called back from a planned attack on Enniskillen.[16] With Schomberg at Chester taking command of 'his Majesty's forces for the relief of Ireland',[17] the situation appeared much more positive than hitherto.

It seemed that Kirke was awaiting reinforcements from England before making his attempt to relieve Londonderry. In a despatch from Lough Foyle he reported that:

> The enemy are well entrenched on both sides of the river and have batteries of 24-pounders on the narrowest part of it, which is not a pistol shot over. But if that were all, we could pass them with a leading gale, but they have secured the river with a boom cross it, made of cables, chains and timber, and have besides sunk great boats laden with stones in the middle of the channel so that being by a council of war not thought advisable to attempt the relieving the town by the river we are waiting for some more forces in order to land and force our way through the enemy's camp.[18]

The dangers of trying to run upriver were thus many in the minds of Kirke, his army officers and the Royal Navy captains. Believing that boats had been sunk in the channel meant that the naval officers would have been concerned about the safety of their ships as they tried to navigate the narrows. Most of the warships drew too much draught to risk them in such an enterprise, and this fact alone would have made the seamen counsel Kirke against a waterborne assault. (The frigate HMS *Dartmouth* was one of the few with a draught shallow enough to operate in the Foyle river, and it was this vessel that eventually escorted the relief ships.)

Kirke also reported that the besieged were holding out 'very bravely and have placed two guns upon the church steeple, which do great execution'. Although the Irish army had made several attempts on the city, they had been beaten off each time 'with great loss'. He reported on the two attacks on the Windmill Hill positions and noted the friction that existed between the Irish and the French officers, especially the French general. These, he recorded, had a 'cold reception in the camp, tho' a very warm one from the town'. As for his own men, they were 'very hearty and in good health' and their presence on Lough Foyle was, he believed, a great encouragement to the besieged. Finally, he noted that a messenger had succeeded in swimming from the fleet to the town as signals made from there had indicated his arrival.[19]

Other reports coming back to London emphasized the morale and courage of the besieged. HMS *Antelope* had left the Foyle on 5 July and arrived at Highlake (Hoylake) two days later with a report that the 'besieged continue to defend themselves with a bravery and resolve that exceeds all the account that can be put on it'.[20] On 24 July a report reached Whitehall from Kirke stating that 'Londonderry held out with the greatest bravery that can be imagined, and continued to repulse the enemy in all their attempts'.[21] And there was also intelligence on the overall state of the Jacobite army from 'persons in Dublin' who claimed that the main body of that army was before Derry and 'not above two or three regiments' were at Dublin and that many of the soldiers of these units 'wanted clothes and arms'. The Dublin informants also advised that 'the town of Derry, upon the best enquiry they could make, was not yet reduced to any great distress and that the Irish soldiers deserted in great numbers'. [22]

Thus it seemed to Kirke and to his masters that there was no great urgency in relieving the city since the defenders were in a good state and holding out so well that they were inflicting heavy losses on the Jacobites. In addition, the dangers presented by the boom and the boats that were believed to have been sunk in the narrows, never mind the Jacobite batteries along the river, militated against moving upriver towards the city. With the knowledge that further troops would soon be landing in Ireland, Kirke must have felt that his best course of action was to wait for those men to arrive before advancing overland. Those inside the city would not have agreed with him, and their frustration mounted as they looked at the masts and sails of the ships in the lough.

Notes

Most of the information on which this chapter is based is from Richards' *Diary of the Fleet* and these sources are not annotated individually.

1: Powley, op cit, p. 226. A 'large mile' may be a nautical mile, which is 2,025 yards or 1.85 kilometres. In this context it is unlikely to refer to an Irish mile, which is longer than an English mile.
2: Ibid
3: Ibid, pp. 226–7
4: Powley, op cit, p. 229
5: Mackenzie, op cit, p. 56
6: John Rylands Library, Manchester; Bagshawe muniments, B3/2/38(i) & (ii); B3/2/38; Cunningham & Whalley, *Queries Against Major General Kirke, Irish Sword*, Vol. XVI, No. 64, pp. 208–16
7: Gebler, op cit, p. 256
8: *London Gazette*, 25–29 July 1689
9: NA Kew, ADM52/9, Captain's log, HMS *Bonadventure*; Richards, op cit, p. 34
10: *London Gazette*, 29 July–1 August 1689,
11: Ibid, 1–5 August 1689
12: Gilbert, op cit, p. 54
13: *London Gazette*, 1–5 August 1689
14: Powley, op cit, pp. 239–43; NA Kew, ADM52/9, Captain's log, HMS *Bonadventure*
15: Richards, op cit, p. 38; Walker does not record sending the letter to Kirke.
16: *London Gazette*, 1–5 August 1689
17: Ibid, 18–22 July 1689
18: Ibid, 11–15 July 1689
19: Ibid
20: Ibid, 15–18 July 1689
21: Ibid, 25–29 July 1689
22: Ibid, 1–5 August 1689

CHAPTER EIGHT

Knocking on the Gates of Derry

While Kirke was waiting in Lough Foyle and deploying most of his force to Inch, the situation in the city was worsening. Earlier in this study of the siege we saw how Robert Lundy felt frustrated at the failure of those in authority in England to provide support for the garrison of Londonderry. By now, had he remained, he would have been confirmed in his attitude to those same authorities while his feelings for his former comrade-in-arms Percy Kirke can but be imagined. His successors as governors, Henry Baker and George Walker, must also have felt frustration, but Baker died before the siege was raised and so left no account while Walker's account leaves as much unsaid as it includes. Walker is much more enthusiastic about relating the defenders' successes, and his part in them, than elaborating on the many difficulties faced by them. Nonetheless, there is much information between the lines in Walker's account that he did not realize that he was imparting.

The completion of the boom was one of the rare occasions on which Walker admits to real concerns. Learning of the work that the Jacobites had just finished he wrote: 'This account, as we had it from the prisoners, did much trouble us, and scarce left us any hopes.'[1] He was also concerned about the epidemic of disease that broke out in the city from early-June onwards.[2] But he does not include any information about the concerns that others felt about him and which we noted in Chapter Five. A further worry was that the Jacobites intended 'some mischief' against him. This information he received from 'a friend in the enemies camp' and, before long, he became aware that some of the garrison suspected that he had considerable quantities of provisions hidden in his house. When this suspicion increased to such a degree that a danger of mutiny was perceived, Walker claims that he then remembered the warning. Thus he suggests that this was the 'mischief', a Jacobite plot to discredit him. He showed his own guile by arranging to have his house searched privately but with the negative results of the search made known to all, after which the garrison returned 'to the good opinion of their governor'.[3] Mackenzie is confident that Walker had something to hide and recorded that a search of the latter's house on 16 June uncovered beer, mum* and butter, which was removed to the store. Rather than the garrison being restored to a good opinion of Walker, it was only the intervention of Baker that saved his fellow governor from being incarcerated or shot.[4]

Walker was also suspected, as we have seen in Chapter Five, of being prepared to betray the city to King James. He recalled that this story surfaced again later in the siege. Among the prisoners taken by the Jacobites in the early days of the siege was one Mr Cole whom Mackenzie refers to as Captain Cole. This individual remained a prisoner of the Jacobites for some time but then fell into conversation with Richard Hamilton, who asked him what kind of person was Walker and with whom was he most intimate. Cole told Hamilton that he counted himself one of Walker's friends 'hoping by this means to be employed on a message to him and to obtain his liberty'. In this hope he was justified when Hamilton asked if he would carry some proposals to Mr Walker; these were proposals that King James had ordered Hamilton to make to the city's leaders. Cole agreed, was granted a pass allowing him to leave the Jacobite lines, and left with his message to Walker. According to Mackenzie, however, Cole returned to the city 'about the 10th or 12th of May' when Baker, suspecting that he might be acting for the Jacobites, had him confined 'till he was satisfied he had no ill design against the city'.[5]

The story now enters the realms of farce for, by Walker's account, Cole reached the town, where he 'was received with great joy' and was so delighted to be free that he simply forgot to deliver his message to Walker. However, he did mention it casually in the course of a later conversation with some members of the garrison who subsequently greeted Walker with what the latter describes as 'some great names and titles'. Now, it seems, Walker realized the danger he was in, saw that it was caused by the 'discourses of Mr Cole' and had the unfortunate Cole confined immediately and interrogated. That interrogation allowed Walker to solve the mystery. Once again, when presented with the explanation from Walker, we are told that this gave 'all people satisfaction, so that they remained in no more doubt of their governor'.[6] Walker's stories seem to be just that: stories. They also seem implausible and the work of a man determined to cast himself in the

---

*A very nutritious beverage.

best possible light. How else can one explain the differences between his and Mackenzie's accounts of the Cole affair?

The day after he intervened to save Walker, Henry Baker's physical condition deteriorated to the point where he was forced to take to his bed. He became dangerously ill, another victim of the fever endemic in the city, and appointed Jonathan Mitchelburne to act in his place while he was ill.[7] It seems that their dispute of the previous month had been forgotten. Baker's distrust of Walker must have been considerable by this time and, in appointing Mitchelburne as his deputy, he was ensuring that a man with considerable military experience governed the defence of the city rather than the clergyman turned amateur soldier.

Before Baker became dangerously ill, a number of citizens 'and others concerned for the public good' held a meeting and called on Captain Alexander Watson, commanding the artillerymen in the city, to order his men to make a search for provisions within the city. Watson ordered such a search to be conducted and the result was enlightening. The gunners dug up cellars and other possible hiding places and unearthed 'much provision under the ground'. Not everyone, it seemed, had entered into the spirit of mutual support and there must have been many who were highly embarrassed to have their private stores uncovered. Some of the provisions that came to light in this search had been hidden by people who had left the city in the early days of the siege, but much was the secret hoard of others who were still within the walls. The degree of embarrassment created is indicated by the fact that the search prompted others, whose provisions as yet remained undisturbed, to bring out their own hidden treasures to add to the communal stores.[8] Thus the garrison was provided with a meagre bread ration from then until the end of the siege.

That Enniskillen was still holding out was well known to those inside the walls, and it was decided to send a messenger or two to the Fermanagh town. This was to be done under cover of a raid on fish houses along the Foyle using the garrison's new boat which by now must have had the position of its oars corrected. The raiding party was commanded by Adam Murray and included Captains Noble and Dunbar, two lieutenants and some twenty soldiers. Walker claims that the party was led by Noble and that its intention was to 'rob the fish house'; his omission of Murray's name and misrepresentation of the aim of the mission would suggest that Walker was keen to play down Murray's role as far as possible. On the night of 18 June the raiding party left the city with the aim of putting the messengers ashore some distance upriver. According to Mackenzie, they were to travel about four miles which would have taken them to the area of the modern village of Newbuildings, but he goes on to state that they went as far as Dunalong, where the messengers were to be put ashore.[9] This is some eight miles by river from the city.

However, although the party must have taken to the water after darkness, there was still sufficient light for the boat to be spotted and a gun at Evans' wood fired on the party but without scoring a hit, although the gunners 'narrowly missed' the vessel. Other Jacobite troops along the river were alerted by this firing and musketeers on both banks fired on them as they rowed along. When they eventually reached Dunalong wood the two boys who were to go ashore and head for Enniskillen were so terrified that they would not quit the boat.[10] Thus the prime objective of the mission was thwarted.

Worse was to follow. With the sky lightening, Murray's men saw two large boats between them and the city. These were manned by Jacobite dragoons whose intent was to cut off the return of the Williamites. Not one to run away from a fight, Murray turned his boat towards the pair of Jacobite boats so that his men could open fire on their pursuers. There was a sharp exchange of gunfire, after which one of the Jacobite boats closed on Murray's. The intention seemed to be to board the Williamite boat and capture it, but this plan was soon foiled when Murray's men seized the initiative and engaged the foe, beating some of them into the water and killing four or five, including a lieutenant. This was too much for the Jacobites, who threw down their arms and surrendered. Thirteen of them were made prisoner. Seeing the fate of their fellows, the dragoons in the other boat made off speedily rather than wait to be engaged by Murray's men.[11]

With their prisoners 'and some small prize', the latter it seems including the dragoons' boat, the party now made for home. Once again they came under fire from both banks of the river but only one of the party had been injured in the entire operation. That single casualty was Adam Murray, 'who received some shots in his head-piece, that bruised his head, and for a time indisposed him for service'. One prisoner was wounded on the return journey, struck by a shot from the riverbank.[12] Murray might have been killed but for that head-piece, which was probably a small skull cap of steel worn under the hat, and known as a 'secret', intended to protect the head from downward slashes from cavalry swords; it more than served its purpose on this occasion.[13]

Murray's raiders were so pleased with their success that, having landed the prisoners and handed them over to the guards, they decided to attack some Jacobites who were 'drawing off one of their guns'. Spotting the Williamites the men at the gun fled, abandoning the weapon. Murray's men then followed until they reached the top of a nearby hill where they spotted a second, strong, party of Jacobite infantry who were using the hill as cover to cut the Williamites off from their boats. The latter withdrew quickly to the water's edge and were just in time to avoid being captured by the Jacobites.[14]

This episode emphasizes the skills and leadership of Adam Murray, but it is also noticeable that his companions on this occasion included Captains Noble and Dunbar, two men who were to be prominent less than two weeks later in the repulse of the attack by Clancarty's men near Butcher's Gate. Soldiers and leaders of such quality are an inestimable asset to any force, and these men must have played a major role in maintaining the confidence of the city's garrison. Both Noble and Dunbar came from County Fermanagh and seem to have shared the aggressive spirit of their comrades who were defending Enniskillen.

But a success such as this could not bring the siege to an end. The garrison was tiring and its numbers were being reduced steadily by disease and casualties, while Mackenzie commented that 'the close siege' began soon after the return to the Jacobite camp of Marshal de Rosen.[15] Action by Kirke was needed, but that seemed to be as far away as ever, and many within the walls must have wondered if the relief fleet would weigh anchor at all to attempt to run upriver to the beleaguered city.

In the previous chapter we looked at Sir James Caldwell's charges against Kirke. Caldwell believed that Kirke was quite willing to change sides and support the Jacobites and that, among other faults, he showed 'a total lack of appreciation or understanding for those who had carried on the struggle for King William in Ireland both before and during the siege'.[16] Although Caldwell was engaged in the actions in County Fermanagh, he seems not to have been aware of the amount of help that Kirke sent to the defenders of Enniskillen which included arms, ammunition and senior officers to take command of the locally-raised regiments. In doing so Kirke was acting on intelligence obtained from Enniskillen, whereas intelligence on the situation within the walls of Derry was lacking, in spite of the fact that the city lay only a few miles from his anchorage point in Lough Foyle. But Kirke's perceived dilatoriness had much to do with the overall strategy for relieving Ireland, which raised many questions about the preparedness for war of both the Royal Navy and the Army.

In Chapter One we saw how the English Army had lost many officers and men in late-1688 when John Churchill switched his support from James II to the Prince of Orange. The manpower loss then sustained had yet to be made good, while the shortage of officers was another major problem. Furthermore, William was not fully aware of the degree of the problems facing his cause in Ireland and was still concentrating on the broader European campaign that faced him. He had not expected to be distracted from that by a war at his back door, and therefore his mind was not focused on Ireland and certainly not on the people besieged in Londonderry. Not only did he have a problem with the English Army but he also had a major crisis to deal with in the Royal Navy. This service had come close to mutiny in the days since James had fled. Not that this was a sign of support for the deposed Stuart king – although James was popular in the navy – but it was a symptom of the chaos that had reigned in the administration of the country since November 1688.

On 16 January 1689 the Prince of Orange issued a proclamation to seamen. This assured sailors that they would receive their pay, the principal cause of unrest in the navy, and urged those who were absent without leave to return to duty. No action would be taken against those currently absent who reported back to their ships, but action was promised against any who neglected their duty.[17] Although this proclamation would have done much to restore discipline in the navy, there continued to be some disarray which lasted until the spring; money and supplies were still short. Not until April was it possible to assemble a force of any strength, and thus James and his entourage was able to sail from France to Kinsale without being intercepted by the Royal Navy. One naval historian notes that King James was escorted to Ireland by no fewer than twenty-five French warships, of which fourteen were ships of the line, eight were frigates and three were fireships; eight merchant ships carried the deposed monarch with his supporters. However, another authority puts the number of warships at twenty-three.[18]

As the fleet that had carried James to Ireland left Kinsale on 17 March for the return voyage to France, the French navy was preparing a second expedition to Ireland carrying supplies for James' forces as well as additional French advisers. This expedition left France on 26 April with the Brest fleet of Admiral the Marquis de Chateaurenault in support and made for Bantry Bay where it unloaded its supplies and dropped the advisers. In addition to Chateaurenault, who commanded the centre of the French fleet, Jean Gabaret, who had commanded the expedition that landed James, led the van, while Job Forant had charge of the rear. This expedition did not have the same clear run as the earlier fleet that took James to Kinsale as Admiral Arthur Herbert, later the Earl of Torrington, had finally obtained authority to engage French warships. This authority was given on 28 April with Herbert being told that he could engage the French 'wherever he meets them' as England and France were now at war.[19]

Herbert had only been given his command as Admiral of the Fleet and Commander-in-Chief in the English Channel and Irish waters by William on 11 March; he was also head of the Admiralty Commission. William seems to have been especially dilatory in this appointment as Herbert, 'a colourful, immoral, heavy-drinking Welshman with a violent temper', had been dismissed by James II in 1687 following his refusal to agree to the repeal of the Test Act and penal laws. It was Herbert who carried the invitation to William to come to England; the Prince of Orange had then appointed the Welshman as commander-in-chief of his invasion force on account of his popularity with the officers of the English fleet.[20]

On his appointment to command in the Channel and Irish waters, Herbert was also given permission to cruise between Ireland and Ushant, in the approaches of the English Channel, to prevent a French landing in either Ireland or Scotland, but it was early April before he was able to put to sea. By then one of his orders was redundant: he had been told to treat James well if he captured him. Even then he had only twelve ships of the line under command, and these were not fitted out to the standard that Herbert would have liked.[21] When he had been at sea for two days, he discovered that the French were already en route to Munster. He set off in pursuit with his fleet reinforced by another four ships.* The French were making for Bantry Bay and it was there that Herbert, following a brief stop at Milford Haven, made contact with them. On 1 May the two fleets joined in battle in the bay. An offshore wind was blowing which allowed Chateaurenault to bring his warships out to sea, thereby covering the transports. Sailing on parallel courses, French and English warships pounded each other in an extremely fierce engagement that caused considerable damage on both sides. Not every ship could engage a foe, one of the characteristics of a sea battle fought in line, and the action was inconclusive. Herbert withdrew to repair the damage sustained by his ships, while his rival

---

*Peter LeFevre suggests that Herbert had twenty-two ships of the line in all against Chateaurenault's twenty-four.

sailed back into Bantry Bay where the transports completed their unloading before setting sail on the return voyage to Brest. Neither side lost a ship in what became known as the Battle of Bantry Bay, the largest naval engagement ever fought in Ireland's coastal waters.[22]

In much the same way as the Great War battle of Jutland discouraged the German High Seas' Fleet from putting to sea again to engage the Royal Navy, this encounter at Bantry Bay seems to have had a similar effect on the French. Herbert, meanwhile, resumed his patrolling of the western approaches of the English Channel with his command increased to forty Royal Navy warships and eleven Dutch ships of the line. William showed his approval of the navy's role by dining on board HMS *Elizabeth* at Portsmouth where he created Herbert Earl of Torbay, later changed to Torrington; he also knighted Cloudesley Shovell and John Ashby, two of Herbert's most outstanding commanders.[23] Although the battle had been a tactical success for the French – they had, after all, landed their supplies and personnel – Chateaurenault had failed to grasp the opportunity to achieve a strategic victory by pursuing Herbert's ships and bringing them to battle a second time. This would have given the French the opportunity to defeat Herbert in detail, thereby gaining control of the Irish Sea. In turn, this would have allowed the French navy to play a role in the siege of Londonderry, both by supplying and supporting the besieging army and denying free passage from England to Ulster for any relief fleet. It was this strategic failure of the French navy that led naval historian A W H Pearsall to note that 'although in the end the fate of Ireland was settled by the outcome of the military struggle, the conditions of that struggle were largely set by the ability of the Anglo-Dutch navies to supply and reinforce their respective armies there'.[24] The truth of that statement applies as much to the local struggle around Londonderry as it does to the overall struggle in Ireland, but the naval aspects of the siege are rarely considered beyond the actions of those few ships that finally brought relief to the city.

Notes

1: Walker, op cit, p. 44
2: Ibid, p. 43
3: Ibid, p. 57
4: Mackenzie, op cit, p. 47
5: Walker, op cit, pp. 57–8; Mackenzie, op cit, p. 45

6: Walker, op cit, pp. 58–9

7: Mackenzie, op cit, p. 47; Simpson, op cit, pp. 129–30

8: Mackenzie, op cit, p. 47

9: Mackenzie, op cit, pp. 47–8; Walker, op cit, p. 47

10: Mackenzie, op cit, p. 47

11: Ibid, pp. 47–8

12: Ibid, p. 48

13: Doherty, op cit, p. 213

14: Mackenzie, op cit, p. 48

15: Ibid

16: John Rylands Library, Manchester; Bagshawe muniments, B3/2/38(i) & (ii); B3/2/38; Cunningham & Whalley, *Queries Against Major General Kirke*, *Irish Sword*, Vol. XVI, No. 64, pp. 208–16

17: *London Gazette*, 14–17 January 1689

18: LeFevre, *The Battle of Bantry Bay*, 1 May 1689, *IS* XVIII, No. 70, p. 1; Molloy, *The French Navy and the Jacobite War in Ireland*, 1689–91, *IS* XVIII, No. 70, p. 23

19: Ibid, pp. 1–6; Pearsall, in Maguire (ed), op cit, p. 93; Powley, op cit, pp. 130–4;

20: LeFevre, op cit, p. 2

21: Ibid, pp. 2–3

22: Ibid, pp. 8–11; Molloy, op cit, pp. 24–5; Powley, op cit, pp. 135–143

23: LeFevre, op cit, p. 11; Powley, op cit, pp. 143–4

24: Pearsall, op cit, p. 92

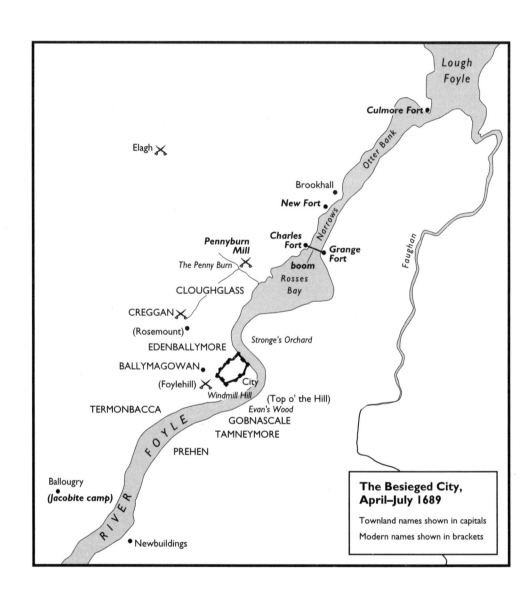

Lough
Foyle

Culmore Fort ●

Otter Bank

Elagh ✕

Brookhall
●

New Fort ●

Narrows

Charles
Fort ●
Grange
Fort ●

Faughan

Pennyburn
Mill
✕

The Penny Burn ✕

boom

CLOUGHGLASS

Rosses
Bay

CREGGAN ✕

(Rosemount) ●

EDENBALLYMORE

Stronge's Orchard

BALLYMAGOWAN ●

(Foylehill) ✕

City

(Top o' the Hill)

Windmill Hill

Evan's Wood

TERMONBACCA

GOBNASCALE

TAMNEYMORE

PREHEN

RIVER FOYLE

Balloughry
●
(Jacobite camp)

● Newbuildings

**The Besieged City,
April–July 1689**

Townland names shown in capitals

Modern names shown in brackets

CHAPTER NINE

Bombs and Great Bombs

As July dawned those within the walls could not be certain what the future held for them. True, they had beaten off Rosen's attempt to storm the city and foiled his plan to hasten their starvation by forcing them to take so many of their fellow Protestants inside the walls. The latter Jacobite plan had even had some beneficial effects for the defenders who had been able to enlist some able bodied men from the ranks of those who had been driven to the walls; these volunteers remained in Derry until the end of the siege. The latters' presence helped steel the resolve of the garrison not to surrender, since many of the newcomers had had protections from either King James or Hamilton which provided evidence to others of the perfidy of the Jacobites.

Of course, the defenders had tried to get some of their weakest citizens out of the city when the gallows was taken down and the hostages were allowed to return home. However, many of these individuals were obvious to the Jacobites who recognized 'them by their colour', a polite way of saying that they were dirtier than the average seventeenth-century citizen. Those so identified were sent back, but there were many, womenfolk among them, who were able to get away from the city. The Jacobite prisoners in the city were returned to their lodgings.[1]

There is an element of black humour in the story of Andrew Robinson, a gentleman who left the city about this time but was intercepted by the Jacobites, who interrogated him. 'Because of some imprudent expressions' he was stripped naked and sent back. Mackenzie does not elaborate on the detail of Robinson's 'imprudent expressions', but the nature of them may be surmised even after the passage of three centuries. On the other hand, Captain Beatty, one of the garrison, was able to leave with a Jacobite protection and go to live at Moneymore in the south of County Londonderry. Beatty, who was probably a native of that village, was allowed to depart because he suffered from 'a violent flux, which rendered him useless to the garrison'. His return home was to aid his recovery which, again, makes one wonder about the policy being pursued by the Jacobites. Beatty was a soldier of some renown, having been involved in all the clashes with the Jacobites from which he had emerged with a reputation for 'great integrity and valour'.[2]

A week into July and the defenders noticed that there were few men about the Jacobite camps. This prompted Mitchelburne to send out a reconnaissance in force from the defensive lines about Windmill Hill. These reconnoitrers opened fire on the Jacobite lines and the enemy returned fire. One Jacobite officer, Colonel Barker, was wounded in the hand and was later reported to have developed a fever from which he died. No major battle developed, although Jacobite reinforcements were seen marching towards the Irish line and some cavalry also made an appearance. However, the Williamites withdrew into their own lines, apparently mistaking the command given to them as being one to retreat. By then it was dusk, and a little later the defenders were surprised to hear much cheering from the various Jacobite camps. This, they learned, was to celebrate the fall of Enniskillen and appeared to be an example of psychological warfare by the Irish army trying to unsettle the defenders. The truth was that Enniskillen had beaten off the most recent Jacobite attack.[3]

The information that the cheering marked the fall of Enniskillen came from Jacobite soldiers in one of many exchanges of information between the two sides. One subject of conversation reported to the garrison commanders was the Irish discontent with their French allies. No love was lost between the common Irish soldier and the French officers. Walker wrote that

> they express'd great prejudice and hatred of the French, cursing those damn'd fellows that walked in trunks (meaning their jack-boots) that had all preferments in the army that fell, and took the bread out of their mouths, and they believ'd wou'd have all the kingdom to themselves at last.[4]

By 8 July the garrison's strength had fallen to 5,520 men. Within another five days it was down to 5,313 and four days later had reduced to 5,114.[5] Meanwhile, on the 11th, the Jacobites called for a parley, sending a messenger to the city to ask if the garrison would be prepared to discuss terms for surrendering the city. Since provisions were very low and most of Kirke's ships had gone, 'we knew not whither', it was decided to gain some time by agreeing to the request which called for six representatives on each side. The defenders were to send the names of their representatives, together with the terms they demanded, to the Jacobites the following day. The latter would reciprocate so that each could consider the other's terms on the 13th, a Saturday.[6]

Representing the besieged were Colonels Hugh Hamilton and Thomas Lance, Captains Robert White, William Dobbin and Matthew Cocken as well as the Reverend John Mackenzie, whom Ash calls McKenny. Escorted by a group of officers of the garrison these six went out to the strand of the river where they met the Jacobite commissioners: Colonels Dominic Sheldon, Sir Neil O'Neill and Gordon O'Neill, Lieutenant Colonel Skelton, Sir Edward Vaudry and Captain Francis Morrow. The city's commissioners were led to a tent, erected for the occasion, where a meal was provided and, according to Ash, they 'were well entertained'. What followed was much less a day of diplomatic negotiation as a demonstration of obstinacy on the part of the garrison. The city's six representatives had been sent out not as plenipotentiaries with freedom to manoeuvre in discussing terms but with a firm agenda that had been set by the governing Council of Fourteen (see Chapter Five, p. 115) and the commanding officers of the city's regiments. However, to ensure that the Jacobites did not conclude that the city was 'a confused multitude without any government', the commissioners were to be seen as representing the governors.[8]

Mackenzie describes the proceedings as a long debate which lasted until nightfall. Whether the Jacobites would have agreed that it was a debate is a matter for conjecture since those facing them had come with a shopping list that they were determined to obtain.[9] One is reminded of Winston Churchill's comment on being told that Sir Alan Brooke was to become the Chief of the Imperial General Staff in late 1941 that Brooke was a stiff-necked Ulsterman who when Churchill would thump the table and shout would simply thump the table harder and shout back. It may well be that these commissioners were the proto-stiff-necked Ulstermen, although Hamilton was under orders from James to bring about the city's surrender no matter what the terms. In the course of the day at the table the Jacobites acceded to all the defenders' demands save for three: the Williamites wished to hand over the city on 26 July but Hamilton insisted that this should happen by midday on the following Monday, 15 July; hostages should be kept in the city and not placed on board Kirke's ships; and, on marching out of the city, only the officers of the garrison would be allowed to bear arms.[10]

The critical point of disagreement was the date of surrender. One cannot help thinking that the defenders had no intention of surrendering at all and that their suggestion of the 26th for an end to hostilities was simply a ploy to gain more time during which, hopefully, Kirke might finally stir himself and come to their aid. For Hamilton, it was imperative that he obtain the surrender as soon as possible before Kirke moved or before another, stronger, force arrived in Ulster from England; the main body of the expeditionary force, under Schomberg, was known to be forming up. In a sense the besiegers were now also under siege since Kirke's force at Inch presented a major threat that could be unleashed at any time. Furthermore there were the troublesome Enniskilleners who had never been content to sit back and take punishment from the Jacobites but had raided the latter's lines of communication, striking almost as far as Dublin, and who might also strike north towards Derry. Combined with an attack from Inch, that would place the Jacobites in a dire situation. Thus Hamilton was as anxious as James to see the garrison of Derry accept terms and march out.

It is much less clear why Hamilton should have displayed obstinacy about the hostages and the carrying of arms by soldiers marching out of the city. We have already looked at the conventions of siege warfare in Chapter Four and noted that what the defenders demanded was within those conventions. However, these were matters that could be resolved with relative ease, and it may be that Hamilton was giving the impression of being difficult because he felt this necessary. Equally, he might well have realized that the Williamites were playing for time and decided to play them at their own game. We shall never know, especially as the matter soon became academic.

The Williamite commissioners returned to the city that night with a promise that they would give the Jacobites an answer by noon on the Sunday. Mackenzie recorded that this time, in which to reach a decision and deliver an answer, had been obtained 'with great difficulty'. On their return the commissioners made a report to the council and a meeting was arranged for 8 o'clock next morning to 'consider what answer they should return'.[11]

But there had been another development that involved George Walker. While the commissioners had been at their meeting with the Jacobites, a small boy had brought a message from the ships to the city. This had been written by a Lieutenant David Mitchell, a soldier who had left the city on 10 May, and included the information that Kirke had sent some of his force to encamp at Inch.[12] Walker decided to amend the letter by changing the details of the size of the force sent to Inch; he increased this to 4,000 horse and 9,000 infantry. It was all the more surprising, therefore, that, on the Saturday night, Walker should advocate surrender by Monday, as Hamilton had demanded. Others of the Council of Fourteen pointed out to him that there was a strong Williamite force, said to be some 13,000 men, on Inch and that this force could reach the city in less than a day. There was, therefore, no reason to surrender when such a reinforcement lay so close. It was then that Walker was obliged to admit that he had amended the letter.[13]

When the council met on Sunday morning there was a debate about the course of action to be followed after which it was decided that 'unless the enemy would give us time until the 26th of July, and secure the hostages in the ships, we would not surrender'. Surprisingly, Walker continued to argue against this which must have aroused among the other members of the council considerable suspicion about his motives. On the other point in dispute, it was agreed to allow the commissioners to debate the manner of surrender and how the garrison should march out. And so the commissioners, as agreed, went out to meet the Jacobites at noon. But their proposals met with refusal and the truce that had been agreed had come to an end.[14]

Mackenzie took this as a sign of providence:

So evidently that gracious God (who had determined our deliverance, and to whose all-comprehending eye that particular season of it that would most illustrate His own glory was obvious) infatuate the counsels and harden the hearts of our enemies. Had they accepted the proposals, the city had been unavoidably surrendered, and we could not have held out three or four days longer than the time we desired.[15]

Although Mackenzie makes no mention of the Jacobite reaction following the breakdown of the truce, Ash tells us that the commissioners had hardly returned to their own lines before the bombardment of the city was renewed, with the Jacobites choosing 'to vent their malice in playing bombs and great bombs against the city, which blessed be God, did little mischief.[16] Later that night, following instructions in the letter from Mitchell, seven rounds were fired from the cathedral's tower, followed by a further three at midnight while a lantern was hung from the flagpole. Throughout that day some eighteen mortar rounds were fired into the city.[17]

The abortive negotiations led to further activity from the Jacobites. On the 15th, eight bombs were fired into the city and, in the evening, some 2,000 Jacobite troops marched to the rising ground beside the Foyle to the south of the city. An attempt to take Windmill Hill seemed to be underway. Orders were issued immediately to some of the garrison to march out and meet the attackers. This brought the attack to a halt. The Jacobites then fired twelve mortar rounds at the Windmill but without killing anyone. Then the cannon emplaced across the river at Tamneymore opened fire on the trenches south of the city, killing a soldier from Captain Gordon's company. Finally, the Jacobite troops marched off, although more bombs were fired after their departure.[18]

The Jacobites returned to the attack next day, during which their mortarmen fired four rounds into the city. Much more serious was a fresh attack on the Butcher's Gate launched, it seems, at about 10 o'clock in the morning. Although the assault was made by a small party of Jacobites, the defenders' positions were unmanned and were quickly in Jacobite hands. However, the new occupants were soon under fire from the walls, to which bombardment the Williamites added stones 'out of the old walls'. Once again the Jacobites were forced to withdraw, having lost some men dead and one captured.[19] Ash states that this attack occurred on the 17th* and that six Jacobites were killed; he names the man taken prisoner as one Robinson who, two days later, took an oath to William and Mary and was given his liberty.[20] Another alarm had been created by the approach of two Jacobite regiments to the out-works on Windmill Hill, but a deployment of the garrison, ordered by Mitchelburne, resulted in the Jacobite units turning about.[21]

By now the garrison's strength had reduced to 5,114 men but Murray seemed still determined to take the fight to the enemy and, taking twelve men with him, sallied out to make a flank attack on the Jacobite trenches before Butcher's Gate. As with the earlier Jacobite attack in the same area, this had all the qualities of a suicide mission. If anything, Murray's mission was more suicidal than that by the Jacobites. It led to a fierce firefight with the Williamites firing until their ammunition was exhausted. One of his men, James Murray – according to Ash, a cousin of Adam Murray – was killed while Adam Murray himself was wounded seriously. He was shot through both thighs and was fortunate not to have died. As it was, he was not recovered fully until November. Ash notes that Murray was shot as his group was withdrawing. Ash adds another Williamite fatality to the story of this encounter, that of Sergeant Lynn, one of the few NCOs or private soldiers to receive a mention in any of the accounts of the siege. Also in the raiding party had been the redoubtable Captain Noble.[22]

At midnight the mortarmen were at their business yet again, firing eight bombs into the city. One of these killed an elderly citizen, Henry

---

*The dates given by Ash conflict frequently with those from Mackenzie and Walker.

Thompson, who was in his bed when the round came through his roof and fell upon him, smashing his body into pieces. The Jacobite artillery continued to pound at the town and the gate, presumably the Butcher's Gate since Ash tells us that the breastwork of the bastion below the gate was broken, but then withdrew the guns under cover of night to redeploy them at Brookhall where they were added to the ordnance supporting the boom. This was a strange move as considerable damage had been done in the Butcher's Gate area and the defenders were carrying out emergency repairs at night using barrels and sods of earth. One explanation for the move could be that the Jacobites were expecting Kirke's fleet to make a run upriver for the city. Ash notes that the last firing at Butcher's Gate took place on the 23rd but, bearing in mind the discrepancy in dates between Ash and other chroniclers, this may have been a day or two earlier than that. Before their move to Brookhall, the battering guns killed a number of people who 'lay in garrets' including two brothers in one such garret in Bishop's Street.[23]

Irrespective of the redeployment of the artillery, the mortarmen continued their punishment of the city; Ash records twenty-two bombs on the 19th with a further twenty-eight two days later.[24] It was around this time that James Cunningham, a merchant, found a way of supplementing the flour in the stores. His discovery was that starch, of which there was a good supply in the town, could be mixed with tallow to bake pancakes. These provided not only good food but also had a medicinal property, being 'physic too to many of those whom weariness and ill diet had cast into a flux'. In other words, these pancakes alleviated the debilitating effects of dysentery. The starch supply provided sufficient ingredients to provide the garrison with these pancakes for six or seven days.[25]

The city's dogs were still providing part of its citizens' diet. One man had killed a dog and was preparing it for cooking when he received a visit from another to whom he owed some money. Eyeing the dead dog, the creditor insisted on having either his money or the dog there and then. The first man, having no money, was forced to part with his dog 'with languishing eye and rueful stomach'. Ash notes the cost of some basic foodstuffs at this time: meal, which cost four pence per peck* at the beginning of the siege, now commanded six shillings while milk cost threepence-halfpenny for a pint and butter was two shillings and sixpence for six ounces. For those with little or no financial means and

---

*A peck was a measure for dry goods and was the equivalent of two gallons, or 9.19 litres. A container of this size was also known as a peck.

with little to barter, the situation was now life-threatening.[26] One way or another, the siege was entering its final phase.

And it was this critical situation that led to a sally from the city on 25 July, the day on which Walker noted that the garrison's strength had been reduced to 4,892 men.[27] This was a foraging expedition, subsequently dubbed the 'battle of the cows', inspired by the sight of cattle grazing just behind the Jacobites' lines 'between this place and Pennyburn'.[28] Whether the Jacobites had intended this to be a piece of psychological warfare we do not know, but the prospect of seizing the cattle for food provided a great incentive to the garrison. A council of war was held on the 24th, at which a plan was made to raid the enemy lines and seize their cattle. The raid was to be launched at 3.00am with 200 men moving out through Bishop's Gate, a similar number through Butcher's Gate and another group of unspecified strength through Ship Quay Gate, while 1,100 men were held in reserve in the ravelin. Such numbers indicate a determination to bring home the desired prize.[29]

In the sleepy hour just before dawn the raiders achieved total surprise. Sir John Fitzgerald's Regiment was shocked to find a mass of Williamites flooding into their trenches. Although the regiment regained its composure and formed up in good order, they remained at a great disadvantage. Fitzgerald's men appear to have been armed only with matchlock muskets and, according to Walker, only three men had their match cord. Although it is more likely that these were three cords that were kept lit so that individuals might light their own from them, the effect was still the same. The Jacobites had no effective means of breaking the attack. Mackenzie tells us that the Jacobites were 'made havoc of' and driven from their trenches. Fitzgerald himself was killed, as was Captain Francis Walsh, while Captain Nugent, Ensign Early and two private soldiers were taken prisoner. According to Walker, some 300 Jacobites, officers and soldiers, were killed but, as ever with Walker, this estimate must be regarded as suspect, especially as it is not supported by either Mackenzie or Ash.[30]

It is from Ash that we have the best account of this incident (and he also agrees on the date with both Mackenzie and Walker), which is hardly surprising as he took part in the raid. He tells us that the raiding party totalled some 500 men drawn from several of the companies in the city – it is interesting to note that the garrison still saw itself as formed in companies rather than regiments – and that it drew up in Shipquay Street, close to the gate, before departing, as we have seen, by the three gates; the sally from Bishop's Gate seems to have been intended to deter any Jacobite attack on the Windmill Hill positions, which would also account for the substantial reserve drawn up in the ravelin.

Captain Wilson, Lieutenant Moor and Sergeant Neely led the attackers who slipped out through Ship Quay Gate while those from the Butcher's Gate were led by Captains Hamilton, Burly and Ash. Their orders were to 'flank the ditches which run through the orchard at both ends'. Shock and surprise allowed these orders to be executed effectively as many enemy soldiers abandoned their trenches and took to their heels 'with great celerity a decision that he confirms was taken because 'most of their matches were out'. Part of the surprise gained by the attackers was due, in Ash's view, to the fact that the Jacobites 'could hardly suppose that a poor hungry starved people would come out upon them in that manner'. In this encounter, Ash puts the Jacobite dead at sixty, far short of the figure claimed by Walker. Even if the same death toll was inflicted by the other attacking party from Ship Quay Gate, the overall toll is still much lower than Walker's figure.[31]

Walker claims that the execution might have been much higher but for the fact that the attackers were so 'much weakened by hunger [that they] were not able to pursue them'. Some were so weak that they fell when they tried to strike blows at their foes. The party that had left by Bishop's Gate had observed what was happening with Ash's group and 'as soon as we were in action came down and did good service'. This group was commanded by Captain Blair, Captain Dixon and Lieutenant Boyd. But the Jacobites on the hill had also been able to see what was happening since, by now, it was daylight and troops were sent forward to restore the situation. This counter-attack was not one that the Williamites could cope with. Exhausted by their efforts and 'weak for want of sustenance', they were forced to pull back and retreat to their own trenches at Bishop's Gate.[32]

The sally had failed in its primary objective, to bring in the cattle grazing between the city and Pennyburn. As soon as the raiding parties left the city, the cattle had been herded over the hill.[33] However, there had been an opportunity to plunder the stores and personal equipment of Fitzgerald's Regiment, and the attackers withdrew with a 'good store of arms and knapsacks, with bannocks of oat-bread, mutton &c. &c. from their camp'. Also included in the booty from the expedition were tools including spades, shovels and pickaxes. The highest-ranking prisoner, Captain Nugent, claimed to have £26 in gold and silver on his person but, in spite of his being searched, only four *louis d'ors*, French gold coins, and a guinea were found. These were shared between Captain Wilson, who had captured Nugent, and Mr Burrel, who brought him into the city. Nugent's sword was given to an English sergeant of the garrison but his scarlet coat, with large plate buttons, was returned to Nugent.[34]

Williamite losses were light, with only three men killed, Lieutenant Fisher and two private soldiers.[35] It was thought that another senior French officer in the Jacobite camp might have perished. This man had been busy organizing the counter-attack when he was struck and killed by a cannon ball from the city.[36] But this was not confirmed and there is no record of a French general perishing at this stage, although a French engineer officer, Massé, had been killed by a cannon ball on 19 July while overseeing the emplacement of a gun in a battery that he had just completed.[37] It is probable that the report of Massé's death became confused within the city with the Jacobite reaction to the sally of 25 July.

The failure of the foraging sally may have been anticipated. A court martial, which had been sitting for several days, had ordered, on the 24th, that 'all the black cattle in garrison, which have been kept in houses this month or six weeks' should now be slaughtered to provide meat for the garrison. There is no indication of the number of cattle involved but it could not have been large since concerns about food persisted. That they had survived so long indicates that these were dairy cows kept to provide milk, butter and cheese for the garrison. Ash notes that, on this same day, a dog was offered for food at a price of six shillings and makes clear that this was not out of the ordinary by adding that dogs, horses and cats were being eaten frequently.[38]

Hunger was not the only problem within the walls although it might have been the root cause of others. There was a dispute in Adam Murray's quarters which resulted in the death of Captain David Ross. It seems that Ross was told to search for saddles belonging to Sir Arthur Rawdon, who had long departed for England, and his search took him into Murray's quarters. There he became involved in an argument about saddles with one of Murray's troopers, Samuel Lindsay. This argument became so heated that Ross, who had been very rude to the soldier, drew his sword and struck Lindsay with it several times. So angered was Lindsay that he took a carbine and fired a round into Ross's chest which killed him immediately. Since Lindsay was fit enough to go for a carbine, Ross must have been striking him with the flat of his sword rather than cutting at him with the edge.[39]

This incident, which occurred on the 23rd, was followed by an attempted mutiny in which 'some turbulent persons' planned to imprison the gunners, spike the artillery and then beat drums to signal to the garrison and the Jacobites that they were prepared to make terms to surrender the city. They believed that once the artillery had been secured they would be able to persuade enough people to support them in their plan to make terms. However, the plotters were overheard, or perhaps one of their number passed on information about the plan, and two of their leaders were incarcerated.[40]

Such problems must have given the court martial considerable business. This military court, effectively an imposition of martial law on the city by the garrison, included thirteen members* whose role was 'to rectify and set right all misdemeanours in garrison'. (Tautologies are not, it seems, a modern phenomenon.) The president of the court was Captain Robert White and the other members were Lieutenant-Colonel Miller, Major J Dobbin, Major Alexander Stuart, Captain J Cook, Captain W Godfrey, Captain David Ross, Captain A Downing, Captain Thomas Ash, Captain John Thompson, Captain J Cochran and Captain Dobbin as advocate. Following Captain Ross's death in the altercation with Trooper Lindsay his place on the court was taken by Captain T Johnston. In addition to dealing with discipline within the garrison, the court martial also oversaw the stores and called the storekeeper to account as well as those 'concerned with the excise and the city rent'. All money raised by the court was to be paid to the treasurer to cover the costs of repairing arms and meeting other liabilities arising from the defence of the city.[41]

The day of the foraging sally appears to have been a very busy one for the besieged. It will be recalled that there had been a fear of a Jacobite attack on Windmill Hill earlier in the day. Although no such attack materialized, some Jacobite soldiers approached the Windmill position and called on the defenders to come out to talk with them. Two men left the entrenchments but when they reached the Jacobites they were killed by them. The defenders had also lost a sergeant and two private soldiers the previous night; these men had deserted, taking their weapons with them. However, they must have been unwelcome additions to the Jacobite army who sent them back to Derry but minus their uniforms and shoes, which were said to be of good quality. Both incidents suggest that the Jacobites were still lacking many necessities, including clothing and footwear.[42]

---

*Ash describes the court-martial board as having thirteen members but then goes on to name only twelve men. It seems that his thirteen includes Johnston who replaced Ross when the latter was killed.

Some time later that day there was an explosion in the guard house which resulted in injury to three members of the guard and three Jacobite prisoners who were being held there. These three had been captured earlier in the day and were allowed to smoke tobacco close to some powder. It was this carelessness that caused the explosion since a spark fell from one man's pipe and landed on some powder grains on the floor. These ignited; but this would not have been a problem had the grains not formed a trail to a half barrel of powder. Inevitably the fire burned along the trail, the barrel exploded, the three prisoners were 'much disfigured' and the floor of the guard house was blown out. This might have led to even more casualties as this was where the court martial usually sat but it was not then in session. Even so, one of the injured guard members died the next day. The wounded Jacobites, Ensign Cartie and two soldiers, were released as they were considered incapable of 'doing us much hurt this campaign'.[43]

Until now there had been a practice of appointing searchers to bring into the city store provisions from those who had a plentiful private supply. The rationale behind this practice was to ensure that those who had come into the city as refugees and had little food or money should not be in need. The court martial ordered an end to this practice on the 26th by demanding of everyone an oath that they would give a true account of what provisions they held. From their store they would be allowed to keep a week's supply, according to their family needs, but the remainder would be requisitioned and taken to the storehouse. It seems strange that this measure had not been taken long before, as it is clear that the commanders were aware that such private stores existed and that some of those in the city were putting themselves before the greater good.[44]

A bizarre attempt was also made to procure food. According to Walker, this occurred after the failure of the foraging sally, but Ash states that it happened on the 26th while Mackenzie writes simply that it occurred 'afterwards'. A cow, the one heifer left alive in the city, which belonged to a Mr Gravet, was taken outside the walls, tied to a stake, smeared with tar and set alight. This must have caused the beast horrendous pain and its cries would have been terrible to listen to. But it was that crying or roaring that the garrison wanted to hear since it was believed 'the enemy's cows which were grazing in the orchard would come to her'. Of course, the pain and panic in the animal's roaring would have had exactly the opposite effect and the other cattle would have stampeded. Obviously, those responsible for this desperate and, to a twenty-first-century mind, exceptionally cruel, plan were town-dwellers with little idea of animal behaviour. Their tethered heifer was given added strength by her pain, broke the rope that held her and ran off in the direction of the orchard. The unfortunate beast was put out of her pain and misery by musket fire from the walls.[45]

The other cattle in the city, plus the few surviving horses, were slaughtered for their meat. Ash notes that there were sixteen cows and twelve horses, which would not have provided much meat even for the garrison at its reduced strength of fewer than 5,000 men. An issue of a pound of meal mixed with Dutch flour, i.e., starch, was made to each soldier and, next morning, every man was given one and a half pounds of horse meat. Blood from the slaughtered animals was offered for sale at four pence per quart for cows' blood and half that price for the horses'. By now there was not a dog to be seen in the city; all had been killed and eaten.[46]

On 27 July the garrison was reduced to 4,456 men and was, in Walker's words, 'under the greatest extremity for want of provision'. Ash agreed with this assessment, writing:

> we never stood in so much need of a supply; for there is not now one week's provisions in the garrison. Of necessity we must surrender the city, and make the best terms we can for ourselves. Next Wednesday is our last, if relief does not arrive before it.[47]

This counsel of despair came on a day when the garrison could hear 'the great guns at or near Inch' but the wind was from the south-west, which would have prevented ships coming up the river to the city. And it was on this day also that Walker records the infamous price list of food in the city. This was taken from an account made 'by a gentleman in the garrison' and is in marked contrast to Mackenzie's note on food on 9 April (see Chapter Four).[48] It makes unpleasant reading.

	1. s. d.
Horse flesh sold for	0–1–8 per pound
A Quarter of a Dog	0–5–6 fatned by eating the bod-ies of the slain Irish
A Dog's Head	0–2–6
A Cat	0–4–6
A Rat	0–1–0
A Mouse	0–0–6

A small Flook taken in the River, not to be bought for Mon, or purchased under the rate of a quantity of Meal.

A pound of Greaves	0–1–0
A poundof Tallow	0–1–0
A pound of salted Hides	0–1–0
A quart* of Horse blood	0–1–0
A Horse-pudding	0–0–6
An handful of Sea wreck	0–0–2
of Chick-weed	0–0–1
A quart of meal when found	0–1–0

Walker emphasizes that the garrison was suffering so much for want of food 'that we had nothing left unless we could prey upon one another'. This suggestion of an imminent resort to cannibalism is strengthened by the anecdote he then includes of a 'certain fat gentleman' who considered himself to be in danger because of the amount of flesh on his body. Thinking that some of the soldiery were looking at him 'with a greedy eye', this individual thought it best to hide himself from the public gaze for three days.[49]

To drink, the garrison and inhabitants of the city had only water; but potable water could be obtained only at great risk, since the wells outside the walls were dominated by the Jacobites. It seems that even this most basic of necessities for life had to be paid for when it was brought into the city. There is no doubt that some of the water for human consumption was contaminated or discoloured, for Walker wrote that ginger and aniseed, 'of which we had great plenty', were mixed with it. However, he confirms that eating the concoction of tallow and starch was not only a source of nourishment but 'was an infallible cure of the looseness', providing a cure for many who were suffering from dysentery and preventing it in others.[50]

To add to the other miseries, two soldiers of the garrison at Butcher's Gate were killed by musket fire from the orchard. It was time, considered Walker, for a sermon intended to maintain the resolve of the garrison. And so, 'finding in himself still that confidence, that God would not (after so long and miraculous a preservation) suffer them to be a prey to their enemies, he went to the cathedral to preach. He spoke of the many instances of providence that they had witnessed since the beginning of the siege and urged them to be constant in their defence of the city and in their belief in the Protestant religion 'and that

---

*quarter of a gallon, about 1.1 litres.

they need not doubt, but that God would at last deliver them from the difficulty they were under'.[51]

That difficulty seemed to be increasing, and Mackenzie notes that Walker's sermon was a discouraging one' rather than one that boosted the morale of soldiers and citizens. He notes that Captain Charleton chose this time, 28 July, to abandon the city and go over to the Jacobites. There is an implication here that Charleton had listened to Walker preach and had not been impressed. Mackenzie's analysis of the morale within the city is probably much closer to the truth than Walker's. The Presbyterian minister commented that 'the desperate necessities that were growing upon us had almost sunk us all into a despair of relief.[52]

Notes

1: Mackenzie, op cit, p. 51
2: Ibid, pp. 51–2
3: Ibid, p. 52
4: Walker, op cit, 59
5: Ibid
6: Ibid, p. 52; Mackenzie, op cit, p. 52; Simpson, op cit, p. 141; Ash, op cit, p. 90
7: Ash, op cit, pp. 90–1; Mackenzie, op cit, pp. 52–3; Simpson, op cit, pp. 141–3
8: Mackenzie, p. 52
9: Ibid
10: Ibid; Ash, op cit, pp. 90–1; Simpson, op cit, pp. 141–2
11: Mackenzie, op cit, pp. 52–3
12: Ibid, p. 52
13: Ibid, pp. 52–3; Simpson, op cit, pp. 143–4
14: Mackenzie, op cit, p. 53; Ash, op cit, p. 91; Simpson, op cit, p. 144
15: Mackenzie, op cit, p. 53
16: Ash, op cit, p. 91
17: Ibid
18: Ibid; Mackenzie, op cit, p. 53
19: Ash, op cit, p. 92; Mackenzie, op cit, p. 53; Simpson, op cit, p. 144
20: Ash, op cit, p. 92
21: Mackenzie, op cit, p. 53
22: Ibid; Ash, op cit, p. 92; Simpson, op cit, pp. 144–5
23: Ash, op cit, pp. 92–4; Simpson, op cit, p. 145; Mackenzie, op cit, p. 53

24: Ash, op cit, p. 93

25: Mackenzie, op cit, pp. 53–4; Ash, op cit, p. 93

26: Ash, op cit, p. 93

27: Walker, op cit, p. 59

28: Ash, op cit, p. 95; Walker, op cit, pp. 59–60; Mackenzie, op cit, p. 53; Simpson, op cit, p. 146

29: Walker, op cit, p. 59; Ash, op cit, p. 95; Simpson, op cit, p. 146

30: Mackenzie, op cit, p. 53; Walker, op cit, pp. 59–60; Ash, op cit, pp. 95–7; Simpson, op cit, p. 146

31: Ash, op cit, pp. 95–7

32: Walker, op cit, p. 60; Ash, op cit, pp. 95–7

33: Ash, op cit, p. 97

34: Ibid, p. 96

35: Ibid; Mackenzie, op cit, p. 53. Mackenzie lists Fisher as the defenders' sole fatality.

36: Ash, op cit, pp. 96–7

37: *Franco-Irish Correspondence*, p. 160

38: Ash, op cit, p. 95

39: Mackenzie, op cit, p. 53; Ash, op cit, p. 94; Simpson, op cit, pp. 145–6

40: Ash, op cit, pp. 94–5

41: Simpson, op cit, pp. 145–6; Ash, op cit, p. 95

42: Ash, op cit, p. 97

43: Ibid

44: Ibid

45: Ibid, p. 98; Mackenzie, op cit, p. 53; Walker, op cit, p. 60

46: Ash, op cit, p. 98

47: Walker, op cit, p. 60; Ash, op cit, p. 98

48: Ash, op cit, p. 98; Walker, op cit, p. 60

49: Walker, op cit, pp. 60–1

50: Ibid, p. 61

51: Ash, op cit, p. 98; Walker, op cit, pp. 61–2

52: Mackenzie, op cit, p. 54

CHAPTER TEN

The Mountjoy *Knew Her Own Way Home*

Mackenzie's comment that the city was despairing of being relieved made all the more wondrous the sighting that evening, at about 7 o'clock, of three ships in Lough Foyle approaching Culmore. Walker wrote that this sighting was made 'in the midst of our extremity' while Ash described the day as one 'to be remembered with thanksgiving by the besieged as long as they live'. Ash and Mackenzie date this day of thanksgiving as 28 July, whereas Walker places it two days later on the 30th. And while Walker and Mackenzie number the ships at three, Ash observed four vessels that 'came swiftly to Culmore without harm'. One other source, the account by Joshua Gillespie, names the fourth ship as being the cutter *Jerusalem*; this vessel was about the same size as the *Phoenix*.[1]

Irrespective of the date, or of the exact number of ships, relief now appeared close at hand. HMS *Dartmouth*, Captain Leake's frigate, was escorting three merchant vessels, the *Mountjoy* of Derry, under Captain Michael Browning, a Derryman, the *Phoenix* of Coleraine, whose master was Captain Andrew Douglas, also of Coleraine but a Scot by birth, and the cutter *Jerusalem*, commanded by Captain Pepwell.[2] We have seen how Richards observed three ships in Lough Swilly being loaded with provisions and setting sail for Lough Foyle on 20 July: these are the same vessels on the final leg of their journey. According to Richards, Kirke accompanied the little convoy in HMS *Swallow*, which does not feature in the accounts from Ash, Mackenzie or Walker, suggesting that Swallow left the others at some point and that only HMS *Dartmouth*, the cutter and the two merchant ships made the run up Lough Foyle as far as Culmore.[3] It seems that *Swallow** drew too much draught to allow the ship to sail up to the city; although the water

---

Swallow was a fourth-rater, i.e., a ship with forty to sixty guns. Both *Deptford* and *Bonadventure* were in the same category: the former had fifty guns with a crew of 280; the latter had forty-eight guns and a crew of 230.

was quite deep at Culmore where the river enters the lough it became shallower on the approach to the city. With Kirke on board, *Swallow* anchored in the lough where she dropped her longboat which was to play a significant part in the breaking of the boom; from the ship's maintop, Kirke was able to watch what was happening, although he was too far away to see in detail the events at the boom.

The choice of the *Mountjoy* and *Phoenix* seems to have been deliberate on Kirke's part since it permitted two local vessels to play the central role in the concluding act of the drama at Derry. According to Mackenzie, Browning had volunteered to make the run for the city before, while both Ash and Mackenzie agree that Kirke chose him to lead the relief because he was a Derryman. Ash wrote that Browning 'had that honour conferred upon him by Major-General Kirke, to be the man who should bring relief to Derry.' Honour it may have been, but it also placed Browning at great risk and he was to pay, with his life, the full price for accepting that risk.[4] Of course, there might have been a more pragmatic reason for Kirke's choice of Browning and Douglas: their familiarity with the waters of the Foyle. As a native of the city, Browning would have known the Foyle better than any of the other captains, and Douglas of Coleraine must also have been very familiar with its waters. One eminent naval historian has commented that 'to Captain Browning the soundings and tidal sets in the River all the way to Londonderry would be thoroughly familiar and *Mountjoy* as it were, knew her own way home!'[5] Whatever the circumstances, Kirke had now heeded the appeal from the city for immediate help;* to its inhabitants the appearance of the relief vessels seemed to be a miracle.

As the ships approached Culmore Fort, HMS *Dartmouth* hove to, 'drew in her sails and cast anchor'.[6] An artillery combat between the ships and the gunners in Culmore Fort then began as *Dartmouth's* role was to attempt to draw the fire of the fort from the two merchant ships while trying to suppress that fire with her own guns; Leake's frigate, a fifth-rater, carried twenty-eight guns, about half of which could be brought to bear on Culmore.** Rather than firing broadsides the frigate would have ripple-fired her guns at the fort, increasing the pressure on the latter's gunners by maintaining a constant fire which would not have been possible with broadsides. Leake had also placed his ship

---

*It will be remembered that he acted on a letter from Walker that suggested that the boom had been broken.

**On her lower deck were sixteen demi-culverins while the upper deck carried eight sakers and there were four 3-pounders on the quarterdeck.

between the fort and the channel that the merchant ships would use. The latter were not helpless since they also carried cannon (Douglas of the *Phoenix* had earlier in the year been issued with letters of marque as a privateer by the Scottish government) and each had forty soldiers on board. Now, as Leake's ship hammered at the fort, Browning, Douglas and Pepwell prepared to take their ships through the narrow channel at Culmore and upriver towards the boom. Leake's orders were that *Mountjoy* would sail with *Dartmouth*, *Phoenix* would not weigh anchor until *Dartmouth* was engaged with the fort and *Jerusalem* would await a signal from Leake that one of the other ships had passed the boom before weighing anchor. It was a well-conceived plan but one still fraught with danger for all the ships.

In a subsequent despatch to London, Kirke noted that

> Captain Leake, commander of the *Dartmouth*, behaved himself very bravely and prudently in this action, neither firing great or small shot (though he was plied very hard with both) till he came on the wind of the Castle, and there began to batter that the victuallers might pass under the shelter of his guns; then lay between the Castle and them within musket-shot and came to an anchor.[8]

Covered at Culmore by the guns of Leake's warship, *Mountjoy* led the way and Browning sailed his ship into the boom in the hope that the force of the vessel striking it would break the structure, thereby clearing the way for the other vessels. But he was unsuccessful. His ship struck the boom, rebounded and ran aground on the east bank. Mackenzie's interpretation of events is slightly different, with the wind dying as the *Mountjoy* reached the boom, the ship failing to strike it in the 'dead calm succeeding' and then running aground.[9] From this version it would seem that it was the tide that pushed Browning's ship aground; other sources indicate that Mackenzie was correct. Whatever the circumstances of the grounding, the result was the same: *Mountjoy* was at the mercy of the Jacobites. And it was then that the ship's redoubtable captain perished. Within sight of his home town, and with his mission almost accomplished, Browning was struck in the head by a musket ball and fell dead on *Mountjoy*'s deck.[10] William R Young, who, in 1932, produced a gazetteer of the principal characters of the siege, wrote this highly imaginative paean on the breaking of the boom:

> Nothing perhaps in the story of the siege is more thrilling than the rush of the *Mountjoy* on the terrible Boom. We can picture the captain, sword

in hand, standing on by the wheel and commanding operations until killed by the fatal shot.[11]

It may be noted that Ash wrote that Browning 'stood upon the deck with his sword drawn, encouraging his men with great cheerfulness' and this is, presumably, Young's source.[12]

With loud cheers large numbers of Jacobite soldiers raced towards the water's edge where some prepared to take to boats from which they might board the stricken *Mountjoy*. Farther along the river, closer to the city, other Jacobites took up the exuberant cheering of their comrades and called to the garrison that their ships had been taken.

We perceived them both firing their guns at them, and preparing boats to board them, [and] this struck such a sudden terror into our hearts, as appeared in the very blackness of our countenances. Our spirits sunk, and our hopes were expiring.[13]

But once again circumstances conspired against the Jacobites. The *Mountjoy* discharged a broadside, obviously from the port side, and this, with the rising tide, freed the ship from the grip of the mud to set her afloat again.[14] According to Ash, it was the inrushing tide that floated the *Mountjoy*.[15] All the while, both HMS *Dartmouth* and the *Phoenix* had been firing at the Jacobites. Restored to her natural element, Browning's ship began to engage the Jacobite batteries and steered once more for the boom. This was to be the crucial test of de Pointis' creation. It will be remembered that the French engineer's first effort had been an abject failure, sinking below the water due to the weight of the oak used in its construction. The boom that now stretched across the Foyle was constructed of fir beams held together with metal clamps, chains and rope and with both ends anchored firmly on dry land.

Walker believed that the *Mountjoy* had broken the boom when first it struck and this version is also included in Gillespie's narrative, but the boom was actually broken by sailors in HMS *Swallow*'s longboat.[16] These men do not feature in any of the indigenous siege narratives, and it appears that, if the writers of those narratives were told the detail of the breaking of the boom, they decided not to tell the full story. The longboat had been lowered from *Swallow* to accompany the ships that would make the run upriver and it was the ten-man crew of that boat who finally broke the boom. Since their part in this episode is so important, it is pleasant to record that the names of these seamen have been preserved in Admiralty records. Boatswain's Mate John Shelley commanded the longboat and his crew were Robert Kells, Jeremy Vincent, James Jamieson, Jonathan Young, Alexander Hunter, Henry Breman,* William Welcome, Jonathan Field and Miles Tonge. And it was Shelley who used the axe, leaping on to the boom to do so and receiving a splinter wound in the thigh in the process.[17] This involvement of the longboat crew is supported by a Jacobite report that indicates that both the *Mountjoy* and *Phoenix* were towed by longboats.[18]

The principal Jacobite account of events suggested that it was actually HMS *Dartmouth* that made the run upriver:

> The ship then aforesaid [*Dartmouth*] took the opportunity on this day of the tide and a fair gale of wind, and so came up to the fort of Culmore, and at all hazards ventured to sail by. The fort made some shots at her, but to no purpose. She, being got clear of that fort, arrived before the next battery, which fired also at her, but the ball flew too high. She came to the last battery; this did her no damage. She struck at the boom, which she forced presently, and so went cleverly up to the quay of Londonderry. What shouts of joy the town gave hereat you may easily imagine.[19]

It should be remembered that *A Jacobite Narrative of the War in Ireland* was written some years after the siege and the author's information came from other individuals. Thus it is not so surprising that he believed *Dartmouth* to have been the vessel that ran the gauntlet of the Jacobite batteries along the Foyle, broke the boom and took relief to the beleaguered city.

Richards also includes an account of how the boom was broken which was delivered to the camp at Inch on 30 July by 'several people . . . from the Irish camp' who had seen the ships pass up the Foyle 'with provisions to Derry quay on Sunday night last past'. These witnesses had seen the man of war lie within Culmore and batter 'all the upper part of the wall down, so that there is now no shelter for men'. But they differed in telling how the ships got up to the city. Two versions of the breaking of the boom were offered, one of which told of Shelley and his fellow seamen in the longboat. This was, however, an exaggerated version which included a 'boat with a house on it' that came to the boom where it stopped 'and of a sudden a man (a witch they say) struck three strokes with a hatchet upon the Boom, and cut [it] asunder, and so passed on' with the ships following.[20] The 'house'

---

*This name may possibly be Brennan.

might have been a form of protection against musket fire, as Kirke indicated by describing the longboat as being 'well barricado'd'.[21] The second version held that the two ships made the run together and struck the boom simultaneously, breaking it so that both were then able to pass on to the city.[22] Kirke's despatch to London noted that it was the weight of the *Mountjoy* that broke the boom after Shelley had wielded his axe. That report also contains the information that there were about four Jacobite guns at the boom 'and 2,000 small shot upon the river'; it also notes that five or six Williamite soldiers were killed, that Lieutenant Leys of Sir John Hanmer's Regiment was wounded and that Shelley was also injured.[23]

The passage of over three centuries has obliterated the stories of most of the individuals involved in the siege and associated operations and this has been the case especially with those who did not hold commissioned rank. Even the small boy who did such sterling service carrying despatches is not named by any of the chroniclers, and we know only the surname of that unfortunate swimmer McGimpsey who volunteered to carry despatches from the city to Kirke. However, there are a few exceptions and these include the men who broke the boom, John Shelley and his shipmates who manned *Swallow*'s longboat. Not only did Captain Wolfranc Cornwall reward them with a guinea apiece, although Shelley received five guineas, but he also wrote to the Admiralty on 8 October recommending each of the men to whom further payments were made, bringing their awards to £10 each.*[24]

Pointis' efforts had been in vain and suggest either that the boom had not been strong enough or that the metal used to hold the beams together had rusted to such an extent that at least one joint had broken when the *Mountjoy* hit. In spite of the first failed effort with the oaken boom, it seems most unlikely that de Pointis would have been guilty of creating a sub-standard defence since he was both an engineer and a naval officer who should have known exactly the pressure that was likely to be put on the boom. Against this, Louis' representative, Comte d'Avaux, considered that the breaking of the boom proved how poor a job de Pointis had done: 'the boom was so badly built that it could not resist the little boats that towed the two small vessels car-

---

*The wording of the resolution to make the reward up to £10 each is interesting: 'resolved that the Navy Board do cause each of the said ten men of the boat crew who shall appear to receive it the money already paid them made up to ten pounds each.' Did this mean that any who did not appear would not be paid?

rying the supplies'. He went on to say that the boom had 'more than once' already been damaged by the wind and the force of the tide. This further comment suggests that maintenance work on the boom had been inadequate, which was probably due to the fact that de Pointis was ill much of the time and unable to exercise the control he might otherwise have done.[25] There is also the fact that Richard Hamilton did not regard the boom as being important which would have reduced the importance given to maintenance when de Pointis was not exercising regular supervision.

However, the boom had never been intended to be the sole counter against Williamite ships coming up the Foyle. It formed part of a defence system in which the artillery batteries along the river were also crucial. We have seen that the Williamite commentators wrote that the Jacobite artillery poured a heavy fire into the relief squadron but the principal Jacobite account, from *A Light to the Blind*, takes a very different viewpoint.

> But it is not so easy to understand how came this ship to pass scot-free by so many batteries, and yet in four or five weeks before, three vessels attempting the same fact were repulsed. The king's soldiers answer that the gunners of the batteries, or some of them, were this morning, the thirty-first of July, drunk with brandy, which caused them to shoot at random. But still there remains a question, whether these officers became inebriated without any evil design, or whether they were made to drink of purpose to render them incapable to perform their duty that day; and whether the English money aboard the fleet in the pool was not working upon them for this effect during the time they lay there on the coast.[26]

The writer of that narrative goes on to state that 'these gunners lost Ireland through their neglect of duty'. His suggestion that the gunners – by which he really means the officers commanding the guns – had been bribed by the Williamites is implausible and more likely to be the result of paranoia than to be based on any real evidence.[27] A similar accusation was made following the Jacobite defeat at Aughrim in 1691: that the Jacobite general Henry Luttrell had, literally, sold the pass to the Williamites. And there is, of course, a parallel with the accusations made about Lundy, Walker and other leading Williamite figures. Both sides in this war were eager to attribute success to the intervention of the Almighty but any failures or setbacks were seen as being the result of human perfidy. The writer was also unaware of the fact that the three vessels that he thought had been trying to sail upriver some weeks before had not been doing so but had been carrying out a reconnaissance.

With the remains of the boom floating useless in the water, the two merchant ships passed through. HMS *Dartmouth* remained on station at Culmore and the *Jerusalem* 'came near the man of war, but no farther that night'. The cutter had been due to weigh anchor and enter the river on a signal from Leake's ship but 'the wind slackened, grew calm and changed about to the SW'.[28] In fact, *Dartmouth* remained on station at Culmore until 8 o'clock next morning 'by reason of the tide' during which time she returned the Jacobite fire five or six shots for one. The ship also endured considerable musket fire from the Jacobites on either side of the river but her casualties were remarkably light with but a single soldier killed and another wounded, while the ship's purser, Mr Lee, suffered a contusion. No serious damage was incurred.[29]

As the other ships 'made their way majestically to the City, to the inexpressible joy of the inhabitants, and to the utter disappointment of the enemy', *Phoenix* took the lead and was first to dock at the city where Captain Douglas was received by Governor Mitchelburne who told him that 'this will be a night of danger'.[30] Both vessels berthed at about 10 o'clock 'not saluted by the turbulent acclamations of the garrison, but with heartfelt and devout gratitude to him who is the unerring disposer of all events'.[31] Young conjectures that

> We can see the arrival of the *Mountjoy* and the *Phoenix* at Derry's quay. We can almost hear the acclamations of the starving population, and we can sympathise with the captain's weeping widow, who was meeting a dead husband.[32]

In *Ireland Preserved*, Mitchelburne attributes the following words to 'Evangelist', or Walker:

> Heaven has heard our prayers, the sighs and groans and shrieks of the distressed have reached the heavens, and has delivered us from the implacable, wicked and designing malice of our merciless enemies.[33]

Of the contemporary accounts, only that from Richards mentions that the merchant ships were towed in by longboats. He claims that these were manned by local people, who came out when the ships were close to Pennyburn,[34] but where the boats came from he does not explain; apart from the locally-built boat and the Jacobite boat captured at Dunalong, there were supposedly no boats in the city. Significantly, none of the local accounts include any mentions of these boats, suggesting that Richards, still on Inch, might have been misinformed. As the ships tied up at the quay the guns in the cathedral tower were fired to let the fleet know that the relief vessels had reached the city safely.[35]

The arrival of this squadron of the relief fleet brought an angry reaction from the Jacobites who opened fire on the quay and the city from across the river. Such was the danger to those unloading the vessels that blinds had to be constructed along the quay; these were improvized from casks and hogsheads filled with earth and built up to form a wall. In the course of the night the blinds were tested fully as the gunners over the river maintained a 'brisk and continued cannonading . . . against the town'.[36]

From the *Phoenix* those acting as stevedores, men detailed from each of the companies in the city, unloaded 800 containers of meal that had been brought from Scotland and for which a petition had been presented to the Scottish government. Browning's *Mountjoy* which could carry 135 tons, had brought 'beef, peas, flour, biscuits etc all of the best kind' which had been sent from England. These were all carried to the store houses.[37] This restocking of the stores brought, in Walker's words, 'unexpressible joy' to the garrison which he reckoned had but two days' rations left 'and among us all one pint of meal to each man'. Nine lean horses were all that remained for meat – where these came from is not made clear; the last horse had supposedly been slaughtered long since – and hunger and disease had reduced the one-time garrison of 7,500 to about 4,300, of whom at least a quarter were unfit for service.[38] The first issues of food from the newly-arrived provisions were made the following morning and must have been as great a boost to the morale of the garrison and people of the city as the sight of the *Mountjoy* and *Phoenix* making for the quay.

The siege was over. Richard Hamilton knew that the arrival of the relief ships would allow the garrison to hold out longer and how he must have rued his decision to countermand de Pointis' plan for a second boom and to carry out maintenance work on the boom that had been completed. He knew also that Kirke had a strong force on Inch and that this might march for Derry at any time while Schomberg was preparing an even larger force that would soon land in Ulster to link up with Kirke's contingent and the Enniskillen garrison. There was no alternative but for the Jacobite army to quit Derry. It had failed in its objective with every plan adopted seemingly doomed. On the day following the arrival of the *Mountjoy* and *Phoenix*, Ash commented that there was 'nothing worth note' although Mackenzie recorded that the Jacobites continued to fire on the city from their trenches.[39]

But the decision to quit was taken that day. According to the writer of *A Light to the Blind*, the decision was made by de Rosen who

> seeing the town relieved with provisions contrary to expectation, and that there was no other way at present to take it, judged it in vain to remain there any longer, and so he commanded the army to prepare for rising the next day, and for marching back into Leinster, and approaching to Dublin.[40]

On 1 August the Jacobite army decamped from Derry. It had lain before the city for fifteen weeks with the loss of some 2,000 men dead, a figure that probably underestimates considerably the true losses.[41] Walker, who wrote that the enemy 'ran away in the night time, [and] robbed and burnt all before them for several miles', also estimated the Jacobite dead at between 8,000 and 9,000 plus a hundred of their best officers. The scorched-earth tactic is confirmed by Ash who wrote that the enemy 'burned a great many houses in the County of Derry and elsewhere' and that, when he went to visit his own farm on 1 August, he found 'the roof of my house was smoking in the floor, and the doors falling off the hinges'.[42] Berwick was later to attain notoriety for his use of the same tactic elsewhere in Ireland, and it is possible that he was also advocating its use at Derry. A deserter from Berwick's camp who arrived at the Williamite base on Inch said that he had been with the duke at Castlefinn when several officers arrived with the news that relief had reached the defenders of the city, An enraged Berwick

> flung his hat on the ground and said, 'The rogues have broken the siege and we are all undone.' He says also, it was at once resolved to immediately quit the siege, and burn, and waste, all before them; but upon second consideration they have despatched a messenger to the late King James at Dublin, of which they expect an answer. In the mean time, they have sent out orders to all the Catholics to send away all their goods and chattels, and to be ready to march themselves whenever the army moves. It is also resolved to drive all the Protestants away before them, and to lay the country in waste as much as they can.[43]

So it would seem that Berwick was the man responsible for ordering so much destruction. The troops at Inch saw several 'great fires' in the direction of Letterkenny, to the south-west, which they believed to be villages set alight by the retreating Jacobites. Under cover of darkness, a company of musketeers, under Captain Billing, crossed from Inch to the mainland near Burt castle and then marched about a mile before surprising a small guard of Jacobite dragoons and securing a safe passage to Inch for several Protestant families with their cattle and whatever other goods were found en route. Confirmation that the Jacobites were quitting the area was provided when several parties of their horsemen were seen 'setting fire to all the neighbouring villages, which gives us great hopes that they don't design any long stay in these parts'. Kirke reported that the Jacobites 'blew up Culmore Castle, burnt Red Castle and all the houses down the river'.[44] By then he had returned to Lough Swilly in HMS *Swallow* and come ashore at Inch.

According to Walker, some of the garrison, 'after refreshment with a proper share of our new provisions', left the city to see what the enemy was doing. Jacobite soldiers were observed on the march and the Williamites set off in pursuit. This proved to be an ill-advised move as they encountered a cavalry unit performing rearguard duty for the Jacobites and the horsemen engaged their pursuers, killing seven of them.[45]

Of course, there had been two wings of the Jacobite army, separated by the Foyle. These made their discrete ways to the nearest point at which a junction could be effected, in the vicinity of Strabane. Retreating from before the city's western and southern defences, the Jacobites made their way to Lifford, back to the area of the fords where they had achieved one of their few real successes of the campaign. Likewise, those who had formed the eastern wing of the besieging force withdrew to Strabane, although some are known to have moved east towards Coleraine. Strabane appears to have been a temporary stop for the army as the commanders awaited further news. What news they received was not good: the Jacobite force in Fermanagh had been defeated at the battle of Newtownbutler where Lord Mountcashel had suffered the greatest defeat yet inflicted on Jacobite arms in Ulster.[46]

On 3 August news reached the camp at Inch that the main Jacobite army was now at Strabane, and Kirke felt confident enough to send Captain Henry Withers to Liverpool on board HMS *Dartmouth* with a despatch for 'King and Parliament [detailing] our great success against the Irish Papists'.[47] Ash recorded that, at Lifford, the Jacobites were in such haste to be away that they 'burst three of their great guns, left one of their mortar pieces, and threw many of their arms into the lake'.[48] By bursting the guns he meant that the Jacobite gunners had destroyed their weapons; this was usually done by dismounting the barrels, filling them with powder and burying them muzzle down before discharging them. This action had been taken following news of the disaster at Newtownbutler which was the final factor in the Jacobite decision to quit Ulster. In their going they dumped many weapons in the river and left behind many of their comrades who were sick. Between the city and Strabane, some groups of Jacobite grenadiers who were engaged in setting fire to houses were taken prisoner by Williamite troops.[49]

A few Williamites were probably fit enough to take part in such forays outside the town, but it is more likely that the patrols were from the fresh troops who had landed in the city with the *Mountjoy*, *Phoenix* and *Jerusalem*, although they would have numbered only about 120 men. Some foragers from the city brought in a 'great number of black cattle from the country for the use of the garrison', but these dairy cattle were restored to their owners the following day. It seems that not everything had been destroyed by the Jacobites and, since these cattle belonged to Williamites, it also appears that those in the vicinity of the city had not suffered too much in the days of the siege.[50] Much of their losses probably occurred as a result of the Jacobite forces venting their anger at failing to take the city.

With the Jacobite army withdrawing, Walker expressed some impatience to see Kirke, whom he described as 'under God and King, our Deliverer'. He sent a delegation of five men, including two clergymen, to Inch to meet Kirke, give him an account of the raising of the siege, convey the city's thanks to him and invite him to come and meet the garrison.[51] The latter invitation was superfluous since Kirke would have intended to come to the city anyway. Richards recorded that Walker's men stayed all night at Inch due to the very wet and windy weather. Following the visit of that delegation, Kirke sent Colonel Steuart and Jacob Richards to the city 'to congratulate our deliverance' according to Walker but, according to Richards, to give the orders necessary for repairs to the city and its fortifications.[52] This was a precursor to Kirke's own arrival which took place on Sunday 4 August. On the same day he had ordered a detachment of seventy-two men from each regiment 'to march over to Londonderry, there to encamp and make up huts for the several regiments against they arrive'.[53]

Windmill Hill had been chosen as the site for the encampment of the relieving forces. The local regiments were to remain within the walls, and the two forces were to be segregated to prevent an outbreak of disease among the newly-arrived troops. The camp at Inch was to be abandoned save for the hospital and a small garrison of 200 men with six artillery pieces commanded by Captain Thomas Barbour. Moving the relief force's supplies and impedimenta required the deployment of the ships to carry them out of the Swilly and around the north of Inishowen into Lough Foyle and hence to the city. That a small garrison was to be left at Inch suggests that there was some concern that not all the Jacobites had departed the region. On the 5th some 'Irish skulking rogues came back to Muff, Ballykelly, Newtown and Magilligan, and burned houses which had escaped' the previous depredations. These 'skulking rogues' would have been from that part of the Jacobite army that was falling back to Coleraine.[54] (The Muff referred to here is the modern village of Eglinton in County Londonderry, while Newtown is Limavady.*)

Kirke was unimpressed by Derry and its defences, writing that

> since I was born I never saw a town of so little strength to rout an army with so many generals against it. The walls and outwork are not touched [but] the houses are generally broke down by the bombs; there have been five hundred and ninety one shot into the town.[55]

The major-general had already had a report from Richards about the state of the city. This had also included the observation that there was 'little appearance of a siege by the damage done to the houses or walls'. However, Richards went on to report that

> the people had suffered extremely, having for 5 weeks lived on horses, dogs, cats etc. They lost not during the whole siege 100 men by the sword, but near 6,000 through sickness and want and there still remained about 5,000 able fighting men in the town, who abound with the spoil of those they have killed or taken prisoner.[56]

When Kirke arrived at Bishop's Gate he was received with courtesy and some ceremony. There Mitchelburne, who would have already known him, and Walker, with other officers of the garrison, members of the corporation and 'a great many persons of all sorts' met him and offered

---

*There were two villages called Muff, one on either side of Lough Foyle, until the villagers of the County Londonderry village petitioned the viceroy to have the name of their village changed. The then viceroy, Lord Eglinton, agreed and the village was renamed in his honour. The name Muff survives in the nearby Muff Glen, a local beauty spot.

him the keys to the city as well as the civic sword and mace, all of which Kirke returned to those who had presented the individual items. Soldiers lined the streets to receive their deliverer while the cannon on the walls fired in salute. Even the city's sick, of whom there were many, made the effort to crawl to their doors and windows to see Kirke and his entourage. Mitchelburne and Walker entertained Kirke to dinner which was described as being 'very good ... considering the times; small sour beer, milk and water, with some little quantity of brandy, was and is the best of our liquors'. Following dinner he went to the Windmill to look at the camp for his soldiers. Ash noted that he rode on a white mare that belonged to Mitchelburne which the latter 'had saved all the siege'.[57] Presumably this was 'Bloody Bones', the charger gifted to Mitchelburne by Clotworthy Skeffington. One wonders that this fine animal had survived, but perhaps she had been kept outside the city?

As Kirke was preparing to return to Inch, three horsemen arrived carrying letters from the governors of Enniskillen. These brought official news of the success of the Williamite forces under Colonel Wolseley and Lieutenant-Colonel Tiffin at Newtownbutler. Details of the battle were included while, later that night, Kirke also received the news that Berwick was decamping from Strabane and that most of the army that had been before Derry had gone to Charlemont en route to Dublin. Kirke then rode back to Inch while Richards remained in the city to make further preparations for the arrival of the remainder of the relief force. Meanwhile Kirke had invited several of the leading citizens to dine with him on Inch the following day. This might not have been the most convivial of occasions for Walker, since Kirke took the opportunity to suggest that it was time for him 'to return to his own profession'.[58]

Kirke's three regiments arrived in the city on the 7th with the major-general at their head; their baggage was en route by sea. Once again there was a rapturous reception, with the defenders coming out in force to give the troops three cheers as well as a salute from their cannon. It also seems that all the garrison's personal weapons were discharged as part of a *feu de joie*. And there was another dinner after which a council of war was held to which only field officers were invited. This meeting discussed regulating the local regiments, the civil administration of the city and 'several other necessary things', which included the market and cleansing the town. The latter task must have been of almost Herculean proportions. It was further decided that the following day would be one of thanksgiving.[59]

And so, on 8 August, the city rejoiced for its deliverance. There was considerable merry-making but the day began with a sermon preached by Mr John Know, who told his congregation, which included Kirke, of the nature of the siege and 'the great deliverance, which from Almighty God we have obtained'. That evening the city's regiments were drawn up around the walls and fired three volleys while the cannon, too, were fired in salute. A proclamation was also issued stating that anyone who was not in the ranks of one of the regiments and had not resided in the city prior to the siege should return to their own homes before the following Monday. Nor were any goods to be taken out of the city without permission. With the Jacobites now far away, the bureaucrats were back in place. And it seemed that the closest Jacobites were at Coleraine 'where they were fortifying themselves'.[60]

Walker took ship for England the next day, there to produce and have published his 'true account' of the siege. Needless to say, this true account would be centred around the activities of Governor Walker, who would thus become the hero of the siege. The *London Gazette* for 19–22 August carried a report from Edinburgh that Walker had reached that city on the 13th with news that the Enniskilleners, under Colonels Wolseley and Tiffin, but whom he called Owsley and Tiffany, had routed the Jacobites on their retreat from Londonderry and caused heavy losses. This was Walker's version of the battle of Newtownbutler which, in fact, had been fought between a different Jacobite force from that retreating from Derry and the defenders of Enniskillen. From Edinburgh he made his way to London and was received at Hampton Court by William and Mary; one report suggests that he received £5,000 'for his service at Londonderry'.[61] For Mitchelburne, Murray and many others their sole reward was to be thanked for their services.

For those left behind in the city there were some indications of what lay in store for them. All who expected pay for their service in defending the city were told to appear in their arms at 10 o'clock on the following Monday. Whatever they anticipated, they were to be disappointed: no payment was ever made. There was a popular belief among the soldiers that Kirke would distribute £2,000 but 'they soon found themselves mistaken, not only in that, but in their hopes of continuing in their present posts'.[62] One man who had provided £1,000 to support the city in its travails was the Stronge who owned the land across the river. When Sir Patrick Macrory was writing his book on the siege he was told by Sir Norman Stronge, a direct descendant of that landowner, that he still held two notes, signed by Mitchelburne, promising that the money would be repaid. In 1980 Sir Norman calculated that the IOUs represented, with interest, some £60m. These notes were lost when republican terrorists attacked Sir Norman's home at Tynan Abbey in County Armagh in 1981, murdering both Sir Norman and his son James before setting fire to and destroying their home.[63]

On the 12th Kirke reduced the garrison's regiments to four. Colonel Monroe's and Colonel Lance's Regiments were amalgamated, Walker's Regiment was given to Colonel Robert White, Baker's to Colonel Thomas St John – the would-be engineer of Inch – and Mitchelburne retained the regiment he had commanded throughout the siege, that which had been Clotworthy Skeffington's.[64] As White died soon after this re-organization his regiment passed to Colonel John Caulfield.[65] No records have survived of the regiment formed by the amalgamation of Monroe's and Lance's Regiments, and so it would seem that the new unit had a very brief existence. This might have been less than a month, as Kenneth Ferguson notes that a royal warrant of 16 September adopted only three Londonderry battalions; Kirke was ordered to treat unplaced officers as supernumerary until vacancies could be found for them.[66] Caulfield's Regiment had been disbanded by 1694 and the surviving regiments, Mitchelburne's and St John's, were disbanded by 1698 by which time the War of the League of Augsburg had ended.[67] In contrast, those regiments formed in Enniskillen had a much longer existence with three of them surviving, albeit in much changed form, to this day: Tiffin's Regiment was the progenitor of the present Royal Irish Regiment while today's Royal Dragoon Guards may be traced back to dragoon regiments raised in Enniskillen in 1689.[68] However, in 1693 some survivors of the siege formed part of a new regiment, Henry Cunningham's Regiment of Dragoons, raised in Ulster. In time, this regiment was ranked as the 8th Dragoons and later as 8th King's Royal Irish Hussars. In 1958 amalgamation with 4th Queen's Own Hussars created the Queen's Royal Irish Hussars,[69] the regiment that led the coalition advance into Kuwait in the Gulf War of 1991; the Hussars' leading tank was called 'Derry' and the regiment was commanded by a Derryman.* Perhaps some of the spirit of Murray's Horse had passed down the centuries to the men who manned the Hussars' Challenger tanks.

To return to 1689, Kirke continued his work on reforming the garrison, but he also organized a force to attack the Jacobites at Coleraine. However, when that force, led it seems by Kirke himself, approached Coleraine, the local garrison decided that it did not want to engage in

---

*A further amalgamation has created the Queen's Royal Hussars (Queen's Own and Royal Irish).[70]

a battle with the butcher of Sedgemoor and the town was abandoned. A plan had been made to destroy the bridge leading into Coleraine, thus at least delaying any Williamite advance if not assisting a Jacobite defence. This had involved coating the timbers of the bridge with pitch which would then be set alight as the foe approached. In the event the Jacobite garrison was so keen to quit the town that the bridge was left standing, those whose assigned task it had been to start the fire showing no heart for the job. The news that Coleraine had been regained reached London at the same time as the news that the town of Sligo had also been abandoned by the Jacobites.[71] The latter information was far from accurate: Sligo did not fall into Williamite hands until 1691, following the battle of Aughrim.

The Williamite army continued its task of clearing Ulster. On 16 August Schomberg sailed from England 'with a fair wind' at the head of the main body of the force that was to be deployed in Ireland.[72] At the beginning of September this army was engaged in the siege of Carrickfergus where Jacob Richards was wounded in both thigh and shoulder.[73] Before long most of Ulster was in Williamite hands, with only pockets of Jacobite resistance remaining in the southern part of the province.

The key element in this campaign had been the siege of Derry. Had the city fallen to the Jacobites in April, or failed to hold out as it did, then the Williamite cause in Ulster would have been lost. Enniskillen could not have held out against a Jacobite army no longer distracted by the task of reducing the recalcitrant city and nor would Sligo have been able to sustain a defence for much longer. That the city on the Foyle was the vital element in saving all Ireland for the Williamites was recognized across the three kingdoms. George Walker, the soi-disant governor of Londonderry, was feted in London and took full advantage of the opportunity to further his own reputation with the publication of his book *A True Account of the Siege of London-Derry*. On 19 November he was thanked by the House of Commons for his services at Londonderry and responded:

> As for the service I have done, it is very little, and does not deserve this favour you have done me: I shall give the thanks of this House to those concerned with me, as you desire, and dare assure you, that both I and they will continue faithful to the service of King William and Queen Mary to the end of their lives.[74]

As the tide of war flowed elsewhere the people of north-west Ulster tried to begin their lives anew, safe from the threats that had so recently beset them. But it would be a very difficult task and one in which many of them would not succeed. The scars of those 105 days in 1689 would never fade and the attitude of the government at Westminster towards the survivors would help to ensure that, as we shall see later.

Notes

1: Walker, op cit, p. 62; Ash, op cit, pp. 98–9; Mackenzie, op cit, p. 54; Simpson, op cit, p. 148
2: *London Gazette*, 1–5 August 1689; Simpson, op cit, p. 148; Ash, op cit, p. 99; Walker, op cit, pp. 62–3
3: Richards, op cit, p. 38
4: Mackenzie, op cit, p. 55; Ash, op cit, p. 99
5: Powley, op cit, p. 274
6: Ash, op cit, p. 99
7: Powley, op cit, p. 241
8: *London Gazette*, 1–5 August 1689
9: Ash, op cit, p. 99; Walker, op cit, p. 63; Mackenzie, op cit, pp. 54–5
10: Mackenzie, op cit, p. 55
11: Young, op cit, pp. 115–6
12: Ash, op cit, p. 99
13: Mackenzie, op cit, p. 55
14: Ibid; Walker, op cit, p. 63
15: Ash, op cit, p. 99
16: Walker, op cit, p. 63; Simpson, op cit, pp. 148–9
17: NA Kew, ADM3/2; Powley, op cit, p. 250
18: *Franco-Irish Correspondence*, letter from Fumeron to Louvois, 13/3 August, p. 165.
19: Gilbert, pp. 83–4
20: Richards, op cit, pp. 49–50
21: *London Gazette*, 1–5 August 1689
22: Richards, op cit, pp. 49–50
23: *London Gazette*, 1–5 August 1689
24: NA Kew, ADM3/2
25: Avaux, op cit, pp. 375–6
26: Gilbert, op cit, p. 84
27: Ibid
28: Ash, op cit, p. 100; *London Gazette*, 1–5 August 1689
29: *London Gazette*, 1–5 August 1689
30: Simpson, op cit, p. 149; Mitchelburne, op cit
31: Simpson, op cit, p. 149

32: Young, op cit, p. 116
33: Mitchelburne, op cit
34: Richards, op cit, p. 50
35: Ash, op cit, p. 100
36: Ibid; Mackenzie, op cit, p. 55; Simpson, op cit, p. 149; Mitchelburne, op cit
37: Ash, op cit, p. 100; Mackenzie, op cit, p. 55
38: Walker, op cit, p. 63
39: Ash, op cit, p. 101; Mackenzie, op cit, p. 55
40: Gilbert, op cit, p. 85
41: Ibid
42: Walker, op cit, p. 65; Ash, op cit, p. 101
43: Richards, op cit, pp. 50–1
44: Ibid; *London Gazette*, 12–15 August 1689
45: Walker, op cit, p. 64
46: *London Gazette*, 19–22 August & 22–26 August 1689; Gilbert, op cit, p. 85; Ash, op cit, pp. 101– 2
47: Richards, op cit, p. 52
48: Ash, op cit, p. 101
49: Mackenzie, op cit, p. 56
50: Ash, op cit, p. 101
51: Walker, op cit, p. 65
52: Ibid; Richards, op cit, p. 52
53: Richards, op cit, p. 52
54: Ibid, pp. 52–3; Ash, op cit, p. 102
55: *London Gazette*, 22–26 August 1689
56: Ibid
57: Ash, op cit, pp. 101–2; Richards, op cit, pp. 52–3; Walker, op cit, pp. 65–6; Mackenzie, op cit, p. 57; Simpson, op cit, pp. 151–2
58: Richards, op cit, p. 53; Walker, op cit, p. 66
59: Richards, op cit, p. 55; Ash, op cit, p. 102
60: Ash, op cit, pp. 102–3; Richards, op cit, p. 55
61: Walker, op cit, p. 66; Ash, op cit, p. 103; Mackenzie, op cit, p. 57; *London Gazette*, 19–22 August 1689; Gilbert, op cit, p 87
62: Ash, op cit, p. 103; Mackenzie, op cit, p. 57
63: Macrory, op cit, p. 214n
64: Ash, op cit, p. 103; Mackenzie, op cit, p. 57
65: Mackenzie, op cit, p. 57; Ash, op cit, p. 105
66: Ferguson, *The Organisation of King William's Army in Ireland, 1689–92*, IS XVIII No. 70, p. 64
67: Frederick, *Lineage Book of British Armed Forces 1660–1978*, p. 392, 403 & 410
68: Harris, *The Irish Regiments 1683–1999*, pp. 283–5 & p. 69

69: Ibid, p. 87
70: Ibid, p. 88
71: *London Gazette*, 29 Aug–1 Sep 1689
72: Ibid, 15–19 August 1689
73: Ibid, 5–9 September 1689
74: HLRO, *HoCJ*, 19 Nov 1689

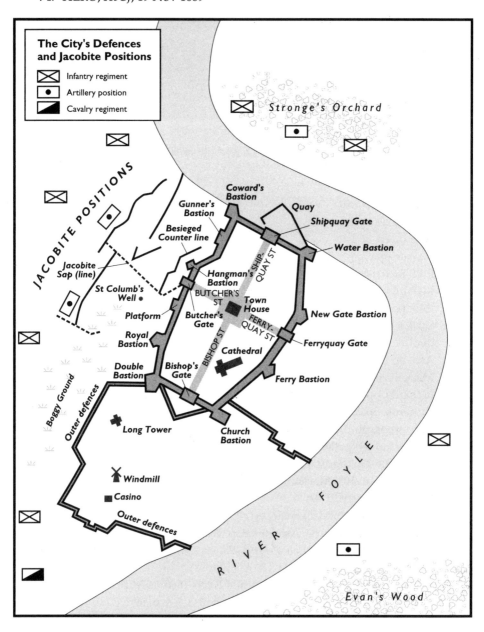

CHAPTER ELEVEN

The Fruits of Victory?

Might the siege have had a different ending? And, if so, what might the results have been? Was there at any time a possibility that the Jacobites might have triumphed? And what was the military and historical significance of the Williamite victory at Derry?

With the benefit of hindsight it is easy to dismiss the possibility of any other ending to the siege; but if we recall the early and middle days of April 1689 there existed then a real possibility of Jacobite success. And that was a possibility that appeared so tangible that it caused a large proportion of the Protestant population of Ireland to flee to England or Scotland for safety. So perhaps it is safe, if paradoxical, to say that the siege might have had a different ending had it never got underway in the first instance. But this leads on to a more pertinent question: why did the Jacobites lose?

For an answer to that question, we need first to examine the Jacobite objectives, the reason or reasons they laid siege to the city at all. It is here that we find one of the first clues to their failure. In warfare commanders must have clear objectives. This was not the case with the Jacobite forces that marched into Ulster and set their faces towards Derry. The failure to define a clear overall objective was inherent in the Jacobite command almost from the start. Remember that Richard Hamilton, who led the first Jacobite army into Ulster, did so with the objective of defeating those who held out against Tyrconnel and, therefore, King James. Hamilton's army, expecting to meet no more than lightly-armed and poorly-trained local forces, marched north for a short, sharp campaign that would bring Ulster into line. Following the battle of the fords in April, the road to Derry was wide open for the Jacobite army. Their cavalry and dragoons had the speed and mobility to race for the city and take it while much of its garrison was still trudging its weary way back to the security of its walls. But Hamilton failed to launch his cavalry and dragoons along that road, thereby denying them the full fruits of the victory they had already gained at Clady, Lifford and Long Causeway.

> This halt gave opportunity to the rebels to get safe into Londonderry, and hindered the loyal cavalry and dragoons to be in with them pell mell, besides their slaughtering of the runaways in the road, and taking of prisoners, which is looked upon to be the first imprudent mismanagement of the northern enterprise...[1]

In doing so, Hamilton ignored that age-old military dictum that the fruits of victory are to be found in the pursuit. Why did he do so? Perhaps he believed that the city would fall anyway and that its defenders were so dispirited that, in common with those at Coleraine, Dromore and elsewhere in Ulster, they would accept defeat. Or had his spies told him that the relief force from England was already in the city? If he believed that two regular infantry regiments were already behind the walls, then he might well have hesitated to send his horsed soldiers off in pursuit and decided that it might be necessary to bring a mixed force of cavalry and infantry to the city to bring about its surrender. Whatever the reason behind Hamilton's strategy, he lost the best opportunity of capturing Londonderry that ever presented itself to the Jacobites.

The overall strategic picture had changed with the arrival in Ireland of King James and that monarch's decision to come north and, specifically, to the rebel city of Londonderry. James had hoped that his arrival outside the city would bring its citizens to their senses, thereby ending rebellion in Ulster. Thus the force that came north with him was not one that was prepared for a lengthy campaign. In common with Hamilton's, it was a light force, deficient in all the weaponry and equipment needed for an extended campaign or for a siege. Even when combined, the two forces were still deficient in terms of all that was needed for campaigning or besieging. Nor did they have the numbers considered necessary to mount a siege: as we have already seen, Vauban held that the besieging force should outnumber the besieged by ten to one but that it should not be less than 20,000 strong although Napoleon later recommended that the superiority should be four to one. Even by that latter guideline the Jacobite army should have numbered 30,000 men at least while, by Vauban's estimate, it should have been over 70,000 strong.

Neither had the Jacobites made their minds up about whether seizing the city was their army's primary aim, or whether that city would be but a stepping-stone for a campaign in Scotland. James' de facto prime minister, Melfort, was among those advocating the use of Derry as a point from which to launch an expedition to Scotland. Once across the sea, the Irish Jacobite army could combine with the Scottish Jacobite army to secure that country for the Stuart cause, after which Scotland could be used as a base for an advance into England. Such a plan appealed to James, but no effort was made to co-ordinate all the elements necessary to launch an expedition. As late as 17 May, James was writing to Viscount Dundee assuring him of support 'as soon as the siege of Derry is over'.[2] Thus he had the Scottish Jacobites continuing to hope that he would cross the North Channel and raise the Stuart flag in Scotland.

Some years later, after the deaths of both James and William, the author of *A Light to the Blind* was arguing that the abandoned Scottish strategy was the one that ought to have been followed. He wrote:

> The affirmative opinion says, that (upon a supposition that Londonderry be early taken, as it might have been done) twenty-five thousand Irish along with the king, in the end of May, transported into the highlands of Scotland, would in their marches so increase by the accession of loyal subjects, that at the time they were got into England the rebellious party would be too weak to make head against the loyal army, because their usurpation was not yet settled in the land. The ten thousand remaining in Ireland would be sufficient to preserve that kingdom in duty, after being made quiet by the expugnation of Londonderry. It is certain that celerity in resolving and in executing is the best medium to conquer an enemy.

As events unfurled, the Jacobite army sat outside Derry for more than three months during which there were times when it seemed uncertain as to whether it was laying siege to the city, conducting a blockade or merely carrying out a pointless exercise. For many of the rank and file the latter might well have appeared to be the case, since there seemed to be little resolution on the part of their commanders. An exception to this latter state of affairs occurred when Conrad de Rosen took charge outside the city for a time.

This illustrates another failure of the Jacobite hierarchy: the apparent lack of a clear line of command. When James departed for Dublin in late-April there were several generals in the Jacobite camp, including the Frenchmen Maumont and Pusignan as well as Richard Hamilton, but there was an absence of clarity about the chain of command. With the presence of the Duke of Berwick, James' natural son, this situation would have been exacerbated; and when Rosen returned in late-June the Jacobite army's chain of command must have been even more smudged. Throughout the siege this absence of a clearly-defined commander-in-chief was a major problem for the besiegers.

There was one major problem with the Scottish strategy: how to transport an army from Ulster to Scotland? James had no navy, although three fifty-gun French frigates – *la Lutine*, *la Jolie* and *la Tempête*, under command of du Quesne Mosnier – had been lent to him by Louis and he would have had to call on the French to provide both the escorts and the merchant ships to carry his troops. Du Quesne Mosnier's small squadron proved a considerable nuisance to Rooke and his command and at one time captured the two Scottish ships, *Janet* and *Pelican*, taking them as prizes into Dublin. They had also landed a small Jacobite force in Lochaber.[4] The achievements of this trio illustrate the difference that more active naval involvement by the French might have made. But the Battle of Bantry Bay had made the French reluctant to risk their 'great ships' in action against both the Royal and Dutch Navies in the waters around Ireland. Thus French support was not to be forthcoming. Nor was there much possibility of requisitioning sufficient civilian vessels to transport an army. The Scottish administration passed an Act for Securing Suspected Persons on 22 March which was followed with an embargo on ships sailing to Ireland. This latter measure was intended to forestall the danger of 'allowing ships and other vessels liberty to pass from this kingdom to Ireland in regard they be made use of in the case of an invasion for transporting forces hither'. Although there is little doubt that James would have gathered considerable support in Scotland and northern England, the difficulty of moving a sizeable Irish Jacobite army across the North Channel without the support of the French navy and without French merchant ships made the Scottish strategy a pipe dream.

The Jacobites were not alone in their need for a clearly-defined commander in chief. Before the siege even began, Robert Lundy had made clear his desire for a general officer to take command of the Williamite forces in the north-west of Ireland. Twice during March he had written to Lord Shrewsbury stressing, inter alia, the need for generals to take command in the region; even when a council of war in Londonderry was making plans to take the field against the Jacobites at the fords, Lundy was elected to command the field force rather than assuming the appointment as might have been seen to be his right as the senior officer present.[6] Why was this? It might be argued that his attitude at the council of war was indicative of a man who was about to betray his comrades and that this was to be expected of 'Lundy the traitor'. Equally it might be argued that this was the action of a man who knew his own limits as a commander. Taken with his two requests to Shrewsbury for general officers to be sent to Ireland, the latter is the much more likely explanation. Lundy knew that he had reached the limit of his ability as a field commander; he was a man who might be happy and confident commanding a battalion in action but not a force of several battalions. That was a task for a more senior officer, a general with experience in such matters. Lundy did not consider himself to be such a man.

Lundy's handling of the battle of the fords supports this argument. One would not expect to see the tactical genius of a Marlborough or a Sarsfield in such an encounter although one would expect to see, at least, the skills of a journeyman commander; but these are sadly missing from Lundy's actions that day. This was an officer who had made dispositions as best as he could on the basis of his understanding of battlefield tactics, but that understanding was restricted by Lundy's own restricted experience of command and of war; the latter was gained mostly in Tangier. He relied on his estimation of the Jacobite army to be as lacking in training, discipline and co-ordination as his own command but in that estimation he had made, as we have seen in Chapter Four, the fundamental error of failing to appreciate that the Jacobite heavy cavalry were trained, disciplined and well led. This error was to be the undoing of Lundy's force and, in all probability, the point at which his own morale began to collapse. And that morale had already been fragile as we have seen from his requests to Shrewsbury. It would seem that Robert Lundy had been placed in a situation in which he had no wish to be. Those, such as Walker, and the anonymous witness to the House of Lords, who espoused faith in him would not have found that faith reflected in Lundy's own mind. Far from being a villain, as many would portray him, Robert Lundy was a victim of circumstances.

Lundy was later exonerated of attempting to betray the city of Londonderry and returned to the military career. (In October 1689 he petitioned the government to allow him to stand trial in London as all the witnesses in his case were then in that city.)[7] He served as Adjutant-General of the Portuguese army some years later although he was paid by Britain. Surely this negates the earlier argument by suggesting that Lundy had the qualities needed for a senior commander? That would be a mistaken conclusion to reach. His role as adjutant-general was a staff post with his work being of an administrative nature rather than of a fighting nature; he had no command responsibilities. One can accuse Robert Lundy of being lacking in confidence, of being a defeatist, of being an incompetent commander, and each of these accusations can be supported with firm evidence, but it is much more difficult to find such evidence to substantiate any accusation of treachery against him. Those who have accused him of being a traitor have done so on evidence that is, at best, only circumstantial, and they also forget, conveniently, the basic fact that Londonderry would not have withstood the siege had it not been for the preparations made for a siege by Robert Lundy. Finally, it should be noted that Lundy was among the names attainted for treason by the Irish parliament in May 1689.

Earlier it was noted that the siege might have had a different ending had it never got underway in the first instance. Since this appears to be a contradictory statement it requires some explanation. The objective of the Jacobite army was to take Londonderry rather than lay siege to it. That army was not prepared for a siege of any duration but was constituted for a campaign of movement in which its opponents would be taken off balance and forced to capitulate. A siege was another matter altogether. Perhaps the best and most succinct description of a siege is that of a prolonged artillery duel. Thus the essence of a siege was something that the Jacobite army lacked: artillery.

We have already noted that a permanent artillery arm had not been added to the army of Ireland until 1684 although there had already been an Irish Board of Ordnance, albeit subordinated to its English equivalent. Until March 1689 the Irish Master-General of the Ordnance had been Lord Mountjoy who, on being sent to France by Tyrconnel, was succeeded by Lord Mountcashel, a man with little experience of artillery. Nor did he exhibit much interest in his post, of him, Rosen commented that he had still not visited the arsenal in Dublin a month after his appointment.[8] The existing disadvantages of the Jacobite artillery, including a considerable shortage of weaponry, was exacerbated by Mountcashel's apparent indolence.

The shortage of weapons was not the principal disadvantage suffered by the Jacobite artillery. There was also a great dearth of trained personnel to serve the guns. Gunners have always been recognized as requiring greater skills than other soldiers, a trait they have shared with engineers. In the British Army the training of artillery and engineer officers was even conducted at a different establishment than that of cavalry and infantry officers until the Second World War. This was the Royal Military Academy at Woolwich, known as 'The Shop', which produced those specialist officers and, from 1922, officers for the Royal Corps of Signals also. To practise the science of gunnery has always required a higher level of education, especially scientific and mathematical, than that required by infantry or cavalry officers. Gunnery was governed by laws that were scientific – although the science of ballistics had yet to be defined – and there were many sets of rules to be learned. Numerous manuals had to be read and understood and thus, although some still considered gunners to be practitioners of black arts, the contemporary gunner was already a member of a military elite.

The establishment of the Irish Board of Ordnance under Mountjoy had numbered fifty-nine, including that worthy himself, with forty-six of those personnel being gunners or mattrosses, the latter being gunners' assistants. These men had all been Protestants and had taken ship to England following Tyrconnel's purging of the army, thus leaving the Irish army without any gunners at all. Within the Irish Catholic community there was virtually no tradition of involvement in artillery and nor was there any grounding in mathematics save for the elite.[9] Hence the Jacobite army faced a real predicament: it needed to recruit gunners quickly but there were very few people with the appropriate educational background. Although some personnel were recruited we have no accurate idea of how many and thus the reliance on French artillery. Those Irishmen who became artillery officers made a poor impression on their French allies, being described as indolent, ill-mannered and lacking knowledge. At Coleraine, Hamilton's Irish gunners were described as being so maladroit that they were incapable of hitting a house.[10] Later, as the *Mounjoy* and the *Phoenix* were being towed up the Foyle only a single round from the Jacobite shore batteries found its mark in the merchant ships, this being attributed to the gunners being inebriated.[11] It is much more a sign of the gunners lacking the basic skills of their profession and suggests that their officers had been negligent in carrying out training. This is the greatest indictment that could be levelled against those officers.

The French gunners who arrived with James were too few in number to perform all the tasks required of them during the siege, even if they had had the requisite number of guns. They also appeared to be given to much disagreement among themselves, since one of them, Macary, was killed in a duel with an Italian gunner called Bada.[12] Avaux also records this incident in a litany of woes relating to the gunners, including the death of Massé, struck by a cannon ball while siting a battery.

Pointis was recovering from his wound at Pennyburn, Dumont was engaged in the field, while Saint Martin, who was later killed at Newtownbutler, was in Dublin. Avaux doubted the ability of Dastier, a fine young man who had done well under Massé's orders, which he had followed to the letter, to act as the chief gunner since he lacked sufficient experience for such a role.[13] The friction between French and Irish soldiers also militated against the latter's gunners learning much from their allies; one cannot imagine the French officers being inclined to spend time on training Irish gunners.

As for the gunners, so also for the engineers. There was no strong engineer tradition in the Irish army and those Irishmen who had become engineers had gone to the English army; these included the Richards brothers, Jacob and Michael. Once again, most of the responsibility for engineering fell on the French officers of whom there were too few to be able to provide the full range of skills and knowledge needed by the Jacobite army. Although Irish soldiers might have served as labourers, or pioneers, the lack of trained engineer officers was yet another major drawback for the Jacobites and contributed to their lack of success at Londonderry.

The Jacobite infantry has come in for much criticism from many writers. While it is true that the army was ill-equipped, poorly-trained and had inadequate leadership in its early days, this did not remain the case, and the army that fought in the later battles of the Irish war showed marked improvements on that which was deployed in the early days of the war, including the period of the siege. Because of these shortcomings it would be easy to assume that the Irish army was composed of unsuitable manpower but this could not be further from the truth. As he travelled through Ireland, Avaux noted the fine physiques of the many Irish peasants he saw along the way, and he was later to recruit Irishmen for French service. They were 'the finest men one could see' with the shortest of the infantrymen being over 5 foot 10 inches in height and the grenadiers and pikemen being about 6 foot 1 inch;[14] this suggests that the Irish peasants were generally well-nourished. While regretting the fact that these men were but half-trained, he recognized their potential, which was to be shown to its full in the Irish Brigade that was formed in the French army. Although the Jacobite infantry at Derry was still in the part-trained phase, it did show signs of the potential that it might have reached: the second attack on Windmill Hill is a good example of this, as is the attack on the Butcher's Gate and the nearby half-bastion. Thus it is worth considering the training of infantry soldiers at this time.

As already noted there were no regimental training depots nor any organized system of training and, in time of war, raw recruits generally learned the trade of soldiering with their regiments. This was not usually a problem if the number of recruits was small since they could be placed under the wing of experienced officers and NCOs from whom they could learn the rudiments of soldiering.[15] Of course, those officers and NCOs needed to be not only conscientious but men with a flair for the job of training; not every good soldier makes a good trainer. The Jacobite army suffered from the fact that the majority of its soldiers were raw recruits with few sufficiently experienced officers and NCOs to train them. Training was complex: everyone had to master foot drill as the basic building block onto which was added the training of a musketeer, pikeman or grenadier. In his specialist training the musketeer armed with a matchlock had to master between thirty-five and forty-four drill evolutions while his comrade with the more modern flintlock still had twenty-six evolutions to learn. A pikeman was trained in thirty-six evolutions while the grenadier had an additional twelve evolutions to do with his role of throwing grenades; he had also to learn the musketeer's role.[16] As may be imagined, training the bulk of an army was no easy task; the wonder is that the Jacobite army was able to function at all. In the circumstances surrounding its creation and taking the field, its performance was really a creditable achievement. Its failure at Derry was due to a host of problems as we have seen, including the lack of the specialized equipment and tools needed to conduct a siege. But it was the arrival of trained and experienced professional soldiers that finally brought about its downfall.

This brings us to the critical question posed in the opening chapter of this book: was there really a siege of Derry at all? For many the question is redundant, as they have no doubt that there was a siege. They will concur with Macaulay's comment that the siege was the most memorable in the annals of the British Isles, which is repeated verbatim by at least one writer on the siege.[17] Others veer towards the opinion expressed by Hilaire Belloc that the lack of adequate siege equipment in the Jacobite army meant that there was no siege and that Jacobite operations amounted only to a blockade of the city. Sir Charles Petrie expanded this argument, or, as Macrory comments, cantered 'happily even further down the trail blazed by Belloc' and claimed that there was not even a blockade. He went on to criticize the commanders of the garrison for allowing themselves to be shut up in the city.[18]

It is possible to argue that there was no siege in the strict military sense since so many of the identifying aspects of a siege were absent. But that begs the question of what the Jacobite army was doing at all. Did it sit around the city and do nothing? We know that not to be the case. If the requisite amount of artillery was missing, if there were insufficient engineers and engineer supplies, if there were not enough foot soldiers, the Jacobite army and its commanders seem still to have considered that they could carry out a siege of the city and bring about its capitulation. When we look at the events of those 105 days we can see many examples of what can only be described as incidents in siege warfare. What else, for example, was Brigadier Ramsey doing when he led the first attack on Windmill Hill other than trying to seize positions from which his artillery could bombard the south-facing wall? What were Skelton and Clancarty doing at the end of June with the attack on the bastion at the Butcher's Gate? With all the preparations that had gone on beforehand – the bombardment and the mining – this was a clear attempt to storm the city through a breach in the walls. And why did de Pointis build the boom if not to deny the river passage to the Williamites? Many other examples could be added to this list. If we look at the contemporary sources from the Jacobite side we see writers such as Avaux and other senior French officers refer to the siege of Londonderry (or Derry: they were quite casual in their use of both names) and the same is true of the author of *A Light to the Blind*.

Those inside the walls had no doubt that they were under siege. Few, if any, of them had any knowledge of what a full-scale siege was like and few would have known what a general would normally have required before sitting down to the business of besieging a city or fortress. But they knew that there was a hostile army outside the walls; they knew that that army's gunners and mortarmen were bombarding their town, destroying the buildings of the city and creating fear in the population. They had no idea that the bombardment was comparatively light – in 1691 Athlone was besieged by the Williamites and destroyed after a ten-day bombardment that saw 12,000 cannonballs, 600 mortar bombs and many tons of stones or rubble, fired from mortars, fall on it;* it remains the most bombarded town in the British Isles[19] – on the scale of such things; but they could see the destruction that had been wrought in the town. In their minds they were under

---

*One cannon round hit Athlone for every minute of the siege while the number of mortar bombs was much the same as that rained down on Derry over a period that was ten times longer than the Athlone siege.

siege and if the Jacobite army created that state of mind then there could be no doubt that there was a siege of Londonderry. In the psychological respect, at least, the Jacobites triumphed.

The siege was to go down in history as we all now know but even at the time it was considered to be a major event with considerable strategic significance. A medal to commemorate the relief of Londonderry was struck bearing the legend 'Wilhelm Maximus in Belgica Liberator in Britannia Restaurator' (William the Most Great, in Holland the Deliverer, in Britain the Restorer). This silver medal bears on its reverse the image of Louis XIV and commemorates the sieges of Mainz and Bonn in Germany, where the French were also defeated in 1689.[21] Linking the three events is an indication of the importance of the raising of the siege in European affairs.

All too often the siege is thought of as an event that was confined to Ireland. But that is not the case. We have seen that small numbers of Frenchmen were involved in the Jacobite force and that Louis XIV was the paymaster for James II's efforts to establish himself in Ireland. However, the French king had no real interest in James being restored to all three kingdoms but rather in James' presence in Ireland distracting the attention of William III, leader of the forces of the Grand Alliance or the League of Augsburg, from the continent where the main battle for domination of Europe would be fought. In that Louis was successful, for the war in Ireland lasted until the end of 1691 and William was forced to take part in events in Ireland during 1690.

The presence of both James and William at the battle of the Boyne on 1 July 1690 tends to focus attention on that encounter since this was the sole occasion on which the two monarchs faced each other in battle. That battle is often seen as the turning point of the war in Ireland, especially as James fled back to France in its aftermath. But the tide of war had already turned inexorably in favour of the Williamites. That turn had happened at Derry, almost a year before the Boyne. Although the Jacobites fought on, and with increasing professionalism, their fate had been decided when the garrison of Derry withstood the siege of 1689. Until that spring day on which King James rode up to the Bishop's Gate, the tide of war had been flowing with the Jacobites. On that day it began to turn and, although the Jacobites might have caught a favourable tide at some point during the next 105 days, by August it was flowing for the Williamites.

It is often only in retrospect that the turning point of any war may be identified with certainty. This is the case with the war of the kings in Ireland. Two monarchs may have faced each other in battle at the Boyne in 1690, and the Jacobite army may have suffered its bloodiest day at Aughrim another year on, but the war began to turn in north-west Ulster in the spring and summer of 1689. Derry's stand gave Dutch William the breathing space he needed to re-organize his forces, to despatch an expeditionary force to Ireland and to deal with the Jacobites of Scotland. In the longer term it also played its part in the checking of Louis XIV's expansionism. That French hegemony over Europe was not established in the closing decades of the seventeenth century owes at least something to those, probably, frightened men who called 'No surrender' to James VII and II in April 1689.

For 105 days in 1689 a small city in the north-west of Ireland, on the very periphery of Europe, became the hinge around which the history of that continent swung. But the siege is more often seen in a narrower historical perspective. William III is remembered as being the sovereign who brought civil and religious liberty to the people of Britain and Ireland but, in the aftermath of the war in Ireland, many in Ireland would not have considered that they enjoyed either form of liberty. While William was no bigot, the political reality was that he, and his queen, reigned at the invitation of parliament. And there were three parliaments to be considered: that at Westminster, the Scottish parliament and the Irish parliament in Dublin. The latter had no desire to see Anglicans, Presbyterians and Roman Catholics all enjoy the same liberties, and it was that Irish parliament that ensured that the civil articles of the treaty of Limerick, which ended the war in Ireland, were overturned and Irish Catholics entered a long period of political and civil limbo. When William died in 1702 – James II had died the previous year – he was succeeded by his late wife's sister Anne, the last of the Stuarts. And it was under Anne that Presbyterians also found themselves excluded from political life and denied religious liberty. This added to the frustrations and anger felt by many Presbyterians at their treatment in the aftermath of the war in Ireland. Those who had helped defend Derry were especially aggrieved. They had been demeaned by Walker, refused recompense by the government and now were to be treated in the same way as the Roman Catholics who had fought against that government. In some ways the penal laws that applied to Presbyterians were worse, since Presbyterian holy orders were not recognized and so marriages in Presbyterian churches were not valid; nor could a Presbyterian minister conduct a funeral service. The Presbyterians reacted not by rebelling or by supporting the exiled Stuarts but by leaving Ireland in large numbers for the new world.

But this migration did lead eventually to rebellion: the American Rebellion or War of Independence, in which Presbyterians of Irish descent played a major role. And they continued to play such a role in the new United States of America. They have produced the largest proportion of US presidents of all the many groups of peoples that make up that nation. There they found the civil and religious liberty that they had craved and fought for but under a constitution that separated state and church.

So what did William III achieve? His gift to history is the survival of the monarchy in its present constitutional form. It was William's ability to work in harmony with parliament that allowed the monarchy to survive and ensured that a second British republic was not established. That harmony between monarch and parliament continues to this day and makes the British monarchy the enduring symbol that it is.

The Stuarts continued to claim the thrones of England, Scotland and Ireland, but there was little Irish involvement in, or support for, the Jacobite risings of the first half of the eighteenth century. Ireland had become disillusioned with the Stuarts, especially with James II, 'with his one shoe English and one shoe Irish'* who had no empathy for the country or interest in its people but had tried to use it for his own ends. Not for nothing was he known in Ireland as *Séamas an chaca*, or James the shit. Over time he was to become a more romanticized figure but that is outside the scope of this work. Today both Anglicans and Presbyterians remember the siege in much the same way. Both faiths are to be found as members of the Apprentice Boys of Derry, although the principal religious services of that organization take place in St Columb's Cathedral which continues to fly Mitchelburne's 'bloody flag' on the anniversaries of the shutting of the gates and the relief of the city. And it was Mitchelburne who summed up the message of the siege for the Protestant people of Ireland when, in *Ireland Preserv'd*, he wrote:

> O brave Derry, thou art the [bulwark] of three kingdoms, thou hold'd out still; if ever thou be reduced, and this Irish army land in Scotland, farewell Ireland.[23]

It was indeed the tenacity of the defenders of Derry who ensured that the Jacobite cause was doomed in Ireland and, therefore, in all three

---

*Séamas an chaca, a chaill Éirinn / lena leathbróg ghallda is a leathbróg Ghaelach. James the shit who, with his one shoe English and one shoe Irish, had lost Ireland.[22]

kingdoms. It was that tenacity that ensured that the new succession with its pattern of constitutional monarchy would take root. And it was that tenacity that helped to ensure that the strategic ambitions of France were to be thwarted.

Notes

1: Gilbert, op cit, p. 46
2: NA Scotland, GD26/8/15, letter from James to Dundee, 17 May 1689
3: Gilbert, op cit, p. 53
4: Powley, op cit, p. 215
5: Kelly, op cit, p. 57
6: NA Scotland, GD26/7/37 – 2: Account of Lundy's proceedings in Ireland since 13 December 1688
7: HLRO, *HoCJ*, 21 October 1689
8: Murtagh, *Jacobite Artillery*, 1689–91, IS XXIII, No. 94, p. 384
9: Ibid, p. 385
10: Avaux, op cit, p. 76
11: Murtagh, op cit, p. 385; Gilbert, op cit, p. 84
12: *Franco-Irish Correspondence*, p. 161; Avaux, op cit, p. 355
13: Avaux, op cit, p. 355
14: Ibid, pp. 8–9
15: Chandler, op cit, p. 102
16: Ibid, pp. 102–3
17: Finlay, *The Siege of Londonderry compiled from the best sources*, p. 30
18: Macrory, op cit, p. 358
19: Story, *A Continuation of the Impartial History of the Wars in Ireland*, p. 108
20: Doherty, op cit, p. 166
21: Guy, *1688: Glorious Revolution? The Fall and Rise of the British Army 1660–1704*, p. 69
22: Quoted in Ó Ciardha, *Ireland and the Jacobite Cause, 1685–1766*, p. 83
23: Mitchelburne, op cit

Epilogue

The physical wounds of the siege took a long time to heal and the scars may be discerned even today in a city that cannot agree on its name. Paradoxically, the combatants of 1689 had no problems with the city's names and from the surviving documents it seems that the Jacobites favoured Londonderry more than Derry while the Williamites favoured Derry over Londonderry. The loyal order that exists to commemorate the siege is called the Apprentice Boys of Derry rather than Londonderry and that anthem of Ulster loyalism 'The Sash My Father Wore' recalls that the eponymous item was worn at Derry. Disputes continue over the Apprentice Boys' marches in August and December but these lack the bitterness that existed only a decade or so ago. An older generation will recall that those marches occurred without rancour in the years before 1969.

The recent innovation of a 'Maiden City Festival' has been a laudable attempt by the Apprentice Boys to try to make commemoration of the siege something that can involve the entire population of the city. And that is how it should be. My memory of being taught about the siege as an eight-year old schoolboy includes the exhortation that it was something that belonged to everyone in the city and there was no sectarian bias, or begrudgery, in the way that the late Danny McLaughlin spoke about the events of 1689 to his pupils of St Eugene's Boys' School.

The Apprentice Boys have chosen to call their programme of commemorative events the Maiden City Festival, evoking one of the soubriquets of the city. That title 'Maiden City' sprang from a belief that the city's walls were never breached, but this is a myth that owes nothing to reality. The reader who has persevered thus far will recall the attack on the walls in the area of Butcher's Gate at the end of June. This was launched only after the walls had been damaged so badly that it would have been possible for a forlorn hope to lead the way through the breach. Accounts from participants of temporary repairs elsewhere – hogsheads filled with earth – also suggest that this may not have been the sole instance of major damage (although both Kirke and Richards commented, caustically, on the relatively undamaged state of the walls following the relief of the city). In spite of all their shortcomings, the Jacobites did come close to bursting into the city, and perhaps the creation of the 'maiden city' myth is a backhanded compliment to those Irish and French soldiers.

Had the Jacobite army made its way into the city in that late-June attack, the conventions of siege warfare would have meant that no quarter would have been given to the garrison. Inevitably, many civilians would also have suffered, especially as it would have been difficult, in many cases, to distinguish male civilians from soldiers. But one of the strange aspects of the siege story is the comparative lack of brutality from either side. True, in the heat of battle Hamilton's soldiers were slaughtering many of the Williamites at the battle of the fords and in the immediate aftermath of that battle while Galmoy's behaviour at Creggan can only be described as brutal, but neither side seemed capable of carrying out threatened acts of brutality: thus neither the Jacobite threat to Protestants from outside the city nor the garrison's counter threat to hang all their prisoners was carried out. But Percy Kirke, already known for his brutality, did send troops ashore to carry out a punitive attack in revenge for Jacobite wrongdoing. Although there was much religious and political friction in the Ireland of the time, it seems that deep-rooted hatred was not a feature of the siege.

A Walk on the Walls

The visitor to the city today can still walk the city's walls which survive as the only intact set of such walls in these islands. Although there have been many alterations since 1689, the walls are still substantially as they were during the siege. The main changes have been the addition of three extra gates: New Gate, Castle Gate and Magazine Gate. A further breach of the original walls has been made at Market Street, which is the only point at which the city wall has been removed, although considerable change has also been made at the Water Bastion. Walking around the walls – a distance of just under a mile – gives a good impression of how confined was the area held by the besieged, even when one takes into account the ground outside the walls to the south and within the outworks on Windmill Hill. From various points on the walls it is also possible to see many of the locations that featured in the siege.

Access to the walls is best made at the Water Bastion on Foyle Street, close to the city's bus depot and beside the Central Library. Across the river from the Water Bastion, against which the Foyle used to flow and hence the name, was Stronge's Orchard. Moving straight ahead with the Millennium Forum on the right, one comes to the sole gap in the walls at Market Street. Crossing over that street there is a steep climb to Ferryquay Gate. Before reaching the gate, however, one of the bastions may be seen. This is the London Bulwark or New Gate Bastion.

From atop the latter an excellent view may be had of the ground around this area of the defences as well as of part of the inner city. Ferryquay Street, originally Gracious Street, runs from the gate towards The Diamond which used to house the Town House, or Market House, and where the city's war memorial now stands. Ferryquay Gate was the first gate shut by the apprentices against Antrim's Regiment in December 1688. Its name signifies that this was the entrance to the city used by travellers who had crossed the river by ferry. The nearby Bridge Street, running beside the Foyleside shopping centre, leads to the site of the original bridge and, before that, the western end of the ferry across the Foyle. This gate also housed the city's gaol.

Continuing the circuit of the walls, the next point of interest is another bastion. This is the Ferry Bastion, previously the Lord Deputy's Bulwark, which was given its name because it stood opposite the ferry. Close by is the modern New Gate after which may be seen, on the left, one of the two guard or sentinel* houses on the walls. Entry is not possible but close inspection will reveal just how claustrophobic duty in such a post must have been. To the right it is possible to leave the walls for a time to visit St Columb's Cathedral through a gate into the cathedral graveyard. One of the most obvious burial places in the graveyard is the Heroes' Mound on which stands a memorial to the defenders of the city. This feature has been renovated recently.

Entering the Cathedral one of the first sights to greet the visitor is a large mortar shell. This is the 'dead shell' in which surrender terms were fired into the city by the Jacobites about the end of June or beginning of July 1689. Within the Cathedral may be seen the memorial to Governor Henry Baker and Captain Michael Browning, of the *Mountjoy* as well as two of the French flags taken at the first battle of Windmill Hill. Although the staffs are original the fabric has been replaced. There is also a small museum in the chapterhouse which includes a number of siege artefacts. These include keys to the original four city gates, locally-made cannon balls, swords and other memorabilia, including an appeal to the government for redress from some of the citizens.

Returning to the walls it is worth taking a look up at the cathedral spire. The original tower was used as a gun platform, for two weapons, during the siege. As well as considering how these guns were lifted to their lofty platform, the visitor should also consider the field of fire enjoyed by the gunners on the tower. Think also of the all-round view to be had from what was the highest point within the walls: from here the relief fleet could be seen in the lough some miles to the north and from here efforts were made to signal to that fleet.

Beside the Cathedral may be seen another bastion. Not surprisingly, this is the Church Bastion which was earlier known as King James' Bulwark – the

---

*Originally 'centinel' meaning one man of a hundred.

sovereign in this case being James I. From the Church Bastion the walk continues towards Bishop's Gate, which involves climbing some steep steps. It was before this gate that King James II appeared in April 1689 expecting to receive the city's surrender. Bishop's Gate was rebuilt in 1789 as a triumphal arch in memory of King William III with the original plans including an equestrian statue of that monarch although this was never completed. It was in front of this section of wall that Lundy's ravelin was built in early-1689. There is now no trace of the ravelin but its outline was unearthed during an archaeological survey and dig in recent years.

Moving along from Bishop's Gate leads the visitor to the Double Bastion, formerly Prince Charles' Bulwark. Its size makes obvious why it was called the Double Bastion; it was here that the defenders erected the gallows from which they threatened to hang Jacobite prisoners in retaliation for Marshal de Rosen's threat to herd Protestants into the city. From here there is an excellent view of the ground to the south, and it is clear why this was the area most under threat from the Jacobites. Looking south (upriver towards Strabane) it is possible, but only between late-autumn and early-spring, to see the remains of the windmill in the grounds of Lumen Christi College. Nearby also is the Long Tower Church, the oldest Roman Catholic church in the city, where Brigadier-General Ramsey was buried after the first battle of Windmill Hill.

Beyond the Long Tower, and looking at an angle, one can see the low-lying ground that was marshy in 1689 and helped protect the city from the Jacobites. Also visible is Foyle Hill where King James retired having been fired on at Bishop's Gate. From there and sweeping round to the north-west the high ground on which the modern Foyle Hill and Creggan estates stand was the area on which many Jacobite troops were encamped during the siege.

Moving yet farther along the walls the next stopping point is the Royal Bastion, formerly Lord Docwra's Bulwark, where may be seen the base on which stood a memorial to George Walker until it was blown up by the IRA in 1973. Between here and Butcher's Gate is another gun platform from where it is possible to look down on the steeply-sloped ground up which the Jacobites attacked at the end of June in Skelton and Clancarty's assault on the city. Looking beyond this to the rising ground to the left of St Eugene's Roman Catholic Cathedral, is the probable location of the gun position from which the Jacobite artillery pounded the wall prior to that attack. It becomes clear, as one looks down on this ground, that the Jacobite soldiers who attacked the walls here on that June night in 1689 were not men who deserved to be dismissed as superstitious drunkards as both Walker and Sir Patrick Macrory have attempted to do.

Inside the walls at this point is St Augustine's Church where also stood a chapel of ease of the same name in 1689 and where was sited the original Augustinian monastery. Nearby is the oldest of the city's Presbyterian churches, First Derry, and between the two is the Apprentice Boys' Memorial Hall, which also houses a small museum. Beside the Memorial Hall is a memorial garden in which stands the statue of George Walker that once adorned the pillar on the Royal Bastion.

Butcher's Gate comes next; and it was in this vicinity that the most resolute attempt was made to penetrate the city at the end of June 1689. The bastion alongside the gate was mined by Jacobite engineers and so much damage was caused to the walls that gabions – large wicker baskets filled with earth or rubble – had to be emplaced before the wall to allow repairs to be carried out and to protect the wall from further damage. Even so, sufficient damage was done to allow the Jacobites to launch an infantry attack on the city. It was here that the walls were breached in spite of the 'Maiden City' soubriquet.

Beyond Butcher's Gate is another of the new gates, Castle Gate, and then the Gunner's Bastion, close to which was the master gunner's house. Below that is the Coward's Bastion, the place furthest removed from danger during the siege, which is beside the final new gate, Magazine Gate. Near here stood the city's magazine and today, just inside the gate, is the award-winning Tower Museum wherein is told the story of the city from earliest times. O'Doherty's Tower or fort, which stands here and gives the museum its name, is a replica built by local enterprise in the early-1980s.

The final stretch of the walls takes the visitor back to the Water Bastion passing over Shipquay Gate. In front of this stretch of the walls the river used to flow and here the relief ships, the *Mountjoy* of Derry and the *Phoenix* of Coleraine, berthed on the night that the boom was broken and the siege was ended. It was on this stretch of wall that, in 1945, Field Marshal Montgomery and Field Marshal Alexander, both from Irish families with connections to the city, were awarded the freedom of Londonderry. Today the city's magnificent Guildhall dominates the area. At ground level the visitor may see the memorial tablet to Michael Browning, captain of the *Mountjoy*, a local man who played a major and fatal part in bringing relief to the city.

As a footnote to the story of the siege, it is interesting to note that plans for improved defences for the city, emphasizing the importance of the ground to the south of Bishop's Gate, were drawn up by the engineer Jean Thomas, a French Huguenot, in 1705. These were never implemented, largely due to the costs involved, which he estimated at £19,752. 12s 2d. The plans were suspended with the act of union between England and Scotland in 1707, which suggests that the city was no longer considered to be under threat. A plan of the proposed fortifications, which would have extended the city walls over an area nearly four times as large as that enclosed by the original walls, as well as building further Vaubanesque fortifications, may be seen in the British Library.

Appendix One

Dramatis Personae

Ash, Captain Thomas: from a local family which is still extant in County Londonderry, Thomas Ash was appointed captain in one of the regiments formed for the defence of the city. He seems to have been a former soldier as his account of the siege includes observations that indicate military experience. Ash is one of the eyewitnesses of the siege from within the walls, but his journal was not written for publication, unlike those of Walker and Mackenzie, and was not published for over a century after the siege.

Avaux, Jean Antoine de Mesmes, le Comte d': Louis XIV's ambassador to the court of James II, Avaux reported on the behaviour of the 'king of England', his plans and policies to his master and tried to persuade James to follow the strategic path that best suited France. A career diplomat, Avaux was born in 1640, fourth son of the President de Mesmes and nephew of Claude de Mesmes, Comte d'Avaux, one of France's most distinguished diplomats. His was a noble and ancient family from Béarn, and the young Avaux followed his uncle into the diplomatic service, where his abilities were soon recognized and he came to the attention of Louis XIV. While still a young man, he was entrusted with several important tasks and was ambassador at Venice from 1672 to 1675 before being chosen, in 1675, as Louis' plenipotentiary at the Congress of Nijmegen. From 1678 until 1688 he was France's ambassador to The Netherlands. His diplomatic gifts and negotiating ability were famous but were sorely tried during his time with James II. However, the latter appointed him a privy councillor in Ireland although the two men never established the mutual trust necessary to work in harmony. Avaux's mission to Ireland lasted only a year before he was recalled to France, but his was the hand that set in motion the recruiting of Irish regiments for French service, the famed Irish Brigade. He had established a high opinion of the soldierly qualities of the Irish peasant, and the subsequent service of the Irish Brigade was to prove the accuracy of his assessment. Avaux died in Paris in 1709. He left a reputation of being one of the finest diplomats of his age and one of the best that France, a nation that had developed diplomacy to a fine art, had produced.

Baker, Colonel Henry: a veteran of Tangier, Henry Baker was a professional soldier of considerable experience. Before the siege he had served in one of the regiments raised in east Ulster and was at the attack on Carrickfergus; he also served at Dromore with Rawdon. He was elected as Governor of Londonderry in succession to Robert Lundy. The Reverend George Walker was elected as his deputy although Walker claimed to be the governor in his own account of the siege. Baker was stricken down by illness in the course of the siege, probably caused by his unstinting attention to the defence of the city, and Colonel Jonathan Mitchelburne was appointed to act in his place. When Baker died, Mitchelburne continued to act as governor. Henry Baker was laid to rest in the north aisle of St Columb's Cathedral.

Berwick, James FitzJames, Duke of: one of the illegitimate Sons of King James II, Berwick was appointed as a general in his father's army. He was a soldier of some skill but became notorious for his ruthlessness, especially for his penchant for the scorched-earth tactic, destroying land, crops and animals to deny them to his enemies. The area around the city and into County Donegal seems to have the first region in which Berwick put this theory into practice.

Browning, Captain Michael: a native of the city, he commanded the merchant ship *Mountjoy* that brought relief to Derry and ended the siege, having earlier volunteered to make the run upriver to the beleaguered city. Browning was killed as his ship was attempting to break the boom across the Foyle. He is buried beside Henry Baker in the north aisle of St Columb's Cathedral and is also commemorated by a tablet on the city walls across from the Guildhall.

Cairnes (or Cairns), David: from County Tyrone, he was a lawyer and one of those urging defiance in the later days of 1688. He later expended much energy in seeking means and funds to strengthen the city's defences including travelling to London on behalf of the corporation to seek the support of the London companies. He died in 1722 and was buried in the churchyard of St Columb's Cathedral.

Cairns, John: also from County Tyrone and possibly a relative of David Cairnes. He is listed as Cairnes in Young's *Fighters of Derry* which also notes that he was from Claremore in Tyrone. John Cairns served as the lieutenant-colonel of Adam Murray's regiment of horse.

Dunbar, Captain: one of the two Fermanagh men who led soldiers out of the city to engage the Jacobite attackers at Butcher's Gate at the end of June. Unlike his fellow officer, Captain Noble, little is known of Dunbar and his subsequent life. Even his first name is not certain.

Hamilton, Lieutenant-General Richard: a member of a Scottish family that came to the English court on the accession of King James I. Richard Hamilton's father was Sir George Hamilton, fourth son of the first Earl of Abercorn who held high office in Dublin castle; he was also related to the Ormondes. Staunch royalists, and Roman Catholics, the Hamiltons chose to accompany Charles II into exile in France, where Sir George was appointed Captain-Lieutenant of a corps of refugees from Britain and Ireland. This appointment was made by Louis XIV who was the captain of the corps. At the time of the restoration some members of the Hamilton family returned to England with Charles II and one was appointed as a maid of honour to Queen Catherine, later marrying Count Grammont. Richard and his three brothers served with the French army before his return to Britain and subsequent mission to Ireland on behalf of the Prince of Orange. When James arrived in Ireland, Richard was promoted lieutenant-general and became one of the commanders of the Jacobite army. He was captured at the battle of the Boyne in 1690.

Kirke, Major-General Percy: another veteran of Tangier, of which he had been governor, Kirke had achieved notoriety for his ruthlessness in suppressing the Duke of Monmouth's rebellion in 1685. He had also commanded the Queen's Royal Regiment, the senior English infantry of the line regiment, who earned the ironic soubriquet 'Kirke's Lambs' for their brutal treatment of Monmouth's rebels at the battle of Sedgemoor in 1685. The paschal lamb of Queen Catherine's coat of arms was the regimental badge. Kirke has been much criticized over the years for his apparent dilatory attitude to the relief of the city.

Leake, Captain John: commander of the Royal Navy frigate HMS *Dartmouth*, Leake played a major and very gallant role in the raising of the siege, positioning his ship to draw the fire of Culmore Fort away from the merchant ships that made the run upriver to the city. The son of the master-gunner of England, he later achieved the rank of admiral.

Lundy, Colonel (later Major-General) Robert: a Scot and a veteran of Tangier where he had served with Kirke, Lundy was known to his fellow veterans Baker and Mitchelburne, which may explain why he was able to avoid the worst

---

*The Royal Regiment was one of the last to submit to William III; it was reformed in December 1688 with Fredriech, Duke of Schomberg as its colonel.

consequences of his perceived treason in the days immediately before the siege. The first record of his military career shows him as a captain in 1684 in the Royal Regiment of Foot which later became the 1st Foot, but was better known as the Royal Scots; but he would have been serving before this as an ensign and then a lieutenant. He is not listed among the officers of the Royal Regiment* in 1685 by which time he was probably with Mountjoy's Regiment in Ireland. During this unit's service at Kinsale, County Cork, Lundy met and married Martha Davies, daughter of the Reverend Rowland Davies, the Dean of Ross. He next appears in surviving records as being appointed Colonel of Colonel Robert Lundie's Londonderry Regiment of Foot on 24 April 1689, by which date he had already left the city. Although imprisoned in the Tower of London, Lundy was cleared of charges of treason and returned to his military career. In the early years of the eighteenth century he served as adjutant-general of the Portuguese army.

Mackenzie, The Reverend John: a Presbyterian minister, the incumbent of Derryloran (Cookstown), who was chaplain to George Walker's Regiment during the siege. He has left us one of the eyewitness accounts of the siege from the defenders' viewpoint which he wrote in response to Walker's narrative, a version that not only withheld credit from the Presbyterians in the city but also included a number of slights and insults to the Presbyterians. Chief among the latter was Walker's claim that he could not recall the names of any of the Presbyterian ministers who were in the city during the siege, including that of Mackenzie. When he wrote his vindication, Walker named the Presbyterian ministers but referred to the Reverend Gilchrist as KilChrist and to Mackenzie as Machiny. Mackenzie's account of the siege is both more detailed and more balanced than Walker's.

Mitchelburne, Colonel Jonathan: an Englishman, born in Sussex in 1648, and yet another veteran of Tangier, Mitchelburne was an accomplished soldier with considerable experience by the time of the siege. His military service appears to have begun in Monck's Regiment, later the Coldstream Guards, before transferring to the Duke of Monmouth's Regiment with whom he served in France. (Zachariah Tiffin, one of the officers with the first relief fleet and later the commanding officer of an Inniskilling regiment, was the adjutant of the regiment.) In 1678 Mitchelburne purchased a commission in Monmouth's Regiment – the commission was dated 10 February – but the following year this regiment was disbanded and he transferred his commission to the Earl of Plymouth's Regiment which became part of the garrison of Tangier in 1680. The regiment's lieutenant-colonel was Percy Kirke, who later became its colonel. Following his service in Tangier Mitchelburne transferred to Mountjoy's Regiment of the Irish army as a lieutenant in the Grenadier Company with which he served on garrison duty in Kinsale and Londonderry. He left the regiment when it was recalled to Dublin by Tyrconnel and entered service with the east Ulster units that fought at Carrickfergus and Dromore. He was appointed major in Clotworthy Skeffington's Regiment with whom he came back to Derry, commanding that regiment at the battle of the fords. Promoted lieutenant-colonel, he retained command throughout the siege. Chosen to act for Baker during the latter's illness, Mitchelburne succeeded his fellow soldier on his death. Also among the dead of the siege were Mitchelburne's wife and children. In the years following the siege he settled in Derry, remarried and seems to have become an adopted Derryman. He campaigned vigorously to have the government fulfil its debts to the defenders of the city but without success. On one of his visits to London to press for reparations he was incarcerated in the Fleet prison as a debtor.

It was Mitchelburne who had the bloody flag of defiance, actually a naval ensign, flown from the cathedral and that colour, known as 'Derry crimson', has become the colour of the Apprentice Boys of Derry, one club of which is named in his honour. In his will Mitchelburne left a sum of money to allow the crimson flag to be flown from the Cathedral. Under the title *Ireland Preserved* he wrote an account of the siege. Following his death, on 1 October 1721, a well on his land at Prehen became a site of veneration for local people, both Catholic and Protestant. He is buried in Old Glendermott graveyard, near the city.

Mountjoy, Lord: William Stewart, of County Donegal, a professional soldier and a major landowner in Ulster, he purchased the position of Master-General of the Irish Ordnance in 1684 and also became the colonel of an infantry regiment, Mountjoy's, which was the Londonderry garrison unit in 1688. Mountjoy had campaigned with the forces of imperial Austria in 1686–7 and was wounded severely during the siege of Buda (part of modern Budapest, which is two cities separated by a river.) Following his unsuccessful involvement in mediation between the opposing parties in Ulster he was sent to France by Tyrconnel and imprisoned on the latter's orders. Following his release he returned to soldiering and was killed at the Battle of Steenkirk in 1692.

Murray, Colonel Adam: a local farmer from County Londonderry, Murray proved to be an inspiring leader and soldier. There are no records to suggest that he had ever been a soldier, although he might have served in the militia which had been disbanded by Tyrconnel. He led a Williamite cavalry unit with considerable distinction at the battle of the fords. Although offered the governorship by acclamation he preferred to remain with his soldiers and commanded the garrison's cavalry regiment. His record during the siege was much better than that of many men who had been soldiers and he remains one of the outstanding figures of the conflict. He received no reward for his service. Although the date of his death is not known he rests beside Mitchelburne in Old Glendermott churchyard. His memory is also invoked by a club of the Apprentice Boys of Derry.

Noble, Captain Arthur: one of the most outstanding of the officers of the city's garrison, Noble was involved prominently in a number of clashes, not least of which was the Jacobite attempt to enter the city at the end of June when he was one of those to lead troops out to attack the Jacobite soldiers in the flank. From Derryrea, near Lisnaskea in County Fermanagh, it was said of him that 'no one has more frequent mention for daring venture and gallant achievement in the sorties of the garrison'. He returned to live in Fermanagh where he died on 29 August 1731 and was buried in Aghalurcher churchyard, near Lisnaskea.

Pointis, Jean Bernard Louis Desjean, Marquis de: a French naval officer with experience of active service in the bombardment of Algiers in 1688, he came to Ireland in early-1689 with an Irish officer called Roth to assess the situation for Louis XIV. As a result Louis decided to support a Jacobite expedition to Ireland. When this arrived, de Pointis was in command of the French artillery and engineers included in the force. As a naval officer he was reluctant to come under army command and therefore sought to be appointed as master-general of the ordnance in which position he would have been answerable only to King James. However, James appointed Justin McCarthy, Lord Mountcashel, to this post. Pointis finally accepted command of the gunners and engineers at Londonderry, where he was also responsible for building the boom, although his proposal for a second boom closer to the city was rejected by Hamilton. Wounded in one of the early engagements of the siege, de Pointis refused to be tended by Irish doctors and thus survived, although the *London Gazette* reported his death. In November 1689, de Pointis returned to France and later (1697) earned a considerable reputation as the commander of the French expedition that captured Cartagena, the Spanish-American port, adding a large store of treasure to the French exchequer.

Richards, Captain (later Colonel) Jacob: born in Ireland, Richards was an engineer and gunner with the Jacobite train of artillery in 1688 but changed his allegiance to William and was first engineer of the expedition to Ireland in 1689. Also during 1688 he had been sent by Lord Dartmouth to Hungary to study Habsburg strategy and tactics, including siege warfare and those aspects of the gunner's and engineer's arts related to such warfare. For this task he was paid £1 per day, a very generous payment for the time. (In 1697 he was sent to Corfu to observe the war against Turkey.) Richards kept a journal of the events that he experienced at Londonderry and Inch which provides us with one of the eyewitness accounts of the siege and has the great advantage of having been written by a professional soldier. Jacob Richards' writings continued after his service in his native Ireland and he is also a major source of information on Marlborough's campaigns in mainland Europe. His younger brother, Michael, also served as both an engineer and gunner.

Rooke, Captain (later Admiral Sir) George: the commander of the Royal Navy's squadron that patrolled Irish waters during the period of the siege, he later became an admiral and one of the most distinguished flag officers of the Royal Navy. It was Rooke who took Gibraltar for Britain in 1704. The presence of Rooke's squadron off Ireland was a major deterrent to the French navy which might otherwise have provided direct support for the Jacobite army besieging Derry. Although his ships supported Kirke's relief fleet, Rooke allowed their captains to take orders from Kirke and took no active part in the operations to relieve the city.

Rosen, Lieutenant-General (later Marshal) Conrad de: described as a Lithuanian while James II once called him a 'bloody Muscovite', de Rosen was almost sixty at the time of the siege. Born in the then-Swedish province of Livonia, he became a mercenary soldier in French service, enlisting as a soldier in 1646. He was commissioned as a cornet in Brinon's Regiment in 1651 and, thereafter, rose steadily through the ranks. Although remembered as a ruthless commander, de Rosen was also a very brave man, which he demonstrated at Lifford during the battle of the fords when he led a small force of cavalry and dragoons across the flooded river against a much superior Williamite force that had the protection of a small fortification and support from some artillery.

Saint-Martin, le Sieur de: a French naval commissary officer who was included in the group of gunner and engineer officers that was sent to Londonderry. He was detached from the army besieging the city to be the artillery commander of the Jacobite army in Fermanagh, where he was killed at the battle of Newtownbutler.

Stewart, William: see Lord Mountjoy.

Talbot, Richard, Duke of Tyrconnel: from one of the most prominent of Irish Catholic families, Talbot became James' Lord Deputy in Ireland and his attitude to the Protestants and Nonconformists of the country, especially in Ulster, was one of the crucial factors that led to war in Ireland and to the eventual defeat of his king and commander. He died of a stroke in 1691 and following his death the Irish army accepted terms for a surrender that became known as the treaty of Limerick.

Tiffin, Major (later Colonel) Zachariah: one of the officers who came to Derry with the first relief fleet in April 1689, Tiffin escaped the censure that brought the careers of the two commanding officers to an end. He returned with Kirke, who sent him to Enniskillen where he took command of one of the regiments raised for the defence of the town. This unit was taken into the Army as Zachariah Tiffin's Inniskilling Regiment and later became the Royal Inniskilling Fusiliers which is now part of the Royal Irish Regiment (27th Inniskilling, 83rd, 87th and UDR). His name also appears as Tiffan or Tiffany.

Walker, The Reverend George: a Church of Ireland rector from Donoughmore near Dungannon in County Tyrone, Walker raised a local regiment that he brought to Derry where he became one of the leaders of the besieged and was elected as deputy governor to Henry Baker at the beginning of the siege. Leaving the city only days after its relief he wrote an account of the siege that became a bestseller but, by failing to give due credit to the Presbyterians who had been in the city, also caused considerable offence. Walker was later appointed Bishop of Derry but never returned to the city as he was killed at the Battle of the Boyne on 1 July 1690. At his widow's request, his bones were brought back to County Tyrone in 1703 for interment in Castlecaulfield Parish Church. Although many accounts describe him as an aged clergyman these confuse him with his father as Walker was in his early forties at the time of the siege. There were many doubts about his loyalty and honesty during the siege and his iconic status as 'Governor Walker' owes more to his own efforts in self-promotion that it does to his real performance during the siege. He is also commemorated by a club of the Apprentice Boys of Derry.

Appendix Two

Declaration of Union made by the Nobility and Gentry of the neighbouring counties, and of the Citizens and Garrison of Londonderry

Whereas, either by folly or weakness of friends, or craft and stratagem of enemies, some rumours and reflections are spread abroad among the vulgar, that the Right Honourable the Lord Blaney, Sir Arthur Rawdon, Lieutenant-Colonel Maxwell, and other gentlemen and officers of quality, are resolved to take protections from the Irish, and desert the general service for defence of the Protestant party in this kingdom, to the great discouragement of such who are so weak as to give credit to so false, scandalous, and malicious a report – For wiping off which aspersion, and clearing the minds of all Protestant friends wheresoever, from all suspicions and jealousies of that kind or otherwise, it is hereby unanimously declared, protested and published to all men, by Colonel Robert Lundy, Governor of Derry, the said Lord Blaney, Sir Arthur Rawdon, and other officers and gentlemen subscribing hereunto, that they, and their forces and soldiers, are entirely united among themselves, and fully and resolutely resolved to oppose the Irish enemy with their utmost force, and to continue the war against them to the last, for their own and all Protestants' preservation in this kingdom. And the Committee of Londonderry, for themselves and for all the Citizens of the said City, do hereby declare and protest, and publish to all men, that they are heartily and sincerely united with the said Colonel Robert Lundy, Lord Blaney, Sir Arthur Rawdon, and all others that join in this common cause, and with all their force and utmost power will labour to carry on the said war. And if it should so happen that our party should be so oppressed by the Irish enemy, that they should be forced to retire into the City, for shelter against them (which God forbid,) the said Lord Blaney, Sir Arthur Rawdon, and their forces, and all other Protestant friends, shall be readily received into this City, and as much as in us lies, be cherished and supported by us.

Dated at Londonderry, the 21st of March, 1688

The declaration was signed by: Robert Lundy, [Lord] Blaney, William Stewart, Arthur Rawdon, George Maxwell, James Curry, John Forward, Hugh McGill, William Ponsonby, H. Baker, Chichester Fortescue, James Brabazon, John Hill, H. Kennedy, E. Brookes, Samuel Norman, Alex Tomkins, Matthew Cocken, Alexander Lecky, [Lord] Massereene, Francis Nevill, James Lenox, Frederick Conyngham, John Leslie, Henry Long, William Crookshanks, Clotworthy Skeffington, Arthur Upton, Samuel Morrison, Thomas Cole, Francis Forster, Edward Cary, John Cowan, Kilner Brasier, James Hamilton and John Sinclare. Against the names of H. Kennedy and E. Brookes was noted the fact that they were sheriffs.

Appendix Three

Articles at a Council of War, at Derry, 10th of April, 1689

Present

Colonels – Robert Lundy, Lord Blaney, James Hamilton, Sir Nicholas Atcheson, Hugh Montgomery;

Lieutenant-Colonels – Whitney, White, Johnston, Shaw, Ponsonby;
Majors – Barry, Crofton, Hill, Phillips, Tubman;
Captain – Hugh McGill.

1. Resolved – That a mutual engagement be made between all officers of this garrison and the forces adjoining, to be signed by every man. That none shall desert or forsake the service, or depart the kingdom without leave of a council of war; if any do so, he or they shall be looked upon as cowards, and disaffected to the service.
2. That a thousand men shall be chosen to be part of this garrison, and joined with the soldiers already herein, to defend the City; the officers of which thousand, and the garrison officers, are to enter into the engagement aforesaid.
3. That all officers and soldiers of any of our forces, in the neighbourhood not of this garrison, shall forthwith repair to their respective quarters and commands.
4. That all colonels and commanders of every regiment or independent troop or company, be now armed and fitted, that so we may take up resolutions for field-service accordingly: the lists to be sent hither by Saturday next.
5. That the several officers in their respective quarters, shall take care to send in provisions to the Magazines of this garrison, for supply thereof and take care that they leave with the owners thereof, some of their victuals and provisions for their own support, and to send in spades, shovels and pick-axes.

6. The thousand men to be taken into this garrison shall have the old houses about the walls and ditches without the gates divided among them to be levelled with all possible speed.

7. That the several battalions and companies in the City shall have their several stations and posts assigned them, to which they shall repair upon any sudden alarm.

8. That all persons of this garrison, upon beating of the retreat every night, shall repair to their several quarters and lodgings.

9. That a pair of gallows shall be erected in one of the bastions upon the south-west of the City, whereupon all mutinous or treacherous persons of this garrison shall be executed, who shall be condemned thereunto by a court-martial.

10. That the Articles of War shall be read at the head of every regiment, battalion, troop, or company: and that all soldiers shall be punished for transgressing them, according to the said Articles.

11. That every soldier of the garrison, and non-commissioned officer, shall be weekly allowed out of the magazines eight quarts of meal, four pounds of fish, and three pounds of flesh for his weekly subsistence.

12. That every soldier and non-commissioned officer shall be allowed a quart of small beer per day, as soon as the same can be provided until some money shall come to allow them pay.

Agreed upon at the said Council of War, and ordered to be copied.

Appendix Four

Richard Hamilton's letter to the governors with proposed terms of surrender; 27 June 1689.

1st – That Colonel O'Neill has a power to discourse with the Governors of Derry, from General Hamilton, as appears by his sending this.

2nd – That the general has full power, does appear by his commission.

3rd – That General Rosen has no power from the king to intermeddle with what Lieutenant-General Hamilton does, as to the Siege, being only sent to oppose the English succour; and that all conditions and parleys are left to the said Lieutenant-General Hamilton; that as to what articles shall be agreed on they may see, by the king's warrant, he has full power to confirm them; notwithstanding, if they do not think this sufficient, he will give what other reasonable security they can demand. As to English landing, such as had commission from the Prince of Orange, there need not be apprehension, since it will be the king's interest to take as much care of his Protestant subjects as of any other, he making no distinction of religion.

4th –As to what concerns the Inniskillen people, they shall have the same terms as those of Derry, on their submission, the king being willing to shew mercy to all his subjects, and quiet his kingdoms.

5th – That the Lieutenant-General desires no better than having it communicated to all the garrison, he being willing to employ such as will freely swear to serve his Majesty faithfully; and all such as have a desire to live in town, shall have protection, and free liberty of goods and religion. As to the last point, such as have a mind to return to their homes, shall have a necessary guard with them to their respective habitations, and victuals to supply them; where they shall be restored to all they possessed formerly, not only by the sheriffs and justices of the peace, but also by the governors and officers of the army, who, from time to time, will do them right, and give them reprisals of cattle from such as have been taken from the mountains.

Appendix Five

Surrender demand from Conrad de Rosen, Marshal-General of all King James's Forces

Declares, by these presents, to the commanders, officers, soldiers, and inhabitants of the City of Londonderry, that, in case they do not, betwixt this and Monday next, at six o'clock in the afternoon, being the first of July, in the year of our Lord one thousand six hundred and eighty-nine, agree to surrender the said place of Londonderry, unto the king, upon such conditions as may be granted to them, according to the instructions and power Lieutenant-General Hamilton formerly received from the king, that he will, forthwith, issue out his orders, from the barony of Innishowen and the sea coasts round about, as far as Charlemont, for the gathering together of their faction, whether protected or not, and cause them immediately to be brought to the walls of Londonderry, where it shall be lawful for those in the town (in case they have any pity for them,) to open the gates and receive them into the town, otherwise they will be forced to see their friends and nearest relations all starve for want of food; he being resolved not to leave one of them at home, nor any thing to maintain them. – And, that all hopes of succour may be taken away, by the landing of any troops in these parts from England, he further declares that in case they refuse to submit, he will, forthwith, cause all the said country to be immediately destroyed, that if any succours should be hereafter sent them from England, they may perish with them for want of food; besides which, he has a very considerable army, as well for the opposing of them in all places that shall be judged necessary, as for the protection of all the rest of his Majesty's dutiful subjects, whose goods and chattels he promises to secure, destroying all the rest that cannot be conveniently brought into such places as he shall judge necessary to be preserved, and burning the houses and mills, not only of those that are in actual rebellion, but also of their friends and adherents, that no hopes of escaping may be left to any man; beginning this very day to send his necessary orders to all governors, and other commanders of his Majesty's forces, at Coleraine, Antrim, Carrickfergus, Belfast, Dungannon,

Charlemont, Belturbet, and Sligo; to Colonel Sarsfield, commanding a flying army at Ballyshanny [Ballyshannon]; Colonel Sutherland, commanding another towards Enniskillen; and the Duke of Berwick, another on Finn water; to cause all the men, women and children who are in any way related to those in Londonderry, or any where else, in open rebellion, to be forthwith brought to this place, without hopes of withdrawing further into the kingdom; that in case before the said Monday, the first of July, in the year of our Lord one thousand six hundred and eighty-nine, be expired, they do not send us hostages and other deputies, with a full and sufficient power to treat with us for the surrender of the said City of Londonderry, on reasonable conditions, they shall not, after that time, be admitted to any treaty whatsoever; and the army which shall continue the Siege, and will, with the assistance of God, soon reduce them, shall have orders to give no quarter, or spare either age or sex, in case they are taken by force; but, if they return to the obedience due to their natural Prince, he promises them, that the conditions granted to them in his Majesty's name, shall be inviolably observed by all his Majesty's subjects; and that he himself will have a care to protect them on all occasions, even to take their part, if any injury, contrary to agreement, should be done them, making himself responsible for the performance of the conditions on which they shall agree to surrender the said place of Londonderry to the king.

Given under my hand this 30th day of June, 1689

Le Marechal de Rosen

Appendix Six

Preparations for a siege

In his work *La défense des places*, Vauban listed fifteen different sizes of towns and provided calculations for the requisite garrison, weapons, munitions and other stores needed to defend those against a siege. He included a six-bastion fortress which is close enough to Londonderry (six bastions and three half-bastions) to give an idea of what the master of siege warfare would have considered necessary to defend the city in 1689 in the face of a forty-eight-day siege (half the length of the siege of Derry). Noting that the fortress ought to have a peacetime garrison of 1,200 infantrymen with 100 cavalry and a skeleton staff, he recommended that, in wartime, this should increase to 3,600 infantry with 360 cavalry, a staff of 200 and 120 gunners, eighty bombardiers and forty miners. It will be seen that the infantry strength was about half of that at Derry in April 1689 although the cavalry strength was about equal to the size of Murray's Regiment.

Vauban would have considered the artillery strength in the city to be too small as his recommendation was for sixty cannon, with a stock of 24,000 cannon balls, thirty mortars with 15,600 bombs and grenades, sixty wall-muskets and 3,000 spare muskets. For the artillery, mortars and muskets a store of 340,000 pounds of powder, 300,000 lengths of match cord and 419,240 pounds of lead was necessary. The rations for this garrison (and civilian mouths are not considered in Vauban's figures) included 366 tons of grain and rice; 71.2 tons of beef, twenty-four tons of mutton (for sick or wounded officers); twenty-four tons of veal (for wounded rank and file); nineteen tons of cheese; about 900 pounds of plums for the sick; 5,051 boxes of onions; 945 gallons of wine; 28,875 gallons of beer and 3,780 gallons of whiskey, the latter to be issued at the rate of two small tots per day. He also recommended a tobacco ration and a regular regime of fast days that would help the garrison prepare for possible hardships in the course of the siege. In addition he recommended that the commanders ensured that water cisterns were kept clean and full, that weaponry was tested and inspected on a regular basis and that close attention be paid to the overall state of the defences. Consider all this in the light of the preparations made at Londonderry in the months before the siege and it will be seen that Robert Lundy did his best for the city with what was available.

Vauban also provided a timetable for the besieging of such a six-bastion fortress. (Interestingly, although the master of siege warfare, he never believed that fortresses should be considered impregnable.) This timetable suggested that a well-appointed fortress, defended by a determined garrison, would fall after forty-eight days. Having allowed nine days for the investing of the fortress, the collection of material and the circumvallation, Vauban reckoned that the attackers should have a fair breach created within a further twenty days and a practicable breach by the thirty-first day. The capture of the breach would then take another two days, followed by an additional two days for the surrender of the town. Even allowing for errors and delays caused by the courage of the defenders and possible sorties, it should be possible to take the fortress by the forty-eighth day.

In another book, *l'Attaque des places*, Vauban stressed the necessity to prepare well in advance for a siege so that all the manpower, artillery and engineer equipment should be available at the appointed time. This the Jacobites were unable to do and this proved their eventual undoing even though it was possible that the city could have been taken by a shock attack, even by a small force, in the immediate aftermath of the battle of the fords.

Appendix Seven

The Gunners' Role

One of the most important elements in siege warfare was the artillery to the extent that a siege may be described as an extended artillery duel. As we have already noted, the guns of the besieging force were usually sited by an engineer, it being accepted that engineers, men of the profession that designed defences, were also best qualified to oversee the destruction of defences. Once appropriate gunsites, or batteries, had been identified, the construction task was undertaken by pioneers; these were labourers, often locally-recruited, who dug out the emplacements, laid firm platforms on which to position the guns and built defences for the guns and their detachments. (The men who man an artillery piece are referred to collectively as a detachment rather than a crew, which is a naval term.) Ditches and gabion walls were the usual forms of defence for the gun platforms; gabion walls were built from large wicker baskets filled with earth. These could be fronted by fascines, or bundles of rods, to provide protection from musket fire for the gunners and their assistants.

The normal practice was that each battery would be commanded by a master gunner, whose role was to direct and co-ordinate the fire of the guns on that site and ensure that nothing went wrong. This master gunner had to be experienced in the science of artillery – it is significant that the defenders had only a single master gunner – but he would have had a small number of men with artillery experience under his command. These were the mattrosses who actually served the guns. Theirs was a dangerous occupation as gunners often perished due to accidents with powder during the loading process, or from poisoning, while enemy musketry or direct cavalry or infantry attacks were also perils of the gunner's life. To try to reduce the latter risk it was a common practice for gun detachments to add their own refinement to their battery's defences by planting sharpened stakes in the ground to deter cavalry attacks – this was the gunners' version of the hedge of pikes.

Veteran gunners were rare since the risks of their profession did not allow too many gunners to achieve the status of veteran. This was one of the problems that the Jacobite army faced during the siege. Most of their gunners were French since there had been no experienced Catholic Irishmen to recruit into the Jacobite artillery. However, the three dozen French gunners who came to the city could not have provided all the manpower needed and so some local personnel would have been included. This would have created a communication problem since the Irishmen would not have been able to speak French and while the latter might have included English-speaking officers it is unlikely that there were any Frenchmen with a working knowledge of Gaelic. Since the pioneers were invariably also locally-recruited civilians, the level of discipline would have been much lower than with professional soldiers. Similar problems existed with the gunners inside the city although there was no language barrier in their ranks. There is no evidence to suggest that the master gunner, Alexander Watson, had many professionals in his gun detachments but it is probable that a few of those Protestants with artillery experience had made their way north.

What was the nature of the gunners' work both within and without the city? An individual gun detachment would have followed the same procedures in either army and the outline below, therefore, applies to both sides. The only real difference between the opposing artillery elements was that the Jacobite guns were mounted on field carriages whereas those inside the city were on garrison carriages. Replicas of the latter may be seen on the cannon on Londonderry city walls today. Sadly, a recent restoration project has seen a number of the city's cannon mounted incorrectly on field carriages while those mounted on garrison carriages lack rear trucks, or wheels; weapons so fitted would have been very difficult to manoeuvre and would have 'dug in' rather than recoiled after firing.

When an artillery piece was emplaced on its battery and brought into action for the first time, the barrel* was pointed in the general direction of the target. If no elevation or depression of the barrel was necessary and the barrel was parallel to the ground, the piece was said to be firing 'point blank'. This would often have been the case with guns firing at relatively short range which is how that term has come to mean close-range shooting. However, there were tasks to be performed before the gun was aimed at the target. The weapon had to be loaded, a procedure that began with a mattross using a powder shovel, or ladle, on the end of a long shaft to place a measured charge of black powder in the barrel. The shaft had to be long enough for the mattross to place the charge at the extreme end of the barrel; when he had the shaft in place he

---

*So called because early gun barrels were made in the same fashion as wooden barrels and bound together with metal staves.

turned it over so that the powder was placed at the 'breach' end. It was a matter of pride that the correct amount of powder was always lifted in the ladle. Likewise, professional pride considered it a 'foul fault for a gunner to commit' to leave even a small amount of grain on the ladle when the weapon had been loaded. Some armies were already using pre-measured linen or canvas bags, or charges, of powder, but this was not so in Britain, although the French had introduced the system. Thus the gunners inside the walls would have used the old system while those outside the walls might have been employing either that or pre-measured charges; however, the former is more likely. There were recommended charges for every type of gun although it was not for almost another four decades, in the 1720s, that these became scientific calculations rather than based on the experience of gunners. While too much powder in the charge created the danger of bursting the barrel or 'bushing' – widening – the touch-hole, too little reduced both the range and the effect of the round.

Powder was usually stored in barrels that held a quintal, or a hundredweight (112 pounds or 50.8 kilos), and was brought to the gun by a civilian labourer or a gunner's assistant. In this era all powder was of the form known as blackpowder. Such was its composition that it led quickly to fouling of either gun or musket barrels and created great clouds of dense black smoke over the battlefield – the fog of war that obscured the field. This also meant that the barrel had to be cleaned out regularly. (English and French powder differed in composition: the former included 75 parts saltpetre, 10 parts sulphur and 15 parts charcoal while the latter included the same proportion of saltpetre but with equal proportions of sulphur and charcoal.)

A wad of rags was then placed in the barrel and rammed tight on top of the charge by the civilian before the round was rolled into the weapon. This latter task was often performed by a boy who might have been the son of a soldier, perhaps of a gunner, and who, if he were not deafened prematurely, mutilated or killed, might even have grown up to be a professional gunner himself. If the gun was firing point blank the round would have been pushed down to rest against the charge; if there was any elevation on the barrel gravity would have performed that task. More wadding, in the form of rags or even a piece of earth, was then placed in the barrel and rammed home by a civilian rammer.

At this stage the gun was aimed by the master gunner. First, it was 'laid' for line, or direction of fire, by sighting along the centre-line of the barrel and then the angle of elevation was set by hammering a quoin*, or wedge, backwards or forwards under the rear end of the barrel. This was before the era of the elevating screw, which would make the process of elevation much simpler and

---

*The contemporary spelling was coyne.

faster. Quoins may be seen on the surviving cannon on the city walls. In fact, most gunners recognized only two methods of aiming: point-blank and elevating the barrel to 45 degrees which was believed widely, but wrongly, to allow maximum range.

Now came the final stage: that of firing the weapon. The master gunner placed priming powder – a finer mix than that in the charge – in the hole on top of the barrel by using a quill and the detachment then stood back while the senior mattross ignited the primer. This was not done by standing alongside the gun. Instead the mattross stood a safe distance from the piece and with a slow match, a length of matchcord, held on a long pole known as a porte-feu (literally fire-carrier) to reduce the possibility of casualties from accidental explosions, ignited the priming powder. The round was discharged to the accompaniment of a great explosion, which pushed the gun back on its carriage. Then the process of readying the gun to fire the next round could begin.

Preparation for each further shot differed in one critical respect. Before the loading drill could begin the barrel had to be sponged out with a long-handled wet sponge which was wormed into it along its entire length. This was intended to ensure that any smouldering remains from the last charge of powder were extinguished – it also cleaned the barrel – and while one gun detachment member was wielding the sponge or scourer another would be holding his thumb, protected by a leather thumbstall, over the touch hole as an additional safety precaution. Failing to take this two-part safety measure might have had fatal consequences for the rammer later. Had the barrel not been sponged thoroughly there was the possibility that, as the rammer shoved home the wadding, ball and charge, smouldering embers from the previous charge might ignite the fresh charge to blow the charge, rammer and ramrod out of the gun position. Thus it is little surprise that rammers were invariably civilians and that many deserted.

Once reloaded, the gun had to be pushed back to the firing position where the aiming process resumed. There was no mechanism to compensate for recoil and so continued accurate firing depended entirely on the skill and experience of the gunner. The sole advantage that arose from the recoil was that it placed the gun in position for reloading.

Contemporary artillery could fire a variety of munitions, including the familiar solid round shot or cannon ball. In addition, there were hollow balls, or 'shells', filled with powder and fitted with a fuse, as well as case shot, a forerunner of shrapnel. The latter was simply a charge of assorted pieces of metal, musket balls or even stones and was devastating when used against formed bodies of infantry or cavalry. Explosive shells were not entirely reliable since the burning time of the fuse, a length of matchcord, was difficult to determine with any real accuracy. It had even become the practice to apply a light to a length of match and recite the Apostles' Creed as it burned. This was then used to estimate the length of fuse needed for each shell that was fused by an offcut of that length of match. The *Text Book of Ammunition* noted that 'In the 17th century the repetition of the Apostles' Creed was one of the Proof-master's favourite measurements of time, and . . . it could scarcely be said to have constituted a standard of accuracy'.

We have already noted (Chapter One) the artillery requirements of a besieging force. Although the Jacobite army of 1689 lacked the full complement of artil-lery required to bring the city of Londonderry under control of King James, it nonetheless made effective use of the ordnance at its disposal. The guns of the attacking force had two basic tasks to perform: crumbling the walls of the city – bombardment – and neutralizing the defenders' artillery – counter-battery fire. Bombardment was the role of the heavier guns, preferably 24-pounders or larger, which would also be used against the enemy's artillery positions in counter-battery fire. Lighter guns could also be used in this latter role as well as against infantry or cavalry. Counter-battery fire involved duelling with the defending artillery in order to draw the attention of those guns from the bombarding pieces and, also, firing at the tops of the walls to force the infantry to keep under cover.

This latter fire was one of Vauban's developments and was known as ricochet fire. It could be used by skilled gunners to ensure that their rounds skimmed the top of the walls and skipped off to create more damage in the buildings within the defences. Alternatively the rounds could ricochet off the rear walls of outworks to cause greater damage to the main defences. The effect was akin to a boy skimming a stone off the surface of a pond. Flying pieces of masonry added to the effect of the bombardment. Meanwhile, the heavier weapons were pounding at the lower part of the walls with the inten-tion of crumbling the stonework and bringing down the upper part of the wall. If those heavier pieces were used for ricochet fire they used a smaller powder charge than for bombardment.

To perform their task effectively, and in the least possible time, the larger guns had to be moved as close as possible to the walls. As noted in the text, this was done by digging parallels and connecting trenches to bring the guns to within some 200 yards of the walls. This was achieved through co-opera-tion between engineers, gunners, pioneers and infantry. There is probably no other aspect of the gunners' role that illustrates so effectively the scientific nature of siege warfare. Bringing the guns to within 200 yards of the walls not only allowed the maximum effect to be achieved from each round but it also made the task of aiming much simpler since each weapon could be fired point-blank. (This method could be used up to about 800 yards.)

Bearing in mind that the gunners who created the breach in the city walls at the end of June that permitted Skelton and Clancarty's attack were firing from ground on a lower level than the walls and at about twice the optimum range, their gunnery must have been excellent since they would have had to fire at an unusual angle of elevation and maintain a high rate of fire; it is possible that the guns, probably 24-pounders, fired about 90 to 100 rounds per day in direct fire at the walls. This achievement has never been acknowledged before in any account of the siege, having been hidden by Walker's account of the event and, more recently, by Macrory's acceptance of Walker's account as accurate. St-Rémy estimated that it would take three batteries – two of ten and one of eight 24- or 32-pounder pieces – two days of steady bombardment to achieve a practicable breach wide enough for thirty men to advance abreast although Vauban believed that two batteries would suffice. A practicable breach was defined as one where enough masonry and earth had been blown into the ditch to permit an attacking soldier to climb it with ease, allowing him the use of both hands to use his weapons. Obviously, the single battery of two guns firing at the Butcher's Gate did not provide the firepower suggested by either St-Rémy or Vauban but, in the space of perhaps three days – we cannot be certain of the exact length of the bombardment – it managed to create a viable breach in the city walls. Paradoxically, these gunners may also have been among those who, a month later, failed in their endeavours to prevent the relief fleet passing through the narrows.

In Chapter Five (page 116) reference was made to the arrival at Derry of six large cannon which had been hauled overland from Dublin. Although there is no evidence to indicate that these were specialised siege pieces it is reasonable to assume that they were. These weapons used larger powder charges than their field artillery equivalents and their carriages had to be proportionately stronger to absorb the forces of those charges. Whereas an English 24-pounder field gun had carriage cheeks, or sides, of nine feet in length and 4.5-inches wide, a 24-pounder siege gun had thirteen-foot-long cheeks which were also twice as thick as those of the field gun; wheel sizes also differed with the field gun having smaller diameter wheels, by eight inches, than those of the fifty-eight-inch wheels of the siege gun.

This made the siege guns more difficult to move, and thus the reason why it was preferred to move them by water. But the reluctance of the French navy to play a full part in the operations at Derry meant that the guns had to be hauled from Dublin on roads that were no more than earth tracks. When the guns were moved, at the end of May, the ground would have begun to dry out but it would have been rutted and any rain at all would have turned the roads into quagmires. The initial part of the journey would not have been as bad as the final stages since the eastern side of Ireland has much less rainfall than the north-west. Once into Tyrone and County Londonderry it can be assumed that travelling became much more difficult.

We have no account of the progress of the artillery train, nor of its composition, but we do know something of the standard operating procedures for a train. By this period, most guns were provided with a limber, known to the French as an *avant-train*, which was a pair of wheels on an axle with either a pole or shafts to which the team of horses would be harnessed. The rear of the cannon's trail was lifted onto the limber to allow easier movement by road. With the weight of the gun distributed over four wheels rather than two it became possible to reduce the number of draught horses needed for each although a single gun, weighing about three tons, needed a team of six or eight horses. In addition to the guns, the train would have included wagons to carry ammunition and stores and had to be escorted by infantry while engineers and pioneers were also included to carry out any improvements needed to the road; at least one wagon was required to carry their tools and equipment. Many civilians had to be recruited as drivers for the horse teams and they were apt to take to their heels at any sign of danger. It took time for the train to get underway each day and it had to stop early enough in the day to make camp for the night and allow an evening meal to be prepared. It is likely that it took as much as two weeks to cover the 140 miles from Dublin to the outskirts of Derry. Had the French navy not been intimidated into virtual inaction following the Battle of Bantry Bay the guns could have been brought by ship in much less time and would have arrived in much better condition.

Bibliography

Anon, *Account of the most material passages in Ireland since December 1688 with a particular relation of the forces of Londonderry* (London 1689)

Anon, *Derriana: A collection of papers relative to the siege of Derry and illustrative of the revolution of MDCLXXXVIII* (Londonderry 1794)

Antrim, Angela, *The Antrim McDonnells* (Belfast 1977)

Avaux, le comte d', *Négociations de M. le comte d'Avaux en Irlande, 1689–90* (Dublin 1934)

Bartlett, Tom & Jeffery, Keith, *A Military History of Ireland* (Cambridge 1996)

Beckett, J C, *The Making of Modern Ireland 1603–1923* (London 1966)

Bredin, Brigadier A E C, *A History of the Irish Soldier* (Belfast 1987)

Buchanan, John, *A Compendious History of the Siege of Londonderry* (Londonderry 1838)

Carman, W Y, *British Military Uniforms from contemporary pictures* (London 1957)

Chacksfield, K M, *Glorious Revolution, 1688* (Wincanton 1988)

Chandler, David, *The Art of Warfare in the Age of Marlborough* (Tunbridge Wells 1989)

Chartrand, René, *Louis XIV's Army* (London 1988)

Chicester, Henry M, & Burges-Short, George, *Records and Badges of the British Army, 1900* (London 1900; reprinted London 1986)

Childs, John, *The Army, James II and the Glorious Revolution* (Manchester 1980); *The British Army of William III 1689–1702* (Manchester 1987)

Clark, Sir George, *The Later Stuarts 1660–1714* (Oxford 1955)

Clifford, Brendan (Ed), *Derry and The Boyne* (Belfast 1990)

Colledge, J J, & Warlow, Ben, *Ships of The Royal Navy* (London, 2006)

D'Alton, John, *King James's Irish Army List 1689* (Dublin 1855)

Doherty, Richard, *The Williamite War in Ireland 1688–1691* (Dublin 1998)

Dwyer A M, The Rev. P (Ed), *The Siege of Londonderry in 1689* (Wakefield 1971)

Finlay, John Edward, *The Siege of Londonderry compiled from the best sources* (Londonderry 1861)

Fortescue, Sir John, *History of the British Army* (London 1879–1930)

Foster, R F, *Modern Ireland, 1600–1972* (London 1988)

Frederick, J B M, *Lineage Book of British Land Forces 1660–1978* (Wakefield 1984)

Gébler, Carlo, *The Siege of Derry: A History* (London 2005)

Gilbert, J T (Ed), *A Jacobite Narrative of the War in Ireland* (Dublin 1892, reprinted Shannon 1971)

Graham, John, *A History of the Siege of Londonderry and the Defence of Enniskillen in 1688 and 1689* (Dublin 1829)

(Ed), *Ireland Preserved; or The Siege of London-Derry together with The Troubles of the North* (Dublin 1841) (originally published London 1708)

Guy, Alan J, *1688: Glorious Revolution? The Fall and Rise of the British Army 1660 – 1704* (London 1988)

Hackett, General Sir John, *The Profession of Arms* (London 1983)

Hamilton, A, *A True Relation of the Actions of the Inniskilling Men* (London 1690)

Harris, R G, *The Irish Regiments 1683–1999* (Staplehurst 1999)

Harris, Tim, *Revolution. The Great Crisis of the British Monarchy, 1685–1720* (London 2006)

Hayes-McCoy, G A, *Irish Battles. A Military History of Ireland* (Belfast 1989)

Hogg, Ian V, *The Illustrated Encyclopedia of Artillery* (London 1987)

Hughes, Major-General B P, *Firepower: Weapons Effectiveness on the Battlefield, 1630–1850* (London 1974)

Hughes, Quentin, *Military Architecture: The art of defence from earliest times to the Atlantic Wall* (Liphook 1991)

Keegan, John, *A History of Warfare* (London 1985);

& Holmes, R, *Soldiers: A History of Men in Battle* (London 1985)

Kelly, William, *The Sieges of Derry* (Dublin 2001)

Lacy, Brian, *Siege City – The Story of Derry and Londonderry* (Belfast 1990);

Discover Derry (Dublin 1999)

Lucy, Gordon (Ed), *Lord Macaulay on Londonderry, Aughrim, Enniskillen and the Boyne* (Lurgan 1989)

Mackenzie, John, *A Narrative of the Siege of Londonderry 1689* (London 1690)

Macrory, Patrick, *The Siege of Derry* (London 1980)

MacLysaght, E, *Irish Life in the 17th Century* (Dublin 1979)

Maguire, W A (ed), *Kings in Conflict. The Revolutionary War in Ireland and its Aftermath 1689–1750* (Belfast 1990)

Milligan, C D, *The Relief of Derry. Browning and the Boom: its making and its breaking* (Londonderry 1946);

History of the Siege of Londonderry 1689 (Belfast 1951);

The Walls of Derry, Part 1 (Londonderry 1948);

The Walls of Derry, Part 2 (Londonderry 1950)

McBride, Ian, *The Siege of Derry in Ulster Protestant Mythology* (Dublin 1997)

McMahon, Sean, *A History of County Derry* (Dublin 2004)

Mulloy, Sheila (Ed), *Franco-Irish Correspondence, December 1688–February 1692* (Dublin 1983)

Norris, John, *Artillery. A History* (Stroud 2000)

Ó Ciardha, Éamonn, *Ireland and the Jacobite Cause, 1683–1766. A fatal attachment* (Dublin 2001)

Parker, R, *Memoirs of the most remarkable Military Transactions in Ireland from 1683 to 1715* (Dublin 1746)

Petrie, Sir Charles, *The Great Tyrconnel: A Chapter in Anglo-Irish Relations* (Cork 1972)

Powley, Edward B, *The Naval Side of King William's War* (London 1972)

Seymour, W, *Great Sieges of History* (London 1991)

Sheane, Michael, *The Great Siege. The siege of Londonderry, 1689* (Ilfracombe 2002)

Simms, J G, *The Siege of Derry* (Dublin 1966);

    Jacobite Ireland 1685–91 (London 1969)

Simpson, Robert, *The Annals of Derry* (Londonderry 1847; Limavady 1987)

Stewart, A T Q, *The Narrow Ground* (London 1977 & 1989);

    The Shape of Irish History (Belfast 2001)

Story, G, *A Continuation of the Impartial History of the Wars in Ireland* (London 1693)

Sword, The Irish XVIII, no. 70 (Winter 1990): Commemorative Issue entitled 'The War of the Kings, 1689–91'

Thomas, Avril, *Derry–Londonderry (Irish Historic Towns Atlas No. 15)* (Dublin 2005)

Tincey, J, & Embleton, G, *The British Army 1660–1704* (London 1994)

Uden, Grant (Ed), *Longman Illustrated Encyclopedia of World History* (London 1989)

Walker, George, *A True Account of the Siege of London-Derry* (London 1690)

Warner, Philip, *Firepower: From Slings to Star Wars* (London 1988)

Wilson, A W, *The Story of the Gun* (London 1944)

Witherow, Thomas, *Derry and Enniskillen in the Year 1689* (Belfast 1913);

    Two Diaries of Derry in 1689, Being Richards' Diary of the Fleet and Ash's Journal of the Siege (Londonderry 1888)

Young, P, & Lawford, J P (Eds), *History of the British Army* (London 1970)

Young, William R, *Fighters of Derry: Their Deeds and Descendants* (London 1932)

Articles

Cunningham, J and Whalley, M, 'Major General Kirke, Queries against', *The Irish Sword* (hereinafter *IS*) XVI, no. 64, pp. 208–16

Doherty, R, 'Robert Lundy', *IS* XVIII, no. 72, pp. 232–4

Ferguson, K, 'Naval Aspects of the Jacobite War', *IS* XV, no. 58, pp. 57–9;

    'The Development of a Standing Army in Ireland', *IS* XV, no. 60, pp. 153–8;

    'The Organisation of King William's Army in Ireland, 1689–92', *IS* XVIII, no. 70, pp. 62–79

Garland, J L, 'Galmoy's Horse', *IS* I, no. 3, p. 228

    'MacElligot, The Regiment of, 1688–89', *IS* I, no. 2, pp. 121–7

LeFevre, Peter, 'The Battle of Bantry Bay, 1 May 1689', *IS* XVIII, No. 70, pp. 1–16

Loeber, R, 'Engineers in Ireland, Biographical dictionary of', *IS* XIII, no. 50, pp. 30–4; no. 51, pp. 106–22; no. 52, pp. 230–55; no. 53, pp. 283–314

Melvin, P, 'Troop Movements and James II's Army in 1688', *IS* X, no. 39, pp. 87–105;

    'Justin McCarthy, Lord Mountcashel', *IS* XII, no. 49, pp. 305–6;

    'Jacobite Infantry, 1691', *IS* II, no. 6, p. 121

Mulloy, S, 'French Engineers with the Jacobite Army in Ireland, 1689–91', *IS* XV, no. 61, pp. 222–32

'The French Navy and the Jacobite War in Ireland', *IS* XVIII, no. 70, pp. 17–31

Murtagh, Harman, 'Jacobite Artillery, 1689–1691', *IS* XXIII, no. 94, pp. 383–400

O'Donnell, T, 'The Siege of Derry, 1689', *IS* II, no. 7, p. 224

Simms, J G, 'Berwick, The Regiment of', *IS* II, no. 6, p. 129;

    'James II and the Siege of Derry', *IS* III, no. 13, pp. 286–7;

    'The Siege of Derry', *IS* VI, no. 25, pp. 221–32

Terrett, W, 'A Biographical Note on Conrad de Rosen (1629–1715), Marshal of France', *IS* XXV no. 101, pp. 268–70

Wauchope, Piers, 'Colonel John Mitchelburne', *IS* XX, no. 80, pp. 137–144

[Facsimile of ms in National Library of Ireland], 'Pike drill mid-17th century', *IS* I, no. 3, p. 180

Unpublished
House of Lords Record Office, London
House of Commons Journals, 1688–1693, 1701
House of Lords Journals, 1688–1691

National Archives, Kew
State Papers, Ireland, 1689–90
ADM1/4080: Admiralty Secretary
ADM3/2: Admiralty Office
ADM2/1743: Admiralty Orders and Instructions
ADM52/9: Ship's Log, HMS *Bonadventure*

National Archives of Scotland, Edinburgh
GD26/8/15: letter from James VII/II to viscount Dundee, 17 May 1689
GD26/9/217: pass from Melfort to allow Captain James Brougham to travel to the king's camp before Derry.
GD26/7/37 (i): case for Lundy and letter with details of preparations at Derry.
GD26/7/37 (ii): account of Lundy's proceedings in Ireland since 13 December 1688.
GD26/7/37 (iii): draft petition to Privy Council defending his conduct.
GD26/9/549: news of the siege from the fleet at Londonderry.
GD406/1/3530: letter from onboard HMS *Swallow* to Duke of Hamilton.
GD406/1/3531: letter from Inch, 4 August 1689
GD406/1/3532: letter from onboard HMS *Swallow* re relief, 29 July 1689.
GD406/1/3533: proclamation, 24 July 1689.
GD406/1/3536: Melville to Hamilton for pass for bearer to meet Kirke, 11 July 1689

British Library Newspaper Library, Colindale
The London Gazette, 1688–90

Index